Contextual Theology and Revolutionary
Transformation in Latin America

# Contextual Theology and Revolutionary Transformation in Latin America

*The Missiology of M. Richard Shaull*

**Angel Daniel Santiago-Vendrell**

PICKWICK *Publications* · Eugene, Oregon

CONTEXTUAL THEOLOGY AND REVOLUTIONARY TRANSFORMATION IN LATIN AMERICA
The Missiology of M. Richard Shaull

Pickwick Publications
An Imprint of Wipf and Stock Publishers
199 W. 8th Ave., Suite 3
Eugene, OR 97401

www.wipfandstock.com

ISBN 13: 978-1-60899-305-5

*Cataloging-in-Publication data:*

Santiago-Vendrell, Angel Daniel

    Contextual theology and revolutionary transformation in Latin America : the missiology of M. Richard Shaull / Angel Daniel Santiago-Vendrell.

    viii + 198 p. ; 23 cm. — Includes bibliographical references and indexes.

    ISBN 13: 978-1-60899-305-5

    1. Shaull, Richard. 2. Revolutions—Religious aspects—Christianity—History of doctrines—20th century. 3. Missions—Latin America. 4. Liberation theology. I. Title.

BT738.3 S3 2010

Manufactured in the U.S.A.

*In loving memory of my parents*
*Antonia "Toñita" Vendrell and Gilberto Santiago,*
*And my father in law Wae-Jae Im*

*For those who are sharing their lives with me*
*My wife Misoon Im*
*My son Daniel Im Santiago*
*My mother in law Hye-Won Park*
*And my brother in law Jinsoon Im*

# Contents

# Introduction

"A Young Man Worth Watching" was the prophetic title of a chapter written by Charles T. Leber describing Richard Shaull, then a young missionary to Colombia, South America.[1] On April 20 1942, The Board of Foreign Missions of the Presbyterian Church in the United States of America appointed Shaull a missionary.[2] This book is an historical and missiological study of the work of Richard Shaull, who was one of the foremost North American Protestant missionaries and ecumenical leaders to and in Latin America in the second half of the twentieth century.

The study of Richard Shaull's life reveals a myriad of connections with significant theological and political issues of the day. He was a pastor, missionary, evangelist, political activist, human rights advocate, theologian, seminary professor, ecumenicist, writer, and editor of different scholarly journals. This range of activities, and his network of acquaintances, raises the following questions: How did Shaull understand God and God's mission? What core beliefs unified and integrated his variety of interests? What associations and influences helped to shape his identity and thought? The interpretative challenge of this book is to find out how Shaull's understanding of mission developed in dialogue with his multiple contexts.

When Shaull arrived in Colombia in 1942, he intended "to build up a weak church, to develop a strong youth movement, and to establish new

1. Leber, "A Young Man," 49–55.

2. The Board of Foreign Missions of the Presbyterian Church in the United States of America, April 20, 1942, Presbyterian Church in the USA. Commission on Ecumenical Mission and Relations. *Colombia Mission, 1882–1972*. The Presbyterian Historical Society, Philadelphia. RG 88, Missionary Record 360.

patterns of evangelistic outreach."[3] Shaull was appointed as an evangelist to the city of Barranquilla and he developed new patterns of evangelization there. For example, he was a firm believer in literacy as a means of evangelization.[4] He worked with factory workers by opening his house for night studies.[5] One of Shaull's first radical decisions in the 1940s was to move to the poorest neighborhood of Barranquilla and make his house a haven for the masses.[6] He was engaged in developing new centers of preaching in the rural areas in cooperation with the youth groups of the region; so, seeing the necessity of trained local leaders, he opened a new training program in his home.

Shaull's role as a Christian political activist was clearly seen in his last two years of ministry in Bogotá, Colombia, where he assumed the pastoral leadership of First Presbyterian Church from 1948 to 1950. A terrible political and religious persecution emerged when the Conservative Party regained control of Colombia.[7] In the midst of religious persecution, Shaull was a bridge figure informing the Colombian government and North Americans of human rights violations.[8]

3. Shaull, "Dying to Live," n.d. Special Collections, Speer Library, The Richard Shaull Papers, Princeton Theological Seminary, Princeton.

4. Laubach, *Forty Years*. Shaull collaborated with the famous missionary to the Philippines in his literacy program in Colombia.

5. Shaull, Personal Report to the Presbyterian Colombian Mission, 1942. Presbyterian Church in the USA. Commission on Ecumenical Mission and Relations. *Colombia Mission, 1882–1972*. The Presbyterian Historical Society, Philadelphia. RG 88. 360 Missionary Profiles.

6. Shaull, *Surpreendido pela Graça*, 45–47. The Shaulls' residence became a community home as persons from all walks of life sought their comfort from the distressing conditions in the poor neighborhood.

7. While the majority of Latin American countries after obtaining independence from Spain broke with the political integration of Church and State, in Colombia such integration continues to exist in some forms until the present. See Bidegaín, *Iglesia, Pueblo y Política*. Politics in Colombia have been polarized in two camps: The Conservative and Liberal Parties. The Conservatives have been committed to strong unitary government, the interest of large landowners, and a dominant position for the Roman Catholic Church. Liberals have fought for decentralized republican government, broader suffrage, free secular schools, and increased commerce through free trade. See Martz, *Colombia: A Contemporary Political Survey*.

8. Shaull was the representative of various Protestant groups to investigate and report cases of violence against Protestant churches. He argues, "I was the only person in Bogotá with an official position within a Protestant church to assume such responsibility. Even if this placed me in a delicate situation, we presume that for being North American, I will not suffer greater threats than a Colombian." *Surpreendido pela Graça*, 65–66.

In 1952, Shaull arrived in Brazil for a new missionary appointment after spending several years in the United States completing a doctoral program under Paul Lehmann.[9] In this country, he understood the difficulties that the church would face in a revolutionary world. The Communist victory of Mao-Tse Tung in China, the Mau Mau revolt in Kenya inspired by nationalism to end colonialism, and the unrest in Southeast Asia and Latin America were clear indicators that the world was going through a revolutionary process.[10] Shaull worked intensively in universities and educational centers in the early 1950s to offer an antidote to Communism in Brazil. He wondered whether perhaps God was using Communism to destroy Christian complacency and to awaken the church to strive for justice in the world.[11]

In 1954, Shaull participated in the early stages of formulating the study guide on "The Church and Responsible Society" for the Evanston Conference of the World Council of Churches. In 1955, partly at his initiative, the Commission on Church and Society was created in Rio de Janeiro. Shaull's involvement with the Confederation of Presbyterian Youth, Christian Union of Brazilian Students, Christian Association of Academics, and ISAL (Church and Society in Latin America) made him one of the leading Protestant theologians in Latin America in the 1950s.[12]

---

9. Shaull left Colombia in 1950. His leadership in denouncing human rights violations caused him to have many enemies. Shaull states, "It is thus not surprising that I have been arrested by the police, that three agents of the secret police are supposed to be watching me, and that an agent of the life insurance company recently suggested that it would be very wise for me to take out a good amount of my life insurance for the sake of my family." Shaull, "Personal Report to the Colombian Board of the Presbyterian Church," September 26, 1950, Presbyterian Church in the USA, Commission on Ecumenical Mission and Relations. *Brazil Mission, 1890–1965*. The Presbyterian Historical Society, Philadelphia.

10. Shaull, *Encounter with Revolution*. Shaull argued, "Not Communism but Revolution is the fundamental fact we face; revolution which is world-wide, in fact, the first truly world-wide revolution in history, the first time that everywhere all institutions of the past seem inadequate and all things appear simultaneously and unprecedentedly out of joint" (3). Shaull pin-pointed four causes of the revolutionary process: "worldwide poverty, the crisis of modern industrial society, the uneasy conscience of the privilege classes, and the revolution of the soul against the religious ideas and moral bonds of the past." (17).

11. Shaull, *El Cristianismo y la Revolución Social*, 7–9.

12. Shaull, *Surpreendido pela Graça*, 93–187.

Shaull challenged the Presbyterian Church to take a stand in the social situation of Brazil. He criticized missionaries and church leaders for their puritanical tendencies and for their concern with the salvation of souls while neglecting the socio-political structures of oppression.[13] He considered that God had called the church to participate in the struggles of human beings in the world through the formulation of new ways to express the gospel at that particular time in Brazilian history. His missiology was rooted in the conviction that God was active in the world through the agency of Jesus Christ and the guidance of the Holy Spirit in the church. Throughout his missionary career in Latin America, the church took a central place in the evangelization of the world.

Shaull spent twenty years as a missionary in Latin America before he returned to the United States. During his last appointment as a missionary in Brazil from 1952 to 1962, he experienced the impact of the Cold War in Latin America.[14] When Shaull return to North America, he became critical of U.S. foreign policy, seeing it as out of touch with the revolutionary processes occurring in Latin America. In a sense he had become a "reverse missionary."[15]

His contribution to the field of missiology was attested to in his editorial role in *Christianity and Crisis, NACLA Newsletter,* and *Cristianismo y Sociedad.* As a member of the political New Left, he was engaged with Herbert Marcuse, and Carl Oglesby (among others) in criticizing American imperialism in the world. Following his doctoral advisor Paul Lehmann, Shaull strived to create a socio-political ethic that would take the concrete actions of God in history as a starting point for formulating options for social transformation.[16] Shaull was one of the first Presbyterian missionaries after WWII who made the social, political, and cultural revolution of his time the fundamental theme of theological reflection.

By the end of the 1960s, Shaull's positions regarding Marxism had changed drastically. He no longer considered Marxism to be a threat, but rather as one of the solutions to the oppression experienced by the Latin

13. Shaull, "The New Challenge Before the Younger Churches," 194.

14. Ralph B. Levering in *The Cold War* argues that "the breakdown of trust following the [Yalta] conference may well be viewed as the beginning of the Cold War" (7).

15. Shaull and Gutiérrez, *Liberation and Change*; Shaull and Oglesby, *Containment and Change*; and Shaull, *Naming the Idols.*

16. Lehmann, *Ethics in a Christian Context*; Shaull, "And a God Who Acts and Transforms History," 57–70.

American masses.[17] In this sense, Christians were called to enter into an ecumenical relationship with Marxists in their quest for a better society. Shaull's missiology was directed toward interrelatedness and solidarity with the revolutionary forces acting in the world.[18] After an early retirement from Princeton Seminary, he dedicated the rest of his life to being an itinerant preacher, lecturer, and church consultant in the U.S. and Latin America.[19]

Shaull's contribution in formulating a missiology of revolution as a response to rapid social changes in Latin America, and his endeavor to create a socio-political ethic that would take the presumed actions of God in history as a starting point for formulating options for social transformation deserve to be examined in light of his ministry and self-identity as a missionary. Despite these facts, Shaull has not been the subject of an in-depth missiological analysis in the United States.

The biggest contribution of this book is to address the interrelationship between Shaull's missionary career and the development of contextual theologies. This book is the first attempt to interpret the life of Shaull in Colombia, Brazil, and the United States through missiological lenses. Because missiology is the "study of the salvific activities of Father, Son, and Holy Spirit throughout the world geared toward bringing the kingdom of God into existence," conversion and discipleship into the Christian

---

17. Shaull, "Christian Participation in the Latin American Revolution," 96–99. Shaull argued that because Marxism was "the movement which succeeds in raising the question of humanization most sharply and dealing with it most decisively... When the Christian awakens to the problem of humanization, he may see this as the work of Jesus Christ in the world" (97). The concept of humanization use in this book is missiological in nature. Shaull used it to accentuate human collaboration in the work of God within the whole area of human historical life in this world. For Shaull, mission was participation in the activity of God in the world which always occurs where God is most dynamically active. See, "The Revolutionary Challenge to Church and Theology," 25–32.

18. Shaull, "The Church in the Modern Diaspora," 276–83. Shaull went as far as saying, "for us in America, it may mean, among other things, the rediscovery of the work of the early Niebuhr and his development of a Fellowship of Socialist Christians." Shaull and Smolik, *Consumers or Revolutionaries*, 23.

19. He closely collaborated with theological centers such as the Latin American Biblical University in San José, Costa Rica, Centro Ecumenico Antonio Valdevieso in Nicaragua, and the Comisión Evangélica Latino Americana de Educación Cristiana (CELADEC) in Lima, Peru, and lectured in many universities and theological seminaries in the United States.

tradition will be integral parts in understanding how Shaull constructed spirituality as a source of social transformation.[20]

In the 1950s and 1960s, Shaull showed through his missionary career how the process of formulating a contextual theology emerged. His own life as a missionary in situations of revolution inspired him to contextualize the gospel based on the "signs of the times." As Shaull interpreted the Brazilian socio-political reality to formulate his missiology that context of revolution began to overwhelm his theology to the point that many critics just saw a political justification for revolution in his thought.[21] Whatever the criticisms against Shaull, he never swerved in his commitment to formulate a new missional methodology to communicate God in a revolutionary world. He points out,

> For this to happen would require something of a revolution in the life and work of the theologian himself. By this I mean several things: the willingness to do theology in the midst of revolutionary praxis; the experience on the part of the theologian of a real *exodus* and *exile* in relation to the prevailing culture and dominant social system; a rich knowledge of our theological heritage combined with a full awareness of the bankruptcy of its traditional terms and systems and of the need for the creation of new paradigms; most important of all, perhaps, a willingness to dare to allow dead theological systems to be buried, to stand before the world empty-handed, and to expect a theological resurrection.[22]

There were at least three ways in which Shaull influenced the movement of contextual theology: the active participation of the theologian in the struggles of the marginalized; the primacy of *praxis* over Church doctrines; and, the formation of small radical communities of Christian faith. Shaull was one of the first missionaries in Latin America who moved to a full-blown contextual methodology and broke epistemologically with the theological establishment of traditional theology, especially neo-orthodoxy.[23]

Before liberation theologian Gustavo Gutiérrez challenged the world to take "Christian *praxis* in light of the Word of God" as a starting point from which to construct theology in the early 1970s, Shaull in the

20. Verkuyl, *Contemporary Missiology*, 5.

21. O'Keefe, "An Analysis and Critique," 86–108.

22. Shaull, "Hacia una Perspectiva Cristiana de la Revolución Social," 3–17.

23. Shaull, "Liberation Theology and Karl Barth," 4.

1950s was inviting Christians in Brazil to participate through their lives in the formation of a new society through the revolutionary processes in order to transform the world. He pointed out, "Our starting point must be in praxis, but praxis of a very special sort: *our own experience of exodus and exile* as we break out of the order of social oppression and personal repression of which we are victims, and move expectantly toward a new land of promise, toward the creation of a new order of social and personal existence."[24] This was not to be accomplished in an individualistic experience but rather praxis was best served when done in community. Throughout his life, Shaull promoted small groups of Christians who were self-conscious of their participation with God in God's redemptive work of transformation in history.

The type of ecclesiology Shaull was promoting was a key factor in his missiology. Even though he was aware of the criticisms against a church-centered model, he did not embrace completely the new kingdom-centered missiology of his time. He was convinced that the church should be the leading voice in directing the world to fullness and salvation though Jesus Christ. His ecumenical vision was rooted in the activity of God in history through the church. But the church for Shaull was more than an institutional organization; it was a community of believers in the Diaspora who made Christ present in the world.

On the basis of a study of the activities and contributions of Richard Shaull, this work argues that he was one of the first missionaries to formulate a contextual theology in Latin America. Shaull developed a holistic missiology that aimed at total social transformation through the power of the gospel and the instrumentality of the Christian church. Shaull felt that the church's integration of the message of Jesus Christ as a living testimony in the midst of society should bring a reorientation of values and that such a reorientation of values would result in social transformation.

---

24. Shaull, "Hacia una Perspectiva Cristiana de la Revolución Social," 13.

*chapter one*

## Early Life and First Missionary Assignment
## of Richard Shaull to Colombia, South America, 1942–1950

> Our action [of becoming a missionary] has been motivated by
> one supreme conviction, that our world is saved and civilization
> preserved only to the degree that men are willing to sit at the feet
> of the teacher of Galilee and learn his plan for their lives, only to
> the extent that they are willing to allow the power of God to purge
> their hearts of selfishness and lead them in pathways of service
> and love. Thus, we may win the war and lose the peace; we may
> defeat our enemies but not destroy the forces of evil, unless we
> have ambassadors of Christ going into the world drawing all men
> to the feet of the Master and challenging them to live according to
> his will. The Protestant missionaries here are perhaps the best am-
> bassadors our country has. Our country is spoken of with respect,
> almost deference. The students speak at least some English and
> dream of going to the States to study. The United States appears
> to them as the savior of modern civilization. Such an attitude has
> not developed in spite of missionaries, but precisely because of
> them.[1]

The previous quotation from Richard Shaull reveals the tension between the justification of the missionary movement to send ambassadors
of Christ to all the world with the missionaries' own cultural presuppositions and ethnocentrism. The need to separate Christ from Western

---

1. Richard Shaull to The Board of Foreign Missions of the Presbyterian Church
USA, October 4, 1942, The Colombia Mission, The Presbyterian Historical Society,
Philadelphia. RG 88: Box 15, Folder 7.

civilization was at the center of the emerging missionary paradigm that developed during the interwar period. The focus on missions during the interwar period began to shift to internationalism and goodwill among the nations.[2] One of the main goals or objectives that the internationalist paradigm promoted was the movement toward cultural indigenization.[3] Many times the evangelistic zeal of the missionaries of presenting Christ as the solution to the world's problems was not separated from their cultural assumptions of Western civilization as the culture to be emulated. The transfer of values was something of which missionaries were barely aware, yet did continually. Even Shaull in his early missionary career could not escape the trend when he conceived the United States as the savior of modern civilization. Nonetheless, the process of separating Christ from Western civilization was most notable in Shaull's own transformation through his life as a missionary.

This chapter traces the life of Richard Shaull from his early childhood to his first missionary assignment to Colombia, South America, and his return to the United States to pursue doctoral studies at Princeton Seminary. In particular the chapter describes Shaull's early childhood in rural Pennsylvania, his high school experience of isolation and marginalization due to his young age, his years in a Mennonite college, and his ministerial training at Princeton Theological Seminary under John A. Mackay, Emil Brunner, and Josef Hromadka. Second, the chapter sketches the ministerial development of Shaull during his first missionary assignment in Colombia. Here Shaull put into practice the major theological and ideological shifts occurring in the theoretical understanding of missiology at that time, advocating for a missiology that addressed all aspects of human life. He worked in industrial evangelism, youth work, literacy, ministerial formation of national leaders, social transformation through Christian spirituality, and the denunciation of human rights abuses.

## Richard Shaull's Early Life

Millard Richard Shaull was born on November 24, 1919, in the small rural community of Felton, York County, PA. Shaull's family consisted of his

2. Dana Lee Robert, "The First Globalization," 50–66.
3. Ibid.

parents Millard Shaull and Anna Brenneman, one brother, George, and two sisters, Jane and June. Richard's childhood was marked by familial fraternity, love, and strong discipline, but he remembered his childhood with mixed feelings. On the one hand, he was loved and cared for by his family; on the other, he did not care for the extreme discipline of his parents and the hard work in the fields. His parents worked together on the farm and shared work responsibilities with their children. "Working in the fields demanded too much," he wrote, "the other houses were not close, and the neighbors did not have much time or interest in approaching their neighbors socially."[4] For this reason, when the time came to begin school, Richard was excited and curious about what his future might hold.

Shaull's time at the small school of Glessic was relatively short because from an early age his intellectual abilities surpassed those of his peers. As the school had only one room and just a few students, and Richard already knew how to read when he began school, he was advanced on the first day of classes to the second grade. He was transferred again in the middle of the year to the third grade because the only other student in second grade moved away. Thus, by the end of the first year he was already in the fourth grade. When he was supposed to be in the fifth grade, the teacher transferred him to the seventh grade and that same year he took the exams to enter high school.[5]

Shaull started Red Lion High School when he was ten years old, and it was there that he felt out of place for the first time in his life. He recollects, "I realized that I was four years younger than everybody else in my class . . . also going to school thirteen kilometers from home was quite a shock."[6] In a class where he was the youngest by four years, he was clearly out of place socially. His rural background meant he had not encountered the social events typical of a bigger town, such as dances, parties, and athletic and recreational activities, and that even in basic matters such as dress he was quite different from his peers. However these experiences of being marginalized and feeling out of place in his social context taught him the ability to be alone which would be indispensable as a missionary,

4. Shaull, *Surpreendido*, 14.

5. Ibid., 16.

6. Ibid., 18.

and helped him identify with people who were experiencing similar issues of marginalization and displacement.

Shaull entered high school in 1929, the year that marked the beginning of the Great Depression. Amid all the hopelessness that the Depression brought, Shaull was hopeful of a future day when things would change for the better. Shaull's hopefulness could be seen in an essay he wrote for a competition in oratory in his senior year entitled "Franklin D. Roosevelt: The Man of the Moment."[7] Roosevelt became president in 1932 and brought with him a new air of confidence and optimism characterized as the "New Deal." He claimed, "the only thing we need to fear is fear itself." With increased regulations and intervention in the economic development of the nation, the new administration sponsored a series of legislative initiatives and new measures to fight poverty, create employment, and provide a social safety net. Thanks to all these, in the midst of all the tribulations and victories, Shaull grew up seeing the self-reliant spirit of North America.

In this context, Cross-Roads Presbyterian Church became one of the few ways Richard could enjoy the company of other children his age. Even though he was not particularly interested in organized religion, early in his life Richard developed a passion for understanding the Bible and its message. His mother gave young Shaull his first Bible, which he read constantly. She also gave Richard Sunday School material and the Brief Presbyterian Catechism.[8] In addition to the constant religious support of his mother, Richard and his father conversed about social and political events prompted by articles they read in the *York Gazette and Daily*, which was the most progressive journal of the region.[9] Yet the biggest influence in his life in this period was the social gospel novel *In His Steps* by Charles Sheldon. Shaull was fascinated by the life of Jesus and the demands of Christian discipleship portrayed by Sheldon; even at his young age, Shaull understood that to be a disciple of Jesus meant living for others and not for oneself.[10]

Shaull graduated from high school at age fourteen. He thought that after graduation he would tend livestock on the farm with his family, but

7. Ibid., 20.
8. Ibid., 16.
9. Ibid., 17.
10. Ibid., 18.

his mother found a small college in a nearby town for him to attend. Shaull applied successfully for one of the scholarships Elizabethtown College offered for rural youth like him, but as a fourteen-year-old college student he found himself even more out of place than he had been at high school. At the time Shaull attended Elizabethtown College was an institution with an Anabaptist tradition that combined a pietistic faith with education and a strong social concern. For a Presbyterian boy who criticized his pastor for delivering boring sermons, Elizabethtown College was a new and refreshing experience.[11] With two-hundred-fifty students enrolled, classes were small and the professors could give attention to the students that guaranteed a good formation in Latin, Greek, and Literature. But what captured Shaull's loyalty was sociology, particularly thanks to George Weller, a new professor who had just graduated from the University of Chicago and promoted the new liberal social theories of the time.[12] Shaull found in Elizabethtown College a religious spirit and a simple lifestyle marked by the radical tradition of non-violence and discipleship. He found a spirituality that was cemented in social justice and a radical decision to follow Jesus.

When Shaull graduated from the sociology department in 1938, he was not sure of what route he should follow. Teaching students of his same age in high school did not seem a good option, nor did going back to the farm. After some reflection, Shaull decided to apply to Princeton Theological Seminary and sample ministry as a vocation.

*Ministerial Training at Princeton Theological Seminary*

At the time Shaull arrived there, Princeton Seminary had gone through a major shift in its theology, following years of faculty dissension about what constituted doctrinal purity. As academic offspring of Archibald Alexander, Charles Hodge, and Benjamin Warfield, the faculty of Princeton was very conservative in their doctrinal standards. President J. Ross Stevenson along with professors Charles R. Erdman, Frederick Loetscher, John Davis, and J. Ritchie Smith placed the unity of the church above strict doctrinal orthodoxy and promoted tolerance of differences

11. Shaull, "Jesus e Marx," 48.
12. Shaull, *Surpreendido*, 25.

and liberty of interpretations. This inclusive stance increased the antagonism of other more conservative members of the faculty, Gresham Machen, Clarence Macartney, Robert Wilson, Caspar Hodge, William Greene, and Oswald Allis. The resentment in the faculty of the seminary increased to such a degree that the General Assembly of 1926 appointed a special committee to investigate the cause of the schisms within the seminary.[13]

After many years of turmoil and controversy, Princeton Seminary adopted a more inclusive position regarding doctrinal matters. President Stevenson's vision that the seminary would serve the entire church, rather than a sectarian group within it, prevailed. Many members of the faculty resigned from their positions in uproar over the decision for a more inclusive seminary and went on to form their own theological institution, Westminster Theological Seminary.

Shaull went to Princeton Seminary with enthusiasm but without a clear sense of vocation. He hoped to discover how to live his life as a Christian in the world and to be challenged by the intellectual vitality of the faculty. Nevertheless, the first year of studies turned out to be a disappointment to Shaull: "In the midst of that general despair Princeton in the main gave me little help. With notable exceptions, its attempts to force things down my throat and its tacit assumption of things I could not believe bored me. I was disgusted with it all."[14] Shaull began to look for other alternatives. He started attending classes and extracurricular activities at Princeton University and began to travel to New York during the weekends. Yet in the midst of his unhappiness with his studies in the first year, Shaull noticed that the new President wanted to improve the quality of the seminary. It was in John Alexander Mackay that Shaull encountered what he was looking for so desperately. Mackay's attitudes towards

---

13. Longfield, *Presbyterian Controversy*, 162; and Rian, *Presbyterian Conflict*, 71–80. Longfield points out, "The appointment of a special committee to study the 'conditions affecting the welfare of Princeton Seminary and the concurrent suspension of a decision on Machen's appointment to the chair of apologetics was but the culmination of the tensions growing at the seminary since 1920. Differences between the faculty, manifested in disagreements over the 1920 Plan of Union, the Van Dyke incident, the League of Evangelical Students, and the controversy in the church at large, threatened to undo the institution."

14. Shaull, "Application" The Colombia Mission, The Presbyterian Historical Society, Philadelphia. RG 360, Missionary Applications.

missions captivated him; he showed Shaull how the gospel of Jesus Christ was relevant to all areas of life. Shaull subsequently took both of the two courses Mackay taught: Christianity in Latin America, and Ecumenics. These in addition to Mackay's writings became the standard by which Shaull sought to measure himself.

Mackay had an impressive resume already before he arrived at Princeton Seminary as president. He had graduated from the University of Aberdeen in 1912 with a concentration in philosophy, received a fellowship to attend Princeton Theological Seminary, and graduated in 1915 from that institution. He wanted to pursue further studies in Germany, but due to the First World War it was impossible for him to make any arrangements to study there. One of his mentors at Princeton, B. B. Warfield, advised him to consider Spain as an option because Mackay had expressed his desire to be a missionary in Latin America. Mackay went to Spain and studied under one of the greatest Spanish existentialists and mystics, Miguel de Unamuno. In 1916 he married Jane Logan Wells. Soon after that Mackay and his bride went to Lima, Perú, where he served as an educational missionary. There he founded the prestigious school Colegio Anglo-Peruano later named Colegio San Andrés. In Perú he was invited to be a professor of philosophy at the oldest Latin American university, San Marcos University, which had been established in 1551. From 1925 to 1929, Mackay was a Christian worker for the YMCA, which allowed him to write and lecture constantly throughout Latin America.[15] In 1936, Robert Speer, chair of the Board of Trustees, invited him to become the new president of Princeton Theological Seminary.

Mackay struggled with whether he should leave the mission field to be involved in administrative work. Nevertheless, a "Methodist friend" persuaded him to envision the theological seminary as a new kind of mission field, which he did.[16] His presidential inaugural address revealed Mackay's agenda for theological education at Princeton Seminary: "The primary and most important function of a theological seminary is to prepare heralds of the Gospel and shepherds of souls. This function is worthily discharged when the seminary makes adequate provision for the progress of its students in bearing piety and learning . . . Neither of these

15. Latourette, *World Service*, 211.
16. Gillette, "John A. Mackay," 33.

can be a substitute for the other in a Christian minister."[17] The emphasis of piety and service, of prayer and action, of evangelism and social concern marked the new administration of Mackay at Princeton. His emphasis on piety and learning for the service of the church created a vision of the seminary as an ecumenical community dedicated to the purposes of God in missionary activity.

Shaull remembered that Mackay in his course on ecumenics treated all aspects of the life of the church in light of his calling to participate in the mission of God in the world.[18] More than anything else, it was the course on ecumenics that inspired Shaull to become a missionary to Latin America. Admitted Shaull, Mackay's "amazing vision and understanding of the dimensions of God's redemptive activity provided me with a new perspective for understanding the Gospel, the Church and the world, and I was gradually led to discover my own vocation in the mission of the Church by the irresistible logic of his argument and by the power of the conviction which he himself lived."[19]

When Shaull was in his second year of studies at Princeton Seminary, he enrolled in a course on Revelation offered by the visiting Swiss theologian Emil Brunner. Brunner was a prominent figure in the ecumenical movement and also worked as theological advisor for the Young Men's Christian Association. Brunner captured Shaull's attention by making Christianity real and appealing. Said Shaull, "He knocked down my little idols, showed me that I should not judge a religion by the exaggerations of its great truths, and challenged me to a decision."[20]

Brunner was best known for his collaboration in the formulation of dialectical or crisis theology. After the First World War, the hopes of the liberal program based on the "Fatherhood of God" and the "Brotherhood of man" were shattered. A new historical consciousness known as neo-orthodoxy emerged in the theological movement. For Brunner the crisis of theology was the liberal understanding of the immanence of God in the world. Such crisis was an illness but also a turning point. Against the liberal theology constructed in Germany that saw the successful and self-confident democratic, industrial, and scientific revolutions as the highest

17. Mackay, "Role of Princeton," 1.

18. Shaull, *Surpreendido*, 31.

19. Shaull, "John A. Mackay," 22.

20. Shaull, "Application," RG 360, Missionary Applications.

accomplishments of humanity, Brunner perceived that such cultural accomplishments should not dictate the course of theological discourse.

Brunner perceived the substance of Christian theology, the content of Christian faith, to be in complete disarray. He insisted that "Christianity is either faith in the revelation of God in Jesus Christ or it is nothing."[21] Brunner emphasized the transcendence of God as opposed to any real knowledge of God in nature. He developed a natural theology, but it was absolutely subordinated to the revelation of God in Jesus Christ. As God created the world, every living thing revealed its creator. There was a God-given imprint in all of creation, the *imago Dei*. Believing that the *imago Dei* had been destroyed in human beings, and that the possibility of goodness was absent from humans, Brunner insisted that the doctrine of the image of God was subject to two interpretations: "one formal and one material."[22] Since humanity was the measurement of the formal imprint of God, humans had not ceased to be the central demonstration of love in the action of creation, even if they were sinners. All that God made was impressed by God with the stamp of God's being; creation was at the same time the revelation and the sharing of God. Nevertheless, natural theology was barren in the face of God's revelation in Jesus Christ.

According to Brunner, the revelation of God in Jesus Christ was not rooted in the historical Jesus, but rather in the Christ of faith. In this sense, Christ provided the total meaning for human existence in the faith of the resurrected one who was conscious of the love of God in his being. It was evident that neo-orthodoxy was a reaction against liberalism, but it did not break completely with that tradition because it accepted the scientific methods of the times in interpreting Christianity. In this sense, scholars were interested in the preaching of the church about the risen Jesus who could only be known by faith. Brunner stated, "It has been clearly shown that the liberal portraits of Jesus are not true to the facts in the sources . . . We accept the historian's portraits of him, well knowing that a generally accepted portrait does not yet exist."[23] For Shaull the encounter with the resurrected Christ challenged him to deepen his faith, not in the picture of the man from Nazareth who came to do good, but in the figure of the Jesus who was convinced that he was the Messiah, the Son of God, sent by

21. Brunner, *Theology of Crisis*, 2.

22. Brunner, *Natural Theology*, 23.

23. Brunner, *Theology of Crisis*, 11.

God the Father as the Savior of the world.[24] It was the Christ of faith who confronted Shaull to make a decision to follow him in faith for the rest of his life. In this sense, neo-orthodoxy would be one of the theological tools Shaull used to interpret the world in Latin America.

Even though John Mackay and Emil Brunner influenced the theological and ministerial formation of Shaull in his second year of seminary, Shaull's most influential encounter was with Josef L. Hromadka, a Czech pastor and theologian from the University of Prague. Josef Hromadka was born in Northern Moravia on June 28, 1889, and studied theology from 1907 to 1912 in the universities of Vienna, Basel, Heidelberg, and Aberdeen. He obtained a PhD from Charles University in 1920. From 1920 to 1938 he was the first professor of theology at the newly established Hus Faculty of Protestant Theology in Prague.[25] Due to his opposition to German Nazism, he had to leave Czechoslovakia in 1939, traveling via Geneva to the United States. In the United States, Hromadka was appointed as guest professor in the Stuart Chair of Apologetics and Christian Ethics at Princeton Seminary.

The missionary approach in theological education that began with Brunner's course on Revelation continued with Hromadka's courses on the Theology of Crisis, which he offered every year until his departure in 1947. Shaull enrolled for all the courses taught by Hromadka, appreciating that what he taught his students also formed the foundation of his own life and struggle. One of the distinctive aspects of Hromadka's theology, according to Josef Smolik, was its contextual character.[26]

Shaull remembered that in 1940 he and some of his classmates were becoming aware of the magnitude of the disruption occurring in Europe. He was alarmed by the growing influence of Fascism and Nazism there. Hromadka was influential in explaining to his North American students the developments that had caused the First World War, and when they were not resolved, how they led to the Second World War. For Hromadka there was a far deeper reality than just the division of the world between Western liberal democracies and Eastern theocratic empires: namely, the division between the poor and rich, between the haves and have-nots, be-

24. Shaull, *Alternativa ao Desespêro*, 28.

25. Opocenský, "Profile of a Teacher," 11.

26. Smolik, "Josef Lukl Hromadka," 7–10.

tween the victors and the vanquished. Poverty with its cruel degradations was the real beast that was fomenting a world revolution.

Hromadka helped Shaull to look critically, as a Christian, at his own North American culture, politics, and society, as well as the system of values undergirding them. Shaull's ecclesiology also was strengthened by Hromadka's theology. For Hromadka, the church was called to face the world in its ambiguity and show it a new direction. Hromadka was a theologian who understood that theology and the church were called to struggle for humanity in its deepest longings for liberation and self-realization.[27]

After finishing his ministerial training, Shaull decided to give his life in missionary service to Latin America. However, because Shaull was too young, the Board decided to appoint him to a one year pastoral internship to a Mexican-American congregation in Wink, TX. It is not clear when Shaull married his college girlfriend, Mildred Miller, but she was already with him in Wink.[28] It was probable that they married right after Shaull finished his studies at Princeton Seminary. After a year at Wink, in 1942 the Shaulls were sent to the Colombia Mission.

## Richard Shaull's First Missionary Assignment to Colombia, 1942–1950

David W. Hamblin in his dissertation points out that "a template personality is required in order to leave one's relations, culture and nation for the sake of promoting an ideology on foreign shores."[29] What Hamblin meant by "template personality" was the qualities modeled and guided by a person with a particular vision of how to change the world. Richard Shaull represented that special personality. Shaull's life was profoundly marked from the beginning by a radical acknowledgement of the sovereignty of God in history. From his early adolescence, Shaull experienced in his Bible readings a God who was present in the affairs of the world. Together with the Bible, the social gospel novel *In His Steps* generated in him a deep conviction of Jesus' radical call to discipleship, and the neces-

27. Hromadka, *Thoughts of a Czech Pastor,* 62–65.

28. Shaull, *Surpreendid,* 32–33.

29. Hamblin, "Social History," 71.

sity for humanity's total surrender to that call. Shaull had suffered first hand from the lack of material possessions during the Great Depression. This opened his eyes to the reality of poverty in the world, and challenged him to struggle to create conditions of justice. His college years with the Mennonites helped him to understand the church as a community of believers more than as a mere institution. His studies of sociology facilitated an understanding of how society works politically and economically. Shaull's seminary training under Mackay, Brunner, and Hromadka prepared him to face the world with the conviction that the heart of the universe was the grace of God, and that such grace was God's presence and activity in the midst of human life.

When Shaull arrived in Colombia in 1942, he intended "to build up a weak church, to develop a strong youth movement, and to establish new theological initiatives for evangelistic work."[30] In 1942, there were only three single female missionaries in Barranquilla: Ruth W. Bradley, Miriam B. Dickason, and Lois Blair. Together with the other new missionaries, the Van Eatons, the mission now had seven workers. Shaull's first assignment was to teach religion at the boys' school, but because he wanted to work in the churches, the Mission commissioned him to be a missionary-evangelist and pastor of the Barrio Arriba church.

One thing that differentiated Shaull from the rest of missionaries was his sensitivity to the extreme situations of poverty around him. On his first night as a missionary in Colombia, while walking to the hotel, Shaull had to pass by a number of children who were in the street covered with newspapers to protect themselves from the cold. It was an encounter with poverty and deprivation that would stay with him and spur him to create a better world through the gospel of Jesus Christ.[31] For example, when Shaull went to Cartagena, the first thing that impressed him was the poverty of the church members there. Nearly all of them came from the poorest class which would have considered a family income of $50 a month luxurious. Yet, these people with all their hardships built their own chapels, and even though they were without an ordained minister for over ten years they were still faithful to the Presbyterian Church.[32] Early

30. Shaull "Dying to Live," 8.

31. Shaull, *Surpreendido*, 38.

32. Shaull to the Barranquilla Mission, March 16, 1943. The Colombia Mission, The Presbyterian Historical Society, Philadelphia. RG 88 Box 1, Folder 9.

in his life Shaull developed a distrust of his own thought as well as that of others unless it was worked out in the midst of concrete human struggles, and in close association with women and men who were experiencing that reality most intensely.

Incarnational Ministry: Industrial Evangelism to Union Workers

As a student of John A. Mackay, Shaull certainly would have learned about industrial evangelism in the ecumenics class at Princeton Seminary. Industrial evangelism was prompted by the Stockholm Conference of Life and Work in 1925 whose purpose was to unify Christians in a world torn apart by World War I. They proposed to do this through common practical work in which the Gospel would address all realms of life.[33] With this in mind, the Universal Conference of Life and Work was divided into six subjects: 1) the purpose of God for humanity and the duty of the churches; 2) the church and economic and industrial problems; 3) the church and social and moral problems; 4) the church and Christian education; 5) the church and international relations; and 6) methods of cooperation and federative efforts by Christian communities.[34]

As the Stockholm Conference affirmed the Christian responsibility of all believers to engage all realms of life, the increasing problem of industrialism and its aftermath became a prominent concern of Christians.[35] Stockholm was an attempt to erase the false dichotomy between the spiritual and the material realms; many considered the spiritual realm to be exclusively concerned with the salvation of the soul and the material realm to be concerned with the world of business and politics. Rarely had these two realms been considered as complementary but that changed at Stockholm when the church rediscovered its prophetic mandate to be in solidarity with all of humanity. Elie Gounelle, a delegate from France, put out the call: "Let us humanize the social order by the teaching, the life and the spirit of Jesus Christ. To Christianize means humanize in its fullest meaning."[36]

33. Visser't Hooft, "Historical Significance," 1–8.
34. Bell, *Stockholm*, 2.
35. Ehrenstrom, "Movements," 550.
36. Gounelle, "Man and Property," 162.

The theme of industrial evangelism was again extensively considered at the Jerusalem Conference of the International Missionary Council of 1928. Three preliminary papers were written for study before the conference: William Paton, secretary of the International Missionary Council, wrote a long introductory study of industrialism in Asia and Africa.[37] Samuel Guy Inman, Secretary of the Committee on Cooperation in Latin America, wrote an essay on "Missions and Economics in Latin America," while H. A. Grimshaw, Chief of the Native Labor Section of the International Labor Office of Geneva, wrote on "Industrial Revolution among Primitive Peoples."[38] Two addresses on the topic were delivered at the conference, the first by R. H. Tawney, lecturer at the London School of Economics, on "The Bearing of Christianity on Social and Industrial Questions," and the second by Bishop F. J. McConnell, from the Board of Foreign Missions from the Methodist Episcopal Church on "Christianity and Industrialism."[39]

Timothy Yates, a leading figure in British mission studies, referred to Tawney's address as a "masterly piece of advocacy for Christian commitment to the economic and social structures of national and international life."[40] One thing was clear to all these men: Christ was the answer for the increasing problems caused by the inequalities of the industrial revolution. The formal statement on the subject by the council proclaimed,

> The International Missionary Council desires to preface its report on industrial conditions by asserting, with all the power of its command, its conviction that the Gospel of Christ contains a message, not only for the individual soul, but for the world of social organization and economic relations in which individuals live. Christ came that men might have life, and might have it more abundantly.[41]

Following the previous declarations of the Stockholm Conference in denouncing as misleading the antithesis between individual and social regeneration, the participants at the Jerusalem Conference considered

---

37. Paton, "Christianity," 9–114.
38. Inman, "Missions;" 117–45.
39. Ibid.
40. Yates, *Christian Mission*, 66.
41. Council, "Christ the Lord," 181.

that the task of the church was to "carry the message of Christ to the individual soul . . . and to lend its support to all forces which bring nearer the establishment of Christ's Kingdom in the world of social relations, of industrial organizations, and of economic life."[42]

It was in conversation with the ecumenical background of industrial evangelism that Shaull understood the great opportunity that the Montecristo neighborhood presented by being only blocks away from all the major factories of the city. Montecristo was a center of workers' activities and labor unions. Thus, despite the Mission's opposition, one of Shaull's first radical decisions was to move from the comfort of his house in the exclusive Prado neighborhood of Barranquilla to a seven-room house in Montecristo, one of the city's poorest neighborhoods. They divided the house, taking just one bedroom, the living room, and the kitchen for their personal use, leaving the rest of the house to be used for mission purposes.[43] On Monday and Thursday nights they operated a school for adults, offering six English classes. On Friday nights, the Shaulls conducted a religious service to which the entire community was invited. By the end of the first month, the night school had increased from ten attendees to more than eighty.[44] This project was a family affair with Shaull's wife, Mildred, completely involved in the development of the work. Shaull also recruited three youths from Central Church, who took on responsibility and taught English, reading, writing, and arithmetic, and organized clubs for boys and girls. One year later this small initiative had grown to a full-fledged project with its own building and national staff.

From this humble initiative, a whole social program evolved named The Centro Evangélico Obrero. It was not only a place where workers could learn how to read and write; it offered emancipatory possibilities for women as well. Under Mildred Shaull, women took classes on cooking, housekeeping, sewing, child-care, and nutrition.[45] They formed their

42. Ibid., 184.

43. Personal Report of Shaull the Barranquilla Station, January 1943, The Colombia Mission, The Presbyterian Historical Society, Philadelphia. RG 88, Box 2, Folder 6.

44. Ibid.

45. Personal Report of Mildred Shaull to the Barranquilla Station 1943, The Colombia Mission, The Presbyterian Historical Society, Philadelphia. RG 88, Box 2, Folder 6. Mildred was a well educated woman. She earned a B.S. in education and a B.A. in French with a minor in Sociology. Mildred Shaull to Angel Santiago, February 13, 2006. Letter in the authors' files.

own network of women who wanted to increase their possibilities in life. By 1945, the Shaulls had arranged for a doctor to have a permanent office in the building. Mildred attested that "people came from miles to see the doctor, men are enthusiastic to learn how to read, and every night religious services were held with an attendance last night of three-hundred-fifty."[46] From its small beginnings, the Centro Evangélico Obrero grew into a full-blown project that helped the whole community in its particular social context. Shaull went beyond what previous missionaries had done by entrusting much of the leadership of the work to national workers. The center was such a success that Shaull was named honorary president of one of the Workers' Unions of Montecristo.[47] By 1946, the center was completely operated by national workers and the Shaulls had little involvement in it when they went for their furlough. After stabilizing the situation in the three major churches of Barranquilla through a renewal in evangelism and social work, Shaull moved on to new missionary ventures.

Incarnational Ministry: The Presbyterian Youth of Colombia

Shaull worked with the Presbyterian Colombian Youth as a theological advisor. He was a teacher in several camp meetings, conferences, and discipleship programs during his years in Barranquilla. Because he saw in the youth the heart of the Colombian Presbyterian Church and the youth saw in him a person aware of their country's social reality who could guide them in their spiritual journeys, Shaull dedicated his time and energies to strengthen the youth for ministry. Also, the fact that Shaull himself was quite young, probably twenty-four years old in 1944, was a feature that helped him to strengthen ties with the Colombian youth in their evangelistic work.

His plan of action was centered on empowering a new generation of young people who were committed to the radical calling of being a disciple of Jesus Christ. "Feeling that our main task is to challenge men and women to surrender their lives to Jesus Christ, receive his help in

46. Ibid.

47. Leber, "Young Man," 49–55. Leber pointed out that the Shaull's work was, "In fact, so vital and far reaching among laboring men, particularly that, in tribute to Dick's life and influence, a labor union in Barranquilla elected Shaull (a North American Protestant missionary!) Honorary President!"

their problems and give their lives in his service, we have set as our goal the organization of new groups in the various barrios of the city," he wrote.[48] Shaull had organized the youth of the three major churches of Barranquilla, training them to be local evangelists. There was no doubt in Shaull's mind that the local churches should be the center about which all evangelistic work should be organized and directed. As a result, the youth of the three churches followed up most of the evangelistic work that Shaull initiated. Shaull created a strong national leadership, which other missionaries had failed to do.

In efforts to continue to empower Colombian youths he tried to unite them during several camp retreats and conferences. This type of evangelism which gathered youths from different social and economic backgrounds was something Shaull had learned from the Young Men's Christian Association (YMCA).[49] The YMCA was founded in London, England, on June 6, 1844 by a group of clerks in response to the conditions created by the Industrial Revolution. Soon the YMCA expanded to North America, and by 1860 there were 260 chapters throughout the nation.[50] The YMCA played a crucial role in the development of the North American missionary enterprise because in its meeting of 1886 "it launched the late nineteenth century North American student movement for foreign missions."[51]

The post World War II missionary movement had a big emphasis on campus ministry as Christians tried to reconnect with those parts of the world ravaged by war. During this period after the Second World War, a strong emphasis on campus ministry began in the United States not only in the YMCA but also among more conservative evangelical students such as the International Fellowship of Evangelical Students.[52] Interestingly enough, all of Shaull's influential teachers at Princeton Seminary—John Mackay, Emil Brunner, and Josef Hromadka—served in some capacity at the YMCA. Actually, it was the one and only John R. Mott, founder of the World Student Christian Federation and architect of the first ecumenical conference in Edinburgh in 1910, who convinced John Mackay

48. Ibid.

49. Jun Xing, *Baptized*.

50. Ahlstrom, *Religious History*, 742.

51. Robert, *Occupy*, 147.

52. Johnson, *Brief History*, 1964. Also, Escobar, *La Chispa*, 1978.

to assume the responsibility of being the representative of the YMCA for Latin America.[53] During his seven year tenure, Mackay worked tirelessly with students all over Latin America. Mackay said about the work of the YMCA in Latin America:

> They [YMCA and YWCA] were pioneers in teaching young manhood and young womanhood the meaning and necessity of healthy physical recreation. They provided social centers, organized classes on different subjects to meet the needs of their constituency, and arranged for all sorts of cultural events. Work was carried on in inner circles and in camps throughout the continent to make Christ and the Christian life real to youth. Very notable also has been the service both associations have rendered in inspiring their membership and whole communities to launch forth on diverse schemes of social welfare,—the care of delinquent boys, the shepherding of street waifs, and attach on the sexual and alcoholic problems, and interest in lonely immigrants lately arrived in a country. Both organizations have borne witness to a comprehensive and idealistic expression of religion in life. They have helped to give Latin America what Latin America has never had: the idea that all altruistic service is an integral part of the life of a true man or a true woman, and that the great master of all altruism is Jesus Christ.[54]

Once more, Mackay inspired Shaull to put into practice the egalitarian principles of evangelism delineated by the YMCA based on the interplay of Christianity and practical work within four major areas: physical, educational, social, and religious. Thus, Shaull was inspired by an ecumenical type of evangelism that focused in the whole realm of human existence. Committed to the cause of Christ, Shaull transplanted those ecumenical initiatives into the Colombian mission.

On Shaull's initiative, the youth of Cartagena and the Sinú Valley invited the youth of Barranquilla for the First Youth Conference of the Barranquilla station. After great preparations and the financial help of the Board of Foreign Missions in New York, which also sponsored Campus Ministry in the USA, twenty-one young people from the churches of Barranquilla undertook the voyage of their lives. When they arrived in Cartagena after three days of sailing down the Magdalena River, a group

53. Mackay, "Latin America," 1442.
54. Mackay, *That Other America*, 173–74.

of forty young people from Cartagena and the Sinú were waiting for them. The conference centered on the theme of the spiritual life of the youth and how to cultivate it. Shaull was the main speaker at the event.

There are no documents showing his sermons or Bible studies, but we can deduce from the official document of the Conference that the participants tried to discover the process of how conversion affects the life of youth, specially how it begins the spiritual life and a person's total consecration to Christ. Other themes at the Conference were cooperation and interdenominational relations in Colombia, and the responsibility of the Christian youth to face the problems of the contemporary world. Shaull was amazed by the results of this event, as he communicated in a letter to Dr. Seel, a field representative stationed in Bogotá:

> Long have I dreamed of a Christian community in which barriers of race, wealth, and social status would disappear, in which all be one in Christ. Last week I saw members of the three races live together in the same house, university graduates and boys who have never been inside of a school sit in the same class, sons of well-to-do families with boys from isolated rural areas who have never been to the city sleep on the same hard floor and eat of the same meat and rice. For the first time in my life I have really seen the power of Christ change lives of young people like this.[55]

Shaull's ministry was truly conciliatory in nature, and transcended social, economic, and racial lines. In this sense, Shaull took the practices of the YMCA and the whole ecumenical movement and translated them to the Colombian context.

Incarnational Ministry: Evangelism through Literacy

The ministry and vocation of Shaull were directed towards the less fortunate in society. His evangelistic techniques were rooted in the conviction that God was active in history redeeming humanity. Because of that conviction, he insisted that human beings could change their lot in life if they trusted the One who could help them to fulfill their potential. Shaull's eagerness to put into practice the gospel led him to collaborate with Frank

---

55. Shaull to Dr. E.G. Seel, August 9, 1943, The Colombia Mission, The Presbyterian Historical Society, Philadelphia. RG 88, Box 5, Folder 13.

Laubach in a literacy campaign for Latin America. Literacy was one of the biggest problems in Colombian society. In 1940, seventy percent of the population did not know how to read or write.[56] In the mind of such missionaries as Frank Laubach, the distinguished missionary to the Philippines, most of the shortcomings of poor people were tied to their incapacity to read or write. Laubach developed a new method and technique to teach reading by employing phonetics as a teaching and learning mechanism. In this system, once a person had learned how to read and write, he or she taught another person what he/she had learned—a principal of "each one teach one."[57]

After fourteen years of working as a missionary in the Philippines, Laubach was commissioned to work among the Muslim population of Mindanao. He soon realized that conventional methods of evangelization would not work with that group of people and decided to explore other methods. It could be argued that Laubach was one of the first proponents of Christian presence and dialogue as the way to evangelize the "Moros" of Mindanao. For example, he sought out the Muslim religious teachers and asked for their teachings on the *Koran*.[58] From there, the great literary campaign to the Moros of Mindanao began. Gowing stated that "by late 1932 the movement was averaging 3,000 new literates a month and Laubach's literary thermometer showed that 45,000 Lanao Moros had at least begun to read and write in Roman letters."[59] The method consisted of teaching the sounds of the letters as represented in the mother language of those learning. Laubach used one Roman letter for each sound in the Maranao language.[60] Even though Laubach talked about the silent billion, his approach was personal.[61] He insisted that the missionaries or teachers using his method should love their students first and foremost: "You must learn to love people, not for what they are now, but for what you know you can help them become. Personally, I tried always to pray for my stu-

---

56. Dr. Edward G. Seel to L.K. Anderson, November 17, 1940. The Colombia Mission, The Presbyterian Historical Society, Philadelphia. RG 88, Box 9, Folder 7.

57. Gowing, "Frank Charles Laubach," 505.

58. Ibid., 503.

59. Ibid., 504.

60. Laubach, *Toward World Literacy*, 3.

61. Laubach, *Forty Years*.

dent, conjuring the finest dream I can imagine for him, wondering what God would make out of this man if he had a perfect chance."[62]

Laubach was invited to the congress of the World's Sunday School in Mexico City in 1941 to present his method in Latin America. The Colombian mission was the first place Laubach visited in his Latin American tour. Shaull lamented that Laubach was in Barranquilla at carnival time. The whole town was involved in the festivities and the government was closed for the week. Nevertheless, Laubach gave a seminar to the youth of the churches in Barranquilla and Cartagena. From this seminar, Shaull organized small groups and sent them into small towns around the city. Once there, the teachers chose from among their students those most qualified to continue the work.

Shaull believed that if that work were successful "it would give us [Presbyterians] a very open field for the propagation of our faith."[63] He was convinced that the Presbyterian Church needed to be at the vanguard of this project. From its inception, Shaull collaborated with government authorities to accomplish his plan. For example, in Cartagena where 65% of adults were unable to read, the local authorities were trying to pass a law forbidding anyone who did not know how to read and write after six or eight months from working in any industry. When Shaull visited the government officials, they were impressed by the Laubach method. They invited Shaull to address all the teachers in Cartagena and organize groups of students in the public and Catholic schools to do the teaching. The government of Cartagena also published 20,000 copies of the literary primer.

In the Sinú region, where 85% of the population was illiterate, and the Presbyterian Church had its biggest constituency, literary work was instituted by a group of young people from Barranquilla.[64] After Shaull's proposal for funds, The Board of Foreign Missions in New York approved a grant of $1200 to the Barranquilla station to be used in literary work. With that money Shaull started a massive campaign and hired Enrique del Real, a Colombian graduate from the boys school, as full-time worker. The work of Shaull was changing from that of an evangelist engaged

62. Laubach, *Toward World Literacy*, 36.

63. Shaull to L.K. Anderson, January 3, 1943. The Colombia Mission, The Presbyterian Historical Society. RG 88, Box 9, Folder 9.

64. Ibid.

in hands-on work to counselor, operating behind the scenes, directing things, and offering suggestions. Del Real continued the campaign visiting government officials, missionaries and national workers from other denominations.[65]

Literacy work in Colombia was a success, generating stories such as the one Shaull told about Margarita, a servant who did not know how to read. "By the end of the week," he reported, "after a total of three hours of classes, she was reading the headlines of the newspaper. But best of all, the poor, shy, retiring girl, ashamed of her ignorance, suddenly began to have confidence in herself."[66] Shaull was confident that God could change the human condition for the better in a holistic way. In this sense, his missiology continued to be guided by the principle that God as revealed in Jesus Christ was the answer for all realms of human existence.

Incarnational Ministry:
Shaull's Plan for the Ministerial Formation of Nationals

The training of national workers was always a big preoccupation and problem for the Colombian mission. Many missionaries took initiatives in solving the problem, including Rev. Candor, one of the pioneers of the Colombian mission, who opened a small Bible Institute that graduated the first class of Colombian leaders in 1919. Then, after the Bible Institute closed, the Industrial and Agricultural Bible Training School opened its doors and graduated its first class in 1929. The failure of the Colombian mission to train national leaders throughout its history could be blamed on the missionaries' inability to establish a first-class training center. There were several reasons for this failure: first, there were few missionaries who could dedicate their time and energy to training national workers since most missionaries were consumed by the work of educating the middle- and upper- classes through their schools named *Colegios Americanos*. Second, there were insufficient funds from the general offices in New York

65. Shaull to The Board of Foreign Missions of the Presbyterian Church USA, June 5, 1945, The Colombia Mission, The Presbyterian Historical Society, Philadelphia. RG 88, Box 6, Folder 1.

66. Shaull to The Board of Foreign Missions of the Presbyterian Church USA, November 15, 1944, The Colombia Mission, The Presbyterian Historical Society, Philadelphia. RG 88, Box 6, Folder 1.

to employ more people. Third, not many people in the local churches wanted to enter the ministry because of the inadequate salaries.

Before Shaull's arrival in Barranquilla, the salaries of national leaders were never discussed in official meetings. The first wave of national workers was extremely frustrated with the missionaries for their lack of vision in creating a fairer financial set-up. For example, when Rev. Libreros, a national worker from the Sinú Valley, told Shaull in 1944 that he was resigning his position, he gave the following reasons: first, he felt that neither the mission nor the national church had taken any interest in his work nor helped him in any way; and second, his wife refused to live in the house unless it was repaired.[67]

The pastor of Barrio Arriba, Rev. Hernández, faced similar economic problems when the Mission refused to contribute half of his salary. He resigned from his post in 1941. This explains why the church of Barrio Arriba was without a pastor for two years before Shaull was appointed as interim minister. Because of the inequalities in salaries, hardly any national worker encouraged the young men of his congregation to enter the ministry. Shaull alluded to the example of Rev. Escorcia who stood up on the floor of the Mission Conference and said, "I would encourage no young men of my church to become a minister."[68] In addition to the national workers' frustration over compensation, the young people lacked confidence in the missionaries' skills as thinkers and teachers. Shaull stated: "The young people are skeptical of a course set up by missionaries. They like to think for themselves, listen to positive teaching and drawing their own conclusions, while they are convinced that nearly all missionaries are terribly dogmatic."[69] Once again using the liberal's tool for social change, Shaull endeavored to create the first center of Protestant higher education in Colombia.

Under Shaull's initiative, a program of studies equivalent to seminary began. In the first year of operations, the Theological Faculty had three students (Gilberto Torres, Fortunato Castillo, and Javier Zárate) and four faculty members (Shaull, Rev. and Mrs. Van Eaton, and Rev. Escorcia).

67. Juan Libreros to Shaull, November 2, 1944, The Colombia Mission, The Presbyterian Historical Society, Philadelphia. RG 88, Box 15, Folder 2.

68. Shaull to L.K. Anderson, November 14, 1944, The Colombia Mission, The Presbyterian Historical Society, Philadelphia. RG 88, Box 4, Folder 14.

69. Ibid.

Van Eaton was the treasurer and Mrs. Van Eaton was the professor of advanced English. The whole training of the new students was under the direction of Shaull. The courses on church history were: History of Christianity, The Reformation, The Spanish Mystics and Reformers, and The Christian Church in the Last Two Centuries. Shaull also taught the following theological courses: Introduction to the Theology of Crisis, Theological Anthropology, Experience and Christian Faith (an analysis of religious experience which forms the basis for theology), The Person and Work of Christ, and Comparative Religions (a comparison of the non-Christian religions and Christian faith, the Catholic Church and the Protestant, and of various denominations and evangelical sects). Shaull also offered two courses on ethics: Principles of Christian Ethics and The Challenge of the Contemporary World to the Church.[70] The other innovation of the course of studies was that students were taught in the morning, with afternoons free for evangelistic work. By the third semester of studies, Gilberto Torres was in charge of Barrio Arriba church and Fortunato Castillo was the pastor of the church of Barrio Boston.

Shaull brought to Colombia a new missiology rooted in the conviction that God was active in history and that therefore it was imperative for new Christians to adopt the same tenacious attitude of self-denial and commitment to the cause of Christ. Shaull's theology tried to put into practice the social implications of the Christian faith not only serving the world, but also bringing new policies into effect that improved the living conditions of national workers.

Incarnational Ministry: Christian Spirituality and Social Transformation

Richard Shaull was convinced that true and full human existence would only be accomplished to the degree to which humans surrendered themselves to Christ, received help from him to confront the struggles of daily life, and then, committed themselves to the service of God who called and confronted individuals to make a decision.[71] Shaull's conviction of the in-

70. Anuncio de la Facultad Evangélica de Teología, Misión Presbiteriana, 1944. The Colombia Mission, The Presbyterian Historical Society, Philadelphia. RG 88, Box 2, Folder 8.

71. Personal Report of Shaull, 1944, The Colombia Mission, The Presbyterian Historical Society, Philadelphia. RG 88, Box 2, Folder 7.

tervention of God in human affairs guided him to construct a spirituality based on the new life in Christ. It was not a surprise that when it was time to leave for the United States for his first furlough, Shaull took a course of study at Princeton Seminary under John Mackay.

His thesis was a comparative study of the spirituality of Teresa de Avila and John Bunyan.[72] Shaull believed that the core of biblical faith was Christian piety. His Reformed perspective on salvation pointed to the encounter of God with humans as a struggle which was destined to end in surrender and forgiveness. Out of forgiveness, humans entered into an intimate fellowship with Christ, and it was out of this fellowship with Christ that humans surrendered completely to the divine power for Christian service.[73]

After a description of Teresa de Avila's book *The Mansions* and John Bunyan's *The Holy War*, Shaull analyzed their concept and practice of piety. Shaull expounded the similarities between the two saints: 1) God confronted them in such a way that they could not escape God's calling; 2) a terrific struggle ensued after this encounter; 3) Christ became for them the central reality of life; 4) Christ developed in them a new quality of life which made them stand out as superior Christian personalities; and 5) both of them lived on a higher plane and did great things for God because a divine power had entered into their souls. At the same time, he contrasted the two saints' understanding of salvation. Teresa saw Jesus Christ as the Lover within a darkened castle and Bunyan saw him as the Lord outside a rebellious town. Teresa followed the traditional Roman Catholic concept of the entrance of the soul into the Christian life, while Bunyan understood the total depravity of the soul in need of redemption as coming from outside itself.[74] Shaull's critique of both saints was "their failure to do justice to the *new men in Christ* to his neighbor and his world."[75] However, a criticism against Shaull could be that he did not take into consideration the historical context of Teresa who was in a convent and Bunyan who was in prison. Both of them were in isolated contexts in which meditation in the inner self was attuned to their reality.

72. Shaull, "Power of God."
73. Ibid., 1–15.
74. Ibid., 59–81.
75. Ibid., 79.

The old individualistic paradigm of pietistic spirituality was not an option for Shaull. He understood that a true spirituality was formed in everyday life with God and neighbor: "We have conceived the spiritual struggle as bipolar—between God and the individual soul, whereas in reality, it is impossible to understand the spiritual life without three poles—God, self and neighbor."[76] Existence for Shaull was existence with and for others. In this sense, the spiritual quest was a communal activity in which individuals were united to Christ and one another. Shaull envisioned the church as a *koinonia*, a group of believers sharing a common cause and goal in life: the Kingdom of God. For Shaull the intimate fellowship of the group of believers stimulated Christians to a higher ethical life.[77] According to Shaull, "true piety will lead not only to the transformation of the individual but also of collective life; that it is, in fact, the most powerful force for the remaking of society and civilization."[78] The mystical experience provided a guideline for the fulfillment of Christian ethics because this represented "the power of God in the life of man."

Incarnational Ministry:
Human Rights Advocate in the Midst of Persecution

When Shaull returned from his furlough in 1946, the political and religious situation was taking a turn for the worse. Liberals had lost the elections and a new Conservative regime was being established. The Liberal party was divided in the nomination of their candidate for the elections of 1946. The right wing of the party wanted to continue the oligarchy and the status quo. In their political quest they supported Gabriel Turbay, a Colombian of Lebanese descent. The party's left wing was headed by Jorge Eliécer Gaitán. For Gaitán, the greatest enemy was not the Conservative party but rather the oligarchy in both parties. According to Bushnell, "Gaitán accused both the Liberal oligarchs and Conservative oligarchs who competed for the spoils and prestige of office while ignoring the needs of the people and were in fact bound to each other in an unwrit-

76. Ibid., 90.
77. Shaull "Conversion," 505.
78. Ibid.

ten, unholy alliance precisely to head off meaningful change."[79] Gaitán's ideology transcended the boundaries of any party system controlled by the oligarchy. For him, class struggle was inevitable because the interests of the dominant class and that of the proletariat were in conflict since the dominant class maintained its power by coercion.

The division among the followers of Turbay and the followers of Gaitán allowed the Conservative party to elect its candidate, Mariano Ospina Pérez with only 42% of the vote. As Gaitán promoted his reformist views within the Liberal party, it was obvious that he would be the candidate for the elections of 1948. Party violence arose as in previous periods, but this time it was mostly instigated by the Conservatives who wanted to settle old scores with the previous administration. As violence increased, on April 9, 1948, Jorge Eliécer Gaitán was gunned down while leaving his office for lunch. The assassination of Gaitán caused a chain-reaction of frenzied violence. The masses were without their leader and they were confused and frustrated with the political conditions of the nation. It is estimated that in the period of La Violencia (1946-1958) more than 200,000 persons lost their lives. Subsequently, the Conservative regime became a semi-dictatorship under Laureano Gómez who ruled the nation until 1957.[80]

Meanwhile, the sentiment of many sectors within the Roman Catholic Church was captured in the dissertation of Eugenio Restrepo Uribe in 1944, "El Protestantismo en Colombia" [Protestantism in Colombia]. In the foreword, Juan Restrepo Jaramillo, Dean of the Theological Faculty of the Universidad Javeriana, described Protestantism as a hazard that affected the safety of the religious patrimony of the Roman Catholic Church in Colombia and its national unity. In the dissertation, Restrepo Uribe presented Protestantism as an infection that needed to be extirpated from Colombian soil.[81] Restrepo offered the following remedies to accomplish the extermination of Protestantism in Colombia: first, the Roman Catholic Church should ask the endorsement of the government to impede its spread; and second, the Roman Catholic Church should form a national anti-Protestant movement.[82] The government was again

79. Bushnell, *Making of Modern Colombia*, 198.

80. Borda, *Violencia*, 23–38.

81. Uribe, "Protestantismo," 129.

82. Ibid., 131–36.

allying itself with the Roman Catholic Church with the purpose of controlling the masses and the political future of the nation. In this context of political and religious turmoil, the Presbyterian Bogotá station was facing serious schisms between religious liberals and conservatives.

In 1946, the situation in the Bogotá station became chaotic when national workers accused a missionary of having corrupted the youth and having promoted doctrinal heresy. The main moral problem was that Rev. Winston W. Thomas was allowing Colombian youth to dance in his house. The doctrinal scandal was that Rev. Thomas did not adhere to biblical inerrancy, the virgin birth of Christ, and the substitutionary death of Jesus as atonement for sins. Pastor Martinez accused Thomas of being a wolf in sheep's clothing. He stated,

> When the enemy attacks openly from without, he is not so dangerous, not so much to be feared. But when the wolf, disguised in sheep's clothing, enters, then is the time to fear. And this very thing is happening in some missions. The enemy is introducing himself so cleverly that in the majority of cases, he has been received with open arms. The greatest enemy of Christ is the one who takes upon himself to publish criticisms in order to ridicule and to blacken the good name of the work others are doing to advance the Kingdom of God.[83]

The real issue that Thomas faced was the old question of the historic tradition of Presbyterian freedom versus ecclesiastical authority to secure conformity and ensure the status quo. Many Presbyterian missionaries were made from the old mold and showed an intransigent spirit of intolerance and doctrinal rigidity. The Board in New York resolved the problem by taking Rev. Thomas out of his missionary post, which left the Presbyterian Church of Bogotá without a youth leader. In this context of increasing political and religious instability, Shaull was called to sort out an effective way to deal with the crisis at the Bogotá station.

Shaull's responsibilities were divided between Barranquilla and Bogotá. He continued in Barranquilla as adviser to the Presbyterian Youth, evangelist, and Clerk of the Synod. His duties in Bogotá were to be the pastor of the First Presbyterian Church in response to the crisis caused by the schism of 1946 over the Thomas incident. When the Board decided to send him to Bogotá to be the pastor of First Presbyterian, he

83. Martinez, "Obstacles," n.p.

was hesitant because "I do not want to see a gringo in that church, and I don't want to leave the coast."[84] Nevertheless, Shaull began an evangelistic campaign in Bogotá with the hope that he would revitalize the faith of its members. In the first year of his pastorate, Shaull received twenty-nine new members in the church with more than twenty who waited to receive confirmation classes.[85] As in Barranquilla, he continued the process of forming small evangelistic communities in the nearby villages with the help of the young people.

As in the nineteenth century when liberal political leaders asked missionaries for their help in forming schools and chapels with a Protestant religious character, modern liberal leaders were asking Shaull for religious advice. Good liberal that he was, Shaull believed in humans' capacities to change provided they had the necessary tools. Shaull formed a new group of businessmen and professional men who met weekly for lunch in the church basement and carried on a program of study, evangelism, and social services. The *Cristófilos* started with fifteen professional members of the First Presbyterian Church of Bogotá.[86] By the end of a year of meetings, more than one hundred men from the highest strata of Colombian society had received moral, ethical, and religious instruction from Shaull.[87] Among them was an ex-president of the nation, members of the National Committee of the Liberal party, one of the principal leaders of the Masonic lodge, and a young woman lawyer and writer who was very prominent in Bogotá.[88] Because this group of professionals had economic resources available to them, Shaull convinced them to invest their money and time in an evangelistic program in the town of El Carmen. They secured a site for night classes, educational movies, cultural conferences, medical consultations, and evangelistic services.[89] Because of his alliance with liberal progressives, Shaull's notoriety increased dramati-

84. Personal Report of Shaull, August 17, 1948, The Colombia Mission, The Presbyterian Historical Society, Philadelphia. RG 88, Box 2, Folder 8.

85. Shaull, "Evangelistic Report of the Bogotá Station 1948" The Colombia Mission, The Presbyterian Historical Society, Philadelphia. RG 88, Box 1, Folder 10.

86. Ordóñez, *Historia*, 50.

87. Personal Report of Shaull 1949, The Colombia Mission, The Presbyterian Historical Society, Philadelphia. RG 88, Box 2, Folder 8.

88. Ibid.

89. Ordóñez, *Historia*, 50.

cally in political circles. He was a friend and counselor to many leaders of the Liberal party who were members of the First Presbyterian Church and belonged to the *Cristófilos*.

One event marked that period of history as the beginning of tremendous unrest in the region. I have already noted that on April 9th, 1948 the leader of the Liberal party, Jorge E. Gaitán, was assassinated in front of his office. This precipitated a torrent of violence in the capital. A collective hysteria took hold of the masses as a result of frustration with the political instability of the nation and people took matters into their own hands. The crowds destroyed much of the infrastructure of Bogotá. Frank Wood, a Presbyterian missionary in Bogotá, stated,

> When the city was able to take stock on Sunday morning, it was found that hundreds of buildings had been gutted by fire, many building being just a shell; hundred of shops had been looted, scores of streets cars burned, and the center of the town today looks like the pictures we have seen of European cities bombed during the war.[90]

Political tensions grew worse and worse after this event and problems continued between Liberals and Conservatives. Because the Roman Catholic Church saw itself as losing ground when the Liberals were in power, the Catholic Church aligned itself with the Conservative party, thereby creating a siege of persecution in Colombia.[91] The master plan Eugenio Restrepo Uribe had outlined in his dissertation for the Universidad Javeriana in 1944 was becoming a reality. The national anti-Protestant movement was emerging with strong impetus in Colombia. The call to exterminate Protestantism was published in journal articles and promoted on the radio waves. Shaull came across a document entitled "Committee to Destroy Protestantism in Colombia" whose purpose was to give instructions to the local priest on how they could cooperate in an anti-Protestant campaign.[92] In the midst of the tragic events

90. Frank Wood, The Tragic Weekend of 1948, The Colombia Mission, The Presbyterian Historical Society, Philadelphia. RG 88, Box 8, Folder 2.

91. Goff, "Persecution."

92. Shaull, "Why Do Catholics Persecute Protestants in Colombia?" March 7, 1950, The Colombia Mission, The Presbyterian Historical Society, Philadelphia. (Unpublished paper) RG 88, Box 8, Folder 1. Shaull gave the following reasons as to why Catholics persecuted Protestants in Colombia. 1) The Roman Catholic Church was desperate. It

against Protestants in Colombia, Shaull accumulated information about cases of human rights violations and presented them to the Colombian authorities.

Shaull was appointed as the representative of the Presbyterian Mission responsible for bringing information on cases related to religious persecution to the Ministry of Justice of Colombia. The first case that Shaull reported to the Ministry of Justice was that of Aristomeno Porras Parada, pastor of the churches of Riomanso and Santa Helena. Both churches were closed by the government and Pastor Porras suffered great hostilities at the hands of the armed forces. The case was investigated by the authorities, who promised to resolve the problem. Shaull continued to gather information on all cases of religious persecution and brought them to the Department of Justice. From February to March 1950, Shaull gathered information on more than sixty cases of religious persecution ranging from the destruction of churches with dynamite, hostility toward evangelical pastors, intimidation by shooting at church buildings, confiscation of several pastors' evangelical books, the murder of an indigenous leader (Ventura Chavez), the closing of Protestant schools, and intimidation to get people to renounce the Protestant faith and embrace Catholicism.[93]

Shaull not only provided information to the Colombian Justice Department, but also to the Board of Foreign Missions in New York. In April, Daniel M. Pattison, Treasurer of the Board of Foreign Missions, circulated among U.S. Senators and the Sate Department the cases of religious persecution provided by Shaull. Suddenly, the United States media ran the story in most of the major newspapers of the nation. For example, the title of a column in the *New York Times* for Sunday, April 16, 1950, read: "Faith Persecution Laid to Colombia: Clerical—Political Attacks on Protestants are charged in Letter to Washington." In this article, Pattison is quoted as saying, "The situation instead of getting better

---

had lost its hold on the masses and was making one last supreme effort to save itself by destroying its enemies; and 2) From the Catholic point of view, Protestants had no right to propagate their faith and it was the responsibility of the civil government to help to control them.

93. Memorandum from the Director of Judicial Vigilance to the Ministry of International Relations about the Complaint of Protestants related with Human Right Violations. The Colombian Mission, The Presbyterian Historical Society, Philadelphia. RG 88, Box 8, Folder 1.

is getting worse all the time and there seems no alternative but to bring these facts before the people of our country, so they will know the true situation in Colombia as it affects religious freedom."[94] *Time Magazine* had the same account of the events, and insisted that the real persecutors were the national police and the armed forces in conjunction with the Roman Catholic Church.[95]

Yet, this high degree of exposure did not change how things were developing in Colombia. The government did nothing to officials who violated the human rights of Protestants. Shaull narrated how after all the promises of the government to intervene in the persecution, nonetheless further atrocities were committed against Protestants:

> In Cunday, Tolima, the police broke into the Presbyterian Church and manse, destroyed the furniture and forced the young pastor and his wife to flee. In Dabeiba, where the church was dynamited on November, 1949, the pastor and the missionary returned several months later and began anew. In Bogotá, last June, police broke up a service in the Presbyterian Church in Restrepo, and shot several times. At Carmen, the police interrupted the Sunday meeting, and in November of last year took all those present at the Sunday morning service to jail.[96]

These cases were typical of many more atrocities committed against Protestants even after the Pattison declarations to the U.S. Senate. Shaull was determined to continue the struggle regarding human right violations against Protestants in Colombia. He proposed several tactics for action: first, to present the facts clearly to the Ambassador of Colombia in Washington, and request action on behalf of Protestants; second, to ask prominent people in Washington to use their influence to stop loans to Colombia while the persecution continued; third, because political Catholicism was a threat to religious liberty, to highly publicize events in the North American media; fourth, to encourage pastors and members of congregations to take up the problems they faced with the congressman of their respective locales, and to discuss the problems of relations with a totalitarian government which denied religious liberty; and fifth,

94. *The New York Times*, Sunday, April 16, 1950. n.p.

95. *Time Magazine*, "Fire in Colombia" April 24, 1950.

96. Shaull, "Report on Persecution in Colombia, 1950" The Colombia Mission, The Presbyterian Historical Society, Philadelphia: 3. RG 88, Box 8, Folder 2.

to find a mechanism within the UN that would handle the complaints at an international level.[97]

Shaull's disclosure of the atrocities taking place in Colombia received more publicity when in September 25, 1950 he was quoted by *Time Magazine* as denouncing the government of Boyacá. The Minister of Education had decreed that all students from private or public schools must attend mass on Sundays and Church festivals. Schools that did not adhere to the decree were penalized by being closed. Protestants were intimidated because the previous year the government had closed six other Protestant schools. Shaull was quoted as saying, "It is very clear. They can close our schools. If it spread to other departments, they will close them all. We must act now!" *Time* went as far as quoting Shaull saying that he would bring suit to the Boyacá Supreme Court to have the decree declared unconstitutional.[98]

Shaull's involvement in declaring human rights violations to the Colombian government and bringing information to the United States made him a subversive figure to many in Colombia. Shaull paid a great price for his involvement in Colombia's human right violations. He was arrested by the police on three occasions; two visitors to his congregation were possibly spies from the Conservative regime; a member of Colombian high society allegedly contracted an assassin to kill him; and an insurance agent advised him to take out a large life insurance policy for the sake of his family.[99]

In addition to his notoriety with the Colombian government, many of Shaull's missionary peers viewed him with disapproval. James Goff complained to the Board of Foreign Missions in New York that Shaull had a favored relationship with the staff officers of the Board. He complained that "favoritism of such sort would be unworthy of the Presbyterian Board." Goff continues, "His belligerent words printed in *Time* had a more

---

97. Ibid., 5–7. It is important to notice that Shaull was already doing thirty-two years earlier what "The Development of Guidelines on Missionary Involvement in Social-Justice and Human-Rights Issues" of the Division of Overseas Ministries of the National Council of Churches in Christ advocated doing in 1982.

98. *Time Magazine* (September 25, 1950) 25.

99. Personal Report of Shaull, 1950. The Colombia Mission, The Presbyterian Historical Society, Philadelphia. RG 88, Box 2, Folder 8.

contrary effect upon the work here than in the United States. The Board should realize that there has been a Shaull problem here for years."[100]

In a letter to *Time Magazine* that was never published, Frank H. Wood contradicted everything for which Shaull had argued. Wood states, "*Time* has been led astray. An hour ago I got the current issue from the newsstand here in Bogotá and was completely disgusted with the article about Colombia. It conveys completely a false impression." After he explained why he thought the article was false, Wood reiterates, "Reverend Richard Shaull speaks nonsense when he speaks of bringing suit about it. He does not speak for the Presbyterian Mission . . . I wish as a Presbyterian missionary to repudiate the 'persecuted Mr. Shaull' and the rest of the small clique of missionaries seeking martyrdom."[101]

Obviously, Wood was a conservative missionary who conceived politics as a dirty game, while Shaull believed that the political order could be affected by the power of God in the lives of believers in positions of power within the government. This time Shaull won the support of the Board in New York. The Board reprimanded Wood's statements to *Time* making it very clear that the new missiology to be followed in the mission field needed to be in touch with every aspect of human life. Shaull left Colombia the next year, never to return. He left a witness of the power of God to transform human lives and daily struggles.

100. James Goff to Charles T. Leber, Chairman of the Board of Foreign Missions of the Presbyterian Church USA, December 6, 1950. The Colombia Mission, The Presbyterian Historical Society, Philadelphia. RG 88, Box 8, Folder 1.

101. Frank H. Wood to the Editor of *Time Magazine*, October 2, 1950. The Colombia Mission, The Presbyterian Historical Society, Philadelphia. RG 88, Box 8, Folder 1.

*chapter two*

# From Within the Storm:
# M. Richard Shaull in Brazil, 1952–1962

Shaull was a missionary who insisted on constructing his theology in concrete situations of brokenness and despair. His missiology was one of the first attempts to construct a contextual theology that took the Brazilian reality as the locus in which to understand the activity of God in the world. His many ecumenical contacts with leaders of the World Student Christian Federation and the World Council of Churches made him a key figure in Brazilian Protestantism in the 1950s and 1960s as the facilitator of new missiological trends in a period when the nation was going through rapid social transformations.

This chapter follows the development of Shaull's missiology in Brazil. It is divided into three main sections which represent Shaull's ministerial areas of responsibility in Brazil. The first section describes Shaull's appointment as professor of Church History at Campinas Presbyterian Seminary and advisor to the Presbyterian youth of Brazil. The second explores his work as theologian in the Sector of Social Responsibility of the Church of the Brazilian Evangelical Confederation sponsored by the World Council of Churches. In these two ministry frameworks Shaull strove to create a missiology rooted in the sovereignty of God and focused on the transformation of society.

Shaull's article in the first edition of *Testimonium,* "Our Immediate Duty in the Face of an Imminent Crisis," reflected on the profound transformation occurring in all social and political structures of Latin America.

Brazil was experiencing a radical transition from a rural and agricultural economy to an urban and industrial one. Nationalism was on the rise as the once colonized nations were exposed to the economic exploitation of the Western nations, and the poor demanded justice and more participation in their own destiny.[1]

## Brazil: A Brief Overview

A knowledge of the economic, social, and political contexts in which Shaull ministered is crucial to understanding his missiology of revolution. In the first two decades of the twentieth century, coffee and other agricultural products were the main source of Brazil's economy. However, the gradual decline of the coffee trade was intensified by the international depression caused by the Wall Street crash of 1929.[2] The gradual decline of the coffee trade brought acute negative effects in the economy of Brazil because coffee was the principal export of the nation and its basis for capital accumulation. With coffee exports in decline, Brazil's economy concentrated on manufacturing other industrial products: refrigerators, radios, televisions, toothbrushes, glass, and automobiles among other items. As the production and distribution of coffee diminished, industrialization and urbanization increased. Also, after World War II, Brazil began to develop other resources such as hydroelectric plants, steel plants, cement plants, and oil refineries. As all these manufacturing new jobs were in city areas, a rapid mass internal migration from the rural areas to the cities occurred.

The transformation from a rural to an industrial economy brought with it intense urbanization. Prior to World War II, only about one sixth of the population lived in cities of over 20,000 inhabitants. By 1980, as agriculture diminished in rural areas, about half of Brazilians had moved to cities.[3] The intense urban transition created problems for the new city-dwellers. One of the main basic problems was housing. The oldest form of working-class dwelling in Brazil was the tenement, which became the

---

1. Shaull, "Nossa Tarefa Imediata," 27–33.
2. Deniz, "Post-1930 Industrial Elite," 106.
3. Katzman, "Urbanization," 101.

main type of housing for workers until the 1950s.[4] It was a building which was divided into many small rooms and occupied by a large number of people who shared toilets, bathrooms, and standpipes.[5] Such unhygienic living in close quarters resulted in all kinds of diseases. Not only that: because the tenements were controlled by the industrial elites, the elites were able to exploit the workers and charge them exorbitant prices for their living space.[6] Overpopulation in small dwelling spaces not only brought a highly infectious atmosphere for the spread of diseases but also increased crime and the perpetuation of poverty.[7]

Politically, Brazil had been governed since the establishment of the Old Republic in 1889 by the elite oligarchies of Sao Paulo and Minas Gerais. However, with the decline of coffee exports, the oligarchies were vulnerable to new challenges from an emergent opposition. In 1930, the Old Republic ended as a military coup installed Getulio Vargas as the new president of the nation. Himself born into the oligarchy, Vargas believed that Brazil could be modernized rapidly through industrialization and social engineering.[8] Under his leadership, Brazil began the process to rapid industrialization and political centralization.[9]

Vargas believed that class conflict and the interest of capital and labor needed to be harmonized as in the cases of Italy and Portugal through the structure of corporatism and fascism.[10] He promulgated a new constitution in 1931 and gave himself authoritarian powers. In 1937, Vargas constituted the New State, Brazil's milder version of Europe's fascist movements. The principal objective of the New State was to regulate the institutional framework to dominate the working class. Fiscal and industrial policy-making powers were transferred from the states to the federal government. The New State declared that economic production was the principal function of the state—thus crushing the independent unions.[11] Vargas continued in power until October, 1945, when he was deposed by

---

4. Kowarick and Ant, "One Hundred," 62.

5. Ibid., 60–61.

6. Ibid., 63.

7. Katzman, "Urbanization," 129–31.

8. Levine, *Father of the Poor?* 4.

9. Ibid., 11.

10. Skidmore, *Politics in Brazi*, 29.

11. Ibid., 31–32.

a military junta. He regained power in 1950 by democratic elections, but his tenure ended when he committed suicide in his presidential office in 1954.[12]

In 1955, Juscelino Kubitschek was elected the new president of Brazil. He promoted a program that would give Brazil "fifty years of progress in five years."[13] His project did not bring the desired results: economic inflation continued and the rising cost of living was unbearable to the masses. One of the most daring projects of his administration was the construction of Brasilia, a new capital city in the interior of the country. However, not even the construction of a new city with all the jobs it generated was able to turn the tide of Brazil's economic problems.

In 1961, Kusbitschek was succeeded by Jânio Quadros, a pro-revolutionary leader who supported Castro when the U.S. launched its Bay of Pigs invasion. Quadros had campaigned on a moralistic critique of bureaucratic and social injustice which he promised to sweep away if elected president.[14] Under Quadros, Brazil's foreign policy wanted to pursued a middle course by simultaneous negotiations with the Russian bloc, Western Europe, and the United States. When the Bay of Pigs invasion of Cuba failed, the United States pursued a more rigid policy to isolate Cuba by cutting ties with the revolutionary island. Quadros wanted an independent foreign policy that would not be determined by the ambitions of the United States.[15] Brazilian politics was moving more and more to the socialist left, and increased the suspicion of the elites, the military, and the U.S. government. After eight months in power, Quadros resigned and blamed hidden forces in the status quo as responsible for his downfall. Quadros was succeeded by Vice-President João Goulart.

At the time of Quadros' resignation Goulart was a special envoy to China establishing relations with the new Communist regime of Mao Tse Tung. During his three years as president, Brazil became increasingly polarized between those who wanted social and economic justice, and those who wanted to continue the status quo. Goulart was categorized as a Communist and with the help of the United States was deposed in 1964

---

12. Levine, *Father of the Poor?* 88.

13. Juscelino Kubischek, quoted in Dulles, *Unrest in Brazil,* 77.

14. Skidmore, *Politics in Brazil,* 191–203.

15. Ibid., 199.

by a military takeover. This event initiated the national security state itself in Latin America.

While all these things were happening, the masses of Brazilian poor became more convinced than ever that a total change in the government was required. Revolution became the only option for a total change in the Brazilian political apparatus. In one decade, Brazil witnessed the suicide of a president, terrible inflation due to the industrialization process, the resignation of a president after only eight months in power, and the deposition of a president with socialist tendencies by a coup in 1964. In this decaying social and political context, Shaull called the church to be completely engaged in the Brazilian reality.

*Professor of Church History at Campinas Seminary*

In what follows I divide Shaull's missiological career into three frameworks of ministry: as a seminary professor and denominational youth leader, as a theologian for the World Council of Churches in their study program "The Common Christian Responsibility Towards Areas of Rapid Social Change," and as a leader of ecumenical ministry with university students at UCEB (União Cristã do Estudantes do Brasil), the Student Christian Movement of Brazil.

Shaull was invited to Brazil to attend the First Latin American Conference of the World Student Christian Federation with no specific idea where he was heading for his next missionary assignment. The Presbyterian Church of Chile had invited him to initiate work with university students, but the plan did not develop as expected, and Shaull was in limbo and waited for a ministerial opportunity. While in Brazil, Philippe Maury, General Secretary of the WSCF from 1949 to 1960, initiated dialogues with Presbyterian leaders regarding their openness for Shaull to stay and work in the Brazilian Student Movement (UCEB). Before the Conference ended, Shaull interviewed with Rev. Benjamin Moraes, Moderator of the Igreja Presbiteriana do Brasil (IPB). Moraes approved Shaull's missionary assignment for Brazil as representative of the WSCF, but as the political questions developed within the IPB (Igreja Presbiteriana do Brasil) as to how they could allow such a remarkable resource as Shaull to be used outside the denomination, they invited Shaull to become professor of Church History at Campinas Seminary.

Philippe Landes, missionary for many years in Brazil, retired from his functions as professor in 1951, and the Board of Trustees of Campinas Seminary appointed Shaull to fill the position. At the Panama Conference in 1916, Campinas Seminary had been spoken of as "the best developed seminary in South America. It had a distinguished faculty in Erasmo Braga, John R. Smith, and Thomas Porter giving a three-year course, corresponding in the main to the curricula of theological seminaries in the United States."[16] Braga resigned from Campinas in 1920 after having been elected Secretary of the *Comissão Brasileira de Cooperação* [Brazilian Commission of Cooperation] and was succeeded by Guilherme Kerr.[17] Under the leadership of Kerr, Campinas moved from the ecumenical vision of Braga to espousing a conservative ultra-Calvinism.

Erasmo Braga was the foremost Brazilian Protestant ecumenical leader of his time. He was a delegate representing Brazil at the Panama Conference of 1916 by the invitation of Robert Speer who was impressed by Braga's intellectual abilities when they met in Brazil in 1909.[18] He was chosen to write a report on the congress about Christian unity, *Panamericanismo: Aspecto Religioso*, which was published in both Spanish and Portuguese.[19] The Brazilian Commission on Cooperation was established by Presbyterians, Methodists, Anglicans, and Congregationalists to coordinate cooperative efforts between the churches and to serve as intermediary between the churches in Brazil and the Committee on Cooperation in Latin America.[20] Braga contributed as a writer for Sunday School material in the Evangelical Council of Religious Education, and on his initiative the Federation of Evangelical Churches of Brazil was formed in 1931.

The plans to establish a Federation of Evangelical Churches in Brazil was first discussed in the Montevideo Conference of Christian Work in South America in 1926 and expanded in the Jerusalem Conference of

---

16. Congress on Christian Work in Latin America, *Panama*, 455.

17. Pierson, *Younger Church*, 171.

18. Matos, "Life and Thought of Erasmo Braga," 177.

19. Pierson, *Younger Church*, 154; and Matos, "Life and Thought of Erasmo Braga," 177.

20. Ibid., 157.

1928, at which Braga was a delegate for South America.[21] The Federation, the Commission, and the Evangelical Council on Religious Education merged in 1934, two years after Braga's death, creating the *Confederação Evangélica do Brasil* [Evangelical Confederation of Brazil.] Braga's co-operation with the ecumenical movement, which included the Federal Council of Churches in the USA, the Commission of Faith and Order, the Commission of Life and Work, and the Committee on Cooperation in Latin America, made him one of the most prominent ecumenical figures of his time. However, the ecumenical legacy of Braga was shattered by the fundamentalism and denominationalism of some leaders within the Presbyterian Church of Brazil. The best example of the anti-ecumenical trend of this time was the opposition of Kerr and other leaders to the formation of Union Seminary in Rio de Janeiro.

Samuel Guy Inman, Executive Secretary of the Committee on Cooperation in Latin America, had a vision to establish in Brazil a united seminary that would partner with the ones in Puerto Rico and Cuba. Alderi Matos, professor of church history and official historian of the Presbyterian Church of Brazil, pointed out,

> Braga had become one of the most enthusiastic supporters of the proposed institution. Endorsing Panama's vision, he taught that a union seminary would not only promote greater integration among the participant churches, but, more importantly, would provide the only chance to prepare a highly qualified ministry— men who would be crucial for a renewed evangelistic effort, and apt to dialogue with educated Brazilians.[22]

However, this vision of a united seminary involved the closure of Campinas Seminary, something that the Presbyterian denomination would not allow. One of the main issues was doctrinal purity: professors from the Congregationalist, Methodist, and Episcopalian churches were deemed to be not as "orthodox" as some sectors of ultra-Calvinists in the Presbyterian Church of Brazil. Kerr pointed out, "The great modern danger is not denominational division or even atheism; it is the ratio-nalism which is born at times within the church. Presbyterianism which is strong and cohesive will offer indestructible resistance to rationalistic

21. "Relations Between National and Foreign Workers: Report of Commission Ten of the Conference of Christian Work in South America, Montevideo, 1926," 238–40.

22. Matos, "Life and Thought of Erasmo Braga," 188.

negations, and its survival depends primarily on a strong denominational seminary."[23] Because Campinas Seminary was an extremely conservative seminary, Guilherme Kerr opposed Shaull's nomination at the General Assembly of 1954. Kerr accused Shaull in the General Assembly of being a pro-communist in his political ideology and a modernist who represented everything that Campinas Seminary opposed theologically.[24] Shaull survived his first encounter with Brazilian fundamentalism and was allowed to continue his job as professor of Church History at Campinas Seminary. In this sense, it was no surprise that Kerr was the person who would oppose Shaull's teachings until Shaull transferred from Campinas Seminary to Mackenzie University in 1960.

From his experience in Colombia, Shaull was convinced that the best Christian contribution to social transformation could be made only through a renewed church. He went to Campinas Seminary with the same conviction of equipping a new generation of church leaders with a dynamic theology oriented toward the world. When Shaull arrived at Campinas Seminary, he found that "the whole atmosphere of the seminary seemed to be sterile in such a theological vacuum that whatever I do or say attracts too much attention."[25]

Theological education in Campinas Seminary was oriented toward the memorization of orthodox doctrines and a puritanical faith that encouraged students to flee from the world, focusing on a personal relationship with Jesus Christ to the end of attaining heaven. The world was the place where vice and corruption abounded; it was a temporary station in the life of believers, one used to test their loyalty to God by not contaminating themselves with its corrupt affairs. Rubem Alves, a former student of Shaull's, described that world as one of "certainty and prohibitions." For Alves, certainty tells us that we have already found the truth; therefore, all searches are over because once people are certain of the truth, they do not have to keep digging for answers in life. In other words, certainty paralyzes the intellect and mortifies the capacity for discovery.[26] Prohibitions

23. Guillerme Kerr, quoted in Pierson, *Younger Church*, 171.

24. Richard Shaull to Stanley Rycroft, September 16, 1954. The Brazil Mission, The Presbyterian Historical Society, Philadelphia.

25. Richard Shaull to Stanley Rycroft, September 16, 1954. The Margaret Flory Papers, Yale Divinity School Library, New Haven, Connecticut.

26. Alves, "Su Cadáver," 91.

tell individuals what they cannot do. When people know what they cannot do they are not free to make a choice because the choice has been made for them already.[27] Human consciousness is a slave to the dictum of truth and prisoner of intellectual structures that foster regulations for the perpetuation of the status quo. In this context of extreme orthodoxy and pietistic ethics, Shaull was in a unique position to open a new theological world to students.

The Brazilian journal *Religião e Sociedade* published in 2003 a special edition celebrating the life and work of Shaull in Brazil to which numerous students of Shaull from Campinas Seminary contributed to give a portrait of Shaull as seminary professor. Áureo Bispo dos Santos changed his ministerial goals in life after listening carefully to Shaull's presentation of the church in the missiology class. Shaull always challenged students to identify themselves with their contexts and with the needs of the less privileged around them. He was the first missionary at Campinas to respond theologically to the cultural, political, sociological, and economical problems of the day. This new orientation prompted Santos to identify himself with his place of origin in the northeast, one of the poorest regions in Brazil. Santos transferred to the Seminary of the North to be closer to the impoverished masses of Brazilians living under inhumane conditions. Santos quotes Shaull as saying in his class, "The Church could only be the people of God if the struggle for the poor is central to its faith and life because the poor have a privileged position as interpreters of God's revelation."[28]

Claude Emmanuel Labrunie suggested that it was Shaull who helped him keep his faith in Christ and ministerial vocation while he was attending Campinas Seminary, specifically because of Shaull's openness to dialogue and commitment to ecumenism.[29] Jether Pereira Ramalho remembered Shaull as always alert and sensitive to the "signs of the times" and open to the guidance of the Spirit in the Church, people, and society.[30] One of the things that Shaull strived for in his teachings was the need to connect theory and practice. While in Colombia, Shaull served as an evangelist committed to the poor and oppressed. One of his initiatives

27. Ibid., 91.
28. Áureo Bispo dos Santos, "Shaull Mudou," 58.
29. Labrunie, "Richard Shaull," 62–63.
30. Ramalho, "Buscando Novidades," 69.

was the development of a center for union workers in one of the poorest neighborhoods of Barranquilla. In Brazil, he helped seminary students grasp the meaning of their studies when faced with the social transformations of the time.

In addition to the support of the Presbyterian leadership, Shaull had the support of Brazil's Minister of Labor, one of many political leaders who admired Shaull's initiatives. In a confidential letter to Stanley Rycroft, Shaull delineated the plan that the Minister of Labor proposed to him:

> The representative of the Minister of Labor told us that they were most concerned about the Communist infiltration in the labor movement and they have come to the conclusion that there was one group of people in Brazil, the Protestants, who might participate in the Unions with a different spirit and seriousness, and whose participation in the movement might be the biggest factor in counteracting Communist infiltration . . . then he went on to say that as long as he has any influence in the Ministry, the Ministry would put at our disposal all the financial aid we would need for the development of the type of institutes which we had planned.[31]

Even though such cooperation by the Brazilian government sounded like the traditional linkage of progressivism and Protestantism in Latin America, in reality it was the right wing of the conservative semi-dictatorship of Getulio Vargas that made the proposal to provide financial aid in four areas or programs: 1) scholarships for evangelical females to study social services and after their graduation placements to work in areas of social crisis; 2) publication of materials concerning social questions from a Christian perspective; 3) scholarships funded by the U.S. government for several outstanding students to go to Puerto Rico or the U.S. to study questions pertaining to industrialization; and 4) monetary support to finance an Institute to train Protestants to engage the labor movement.[32] Even though Shaull was eager to accept the monetary help from the Ministry of Labor, the Board of Foreign Missions in New York was uncertain of the wisdom of doing so. Rycroft cautioned Shaull about accepting any economic remuneration for the project. Shaull resisted the idea of collaborating with the government on this occasion, but his

31. Richard Shaull to Stanley Rycroft, September 21, 1955. The Brazil Mission, The Presbyterian Historical Society, Philadelphia. RG 86, Box 14, Folder 5.

32. Ibid.

project of industrial evangelism continued with the help of the UCEB (Brazilian Christian Movement).[33]

Jovelino Ramos was one of those students who became involved in this initiative of industrial evangelism. Shaull realized that seminary students at Campinas were disengaged from any practical experience related to their studies—though they adeptly parroted doctrinal positions. Shaull's innovation was that he taught his students to deal with the questions that affected the Christian's testimony in the world. Ramos was one of the first students to participate in Vila Anastácio in São Paulo, an industrial neighborhood in which the majority of the workers were immigrants from the rural areas who were ignorant of their worker's rights. Inspired by his work in Barranquilla, Shaull directed a plan of evangelism in this area. Six people participated in this incarnational ministry of presence with industrial workers. The project was discontinued two years after its inauguration for lack of funds. Nevertheless, those who participated in the experiment of industrial evangelism were transformed by the experience.[34]

Even apart from his evangelistic zeal, Shaull was a refreshing voice in theological education. Starting with an overhaul of the seminary library, Shaull brought new theological voices to Campinas. He introduced the students to neo-orthodoxy through the writings of Emil Brunner, Karl Barth, Dietrich Bonhoeffer, Richard and Reinhold Niebuhr, John A. Mackay, Josef Hromadka, and numerous contemporary biblical scholars. For him, neo-orthodoxy assured meaning out of chaos and assurance of an "ultimate transcendent reality."[35] After his studies with Hromadka, Shaull was sure that the philosophical ideas of the Enlightenment had eroded and could not give adequate answers to the present reality of Latin America. Following Karl Barth, he ascribed to the belief that God has revealed God-self in the person of Jesus of Nazareth, and that therefore theology should be based on the affirmation that God is present in history through Jesus Christ.

Shaull also introduced to Latin America Dietrich Bonhoeffer. According to Julio de Santa Ana, a leading ecumenical leader, "Indeed, it was during one of its seminars in Sitio das Figueiras, Brazil, in 1952,

33. Shaull and Araûjo, "Relatório," 41–48.
34. Ibid.
35. Ibid.

that Richard Shaull began to talk about the work of Bonhoeffer; up to that time only his *Nachfolge* was ever mentioned. Shaull's words had a considerable impact on the students, who expressed a strong desire to know more about the life and work of the martyr theologian."[36] He made sure to introduce the work of these figures in ways that were rooted in the students' Brazilian reality. For example, Jovelino Ramos remembered that Shaull said in class discussions, "I am not interested in your version of Jacques Maritain. I am curious to know how you describe the relevance of Maritain for the concrete situation of the people that live and work in Campinas."[37] In that sense, Shaull introduced a new way of doing theology, a theology informed by the particular context of Brazilian reality.

Work with Brazilian Presbyterian Youth Movement

Shaull's work as a Presbyterian seminary professor placed him in a prominent position to engage the denomination's youth. When Protestantism arrived in Brazil in 1859, it encountered people ready to embrace the new form of Christianity. The Bible was distributed, missionaries traveled widely and evangelized the country, new schools were opened, and politicians saw in Protestantism the antidote to a Roman Catholic Church in decline. Brazilians embraced Protestantism because it gave them a vital and transformative faith based in Jesus Christ. Nevertheless, the second and third generation of Protestants did not have the same experience as their forebears. The new generation had more freedom to question the traditional values imposed on them by the church and by society. When the opportunity came to obtain a higher education, second and third generation Presbyterians in the cities faced the challenge with optimism, only to discover later that their faith had nothing to contribute to the daily struggles of the suffering masses. Many young people left the church because they could not make sense of what was happening there.[38] Shaull pointed out, "One of the most serious weaknesses of our pietistic heritage is its inability to show the relevance of the believer's experience of

36. Julio de Santa Ana, "Influence of Bonhoeffer," 188–97.

37. Ramos, "Voce nao Conhece o Shaull," 27.

38. Pierson, *Church in Need of Renewal*, 211–12.

Jesus Christ to the problems which he faces in his life in the world."[39] Nevertheless, other young people who were unsatisfied with the teachings of their local churches were seeking another type of theological orientation that could clarify the meaning of their existence in the midst of rapid social changes.

These Presbyterian youth were concerned about what the Christian faith had to offer to the masses of impoverished society. The youth began to question existing patterns of church life and began to look for other theological and ethical alternatives. The Presbyterian youth formed their own journal in 1944. Titled *Mocidade,* it became a tool of propaganda for new ideas and approaches for the mission of the church. The main topics discussed in the journal were evangelization, the structure of youth work, social problems (illiteracy, war, and social action), ecumenism, and political problems in the church.[40]

In 1946, Miss Billy Gammon was appointed as Secretary of the Youth by the *Supremo Concílio* of the Presbyterian Church of Brazil. She was the daughter of North American missionary Samuel R. Gammon, one of the most influential missionaries in the North of Brazil. Actually, Samuel Gammon had been one of the organizers of the Union of Students for Christian Work in 1926, the first organized student group of Brazil.[41] His daughter was born and raised in Brazil, thus giving her certain advantages in her work. According to Paul Pierson, also a Presbyterian missionary in Brazil, under her leadership the Brazilian youth movement "grew from 150 societies to 600, with approximately 17,000 members by 1958."[42]

The youth movement was sponsored by the *Supremo Concílio* of the Presbyterian Church of Brazil which in its general meeting in 1938 gave the following recommendations for local congregations regarding youth work: 1) the creation in the local churches of groups of young people; 2) the constitution of Presbyterian youth federations; and 3) the constitution of a general confederation that assembled the federations for statistical purposes, the elaboration of programs and the realization of national congresses.[43] According to Pierson, the Mission also aided in financing

39. Shaull and Alves, "Devotional Life of Brazilian Protestantism," 363.

40. Ibid., 22–23.

41. Silva, "Movimiento Ecumenico," 27.

42. Pierson, *Younger Church,* 214.

43. Araûjo, *Inquisicão sim Fogueiras,* 22.

the youth programs and assisting with personnel, as with the case of Billy Gammon.[44] This meant that the offices in New York of the Board of Foreign Missions of the Presbyterian Church were involved in the development of youth work in Brazil.

Many of the leaders of the Brazilian Presbyterian Youth Movement were those second and third generation Christians whose ecumenical spirit welcomed and worked for cooperation among all Brazilian Christians. For example, Paulo and Waldo Cesar, grandsons of Belmino Cesar, a pioneer pastor, and Paulo Rizzo, grandson of Miguel Rizzo, another Brazilian leader from the first generation, were people exposed to the ecumenical movement from an early age. Waldo Cesar described his first experience outside Brazil when he and three other Brazilians participated in the First Evangelical Latin American Youth Congress in Havana, Cuba, in 1946. Then, in 1947, Cesar and seven Brazilians from other denominations were delegates to the International Congress of Christian Youth in Oslo sponsored by the World Student Christian Federation. When they went back to Brazil, they acted as true evangelists—in this case spreading word of the findings of the Conference throughout the country.[45] Shaull participated in youth conferences, spiritual retreats, and worked as editor of the *Jornal Mocidade*. In this capacity, Shaull was invited as the main speaker to the Fourth Presbyterian Youth National Conference and thus became an innovative voice in theological education for the Brazilian Presbyterian Youth Movement.

The second Secretary of the Brazilian Youth movement was Benjamin Moraes who organized the first National Congress of Presbyterian Youth to be held in Jacarapagua, Rio de Janeiro, in 1946. The second National Congress of the Presbyterian Youth was held in Recife, in 1949. The Presbyterian youth invited the Congregationalists to join the event. The ideas of ecumenical collaboration and unity were at the heart of the organization of the conference which proposed the theme based on the prayer of Jesus in John 17:21a "that all of them may be one." This caused some controversy among the leadership of the Presbyterian Church of Brazil which opted to change the theme of the conference to "I want to be a Vessel of Blessing," which represented a more charismatic and pietistic

44. Pierson, *Younger Church*, 214.
45. Cesar, Bueno, Padilla, and Alves, "Juventude Evangelica," 83–85.

orientation. The third congress was held in Lavras under the title "We are co-laborers with God."

After two years of planning, the Fourth National Congress of Presbyterian Youth of Brazil was held in Salvador, Bahia, in 1956. The organizers decided that "evangelization" should be the theme of the congress, taking John 17:18 as its theme: "We are sent into the world."[46] Shaull prepared the study guide for the congress entitled, *Somos Uma Comunidade Missionária: Oito Estudos de Preparação para o Testemunho* [We Are a Missionary Community: Eight Studies in Preparation to be a Witness]. In it, Shaull encouraged the youth to give the beleaguered nation guidance through their faith in the revelation of God in Jesus Christ as expressed in the Bible and in the life of the community of disciples.[47]

Shaull promoted among the participants of the Congress a personal encounter with God in Jesus Christ. He thought that the main activity for the youth was to engage in constant study the meaning of Jesus Christ through the Bible and the Christian community.[48] It was imperative for him that the youth understand the God who revealed God-self in Jesus Christ. The conviction that God was present in the affairs of the world through Jesus Christ represented for Shaull one of the most revolutionary statements of the Bible.[49] He understood God as a missionary God who was always working on behalf of humans. Throughout the Bible, the actions of God to save humanity were revealed with clarity and precision. The most distinguished action of God was the incarnation of Jesus Christ. God's actions in history, according to Shaull, were clearly manifested in Jesus' message of the Kingdom of God. Shaull pointed out, "The dynamic action of God in the world has as its goal the establishment of the Reign of God; that is, the dominion of God over all humans and the entire world."[50] In this sense, the Kingdom of God in this world represented the power of God manifested among humans, a power creating out of chaos new possibilities to make human life abundant on earth. The new life in Jesus he interpreted as offering to individuals a new nature that empowered them

46. Gammon, "Relatorio," The Margaret Flory Papers, Yale Divinity School, New Haven, Connecticut.

47. Shaull, *Somos Uma Comunidade Missionária*, 1957.

48. Ibid., 9–10.

49. Ibid., 11–13.

50. Ibid., 14–15.

to strive for justice in the world. Therefore, the reality of God being a missionary God accomplishing the salvation of the world in Jesus Christ had revolutionary implications for the church as a missionary community.

The expansive view of the Kingdom of God was very important among the student movements. Dana L. Robert argued that "although it resonated differently over time and across cultures, the kingdom vision underlay the internationalization of the major student movements."[51] Robert identified three prominent interpretations of the Kingdom theme in the student movements: first, geographic expansion and world evangelization in the ministries of the YMCA, John Mott, and the Student Volunteer Movement, which conceived the "evangelization of the world in this generation" as a motto of God's plan for the global expansion of Christianity; second, a social program in which the Kingdom of God could be established on earth as seen in the vision of the Social Gospel (especially in the writings of Walter Rauschenbusch), the founding of the Association Press, and the work of the YMCA and YWCA in the non-western world; and third, a universal Christian community in the midst of nationalism, fascism, and another world war.[52] Robert argued that the World Conference of Christian Youth held in Amsterdam from July 24 to August 2, 1939, portrayed the Kingdom of God as a universal community already given by God's grace and love.[53] Robert pointed out, "The World Conference of Christian Youth in 1939 carried the Christian student movements full circle by taking the vision of God's kingdom back to the church."[54]

The church was crucial in the missiology of Richard Shaull. For him, the church should be a dynamic reality in the world. Quite different from the ideas most Brazilian Presbyterians strived to defend against enemies they saw coming in the guise of modernism, ecumenism, and communism, Shaull's missiology opened up new horizons for theological devel-

51. Robert, "Extending the Kingdom: The Universal Visions of Student Christian Movements, 1855–1939" Lecture delivered at the Christian Youth Movements Conference and the Royal Historical Society at the University of Birmingham, England, February 17, 2006.

52. Ibid., 14–35.

53. Ibid., 34.

54. Ibid., 35.

opments in Brazil in those same areas.[55] Shaull conceived the church as a missionary community called to accomplish a special task in the world. The task of the church was to incarnate the Gospel in those areas of society in which suffering and despair were most notable. The church as an incarnate community induced believers to participate in God's activity of redemption in the world and submerged itself in the affairs that were most crucial for Brazilians. Shaull's missiology conceived the church as being in partnership with God to bring the culmination of all things in Christ.

Shaull never denied the importance of evangelism as proclamation. He pointed out, "Every member of the Brazilian Presbyterian Youth Movement has as its major responsibility in life, personal evangelism; this is, the task of sharing the gospel daily with your friends in the factory, school."[56] Nevertheless, this was not enough. Because God related to humans in a definitive way in Jesus Christ, such relationship should be the motivational goal of every believer. Believers demonstrated the love of God through their lives in every situation they faced in the world. The best way to demonstrate such love was to be involved in the basic problems of society. He pointed out, "This means that our witness of the preoccupation of God for the world should urge us to fight for social justice through political action and the movements and groups that today determine the conditions of life in the modern world."[57] Shaull urged the Presbyterian youth to repent, pray, study, and work for the kingdom of God with one thing in mind: the church as a missionary community with the task of making the gospel of Jesus Christ known through all means available for such task. Once again, the division of evangelization into proclamation or social justice was not how Shaull understood missiology.

Shaull's book *We are a Missionary Community* was a key point in his theological development as a missionary in Brazil. Yet while Shaull became a prophet-like figure for the Brazilian youth movement, some leaders from the older generation had begun to regard him with antagonism and caution. Their reasons were obvious: his views were contrary to the previous theological interpretations of Brazilian Presbyterianism which elevated doctrinal presuppositions to the level of inerrant truth. Not only

55. Pierson, *Younger Church*, 220.
56. Shaull, *Somos uma Comunidade*, 40.
57. Ibid., 50.

that, Shaull's theology was rooted in the Brazilian reality, thus making him one of the first missionaries in Latin America to take a particular social, cultural, political, and economic context as *locus theologicus* and to formulate his missiology from it. Furthermore, his popularity in seminary and the youth movement was causing discomfort within the Presbyterian Church of Brazil. This was due to the fact that Shaull lived in the midst of a fundamentalist-modernist controversy within the Presbyterian Church of Brazil.

The Presbyterian Church of Brazil went through a process of "increasing isolation and stagnation" from 1934 to 1946.[58] Initiatives to integrate the Brazilian Presbyterian Church with the World Council of Churches failed, even though Rev. Miguel Rizzo was a representative of the Presbyterian Church of Brazil in the first Assembly of the WCC in Amsterdam in 1948. Pierson noted two principal reasons why the Presbyterian Church of Brazil did not join the WCC. First, the attitude against Roman Catholicism was the major objection. Leaders of the WCC did not understand the decades of conflict between Protestants and Roman Catholics in Latin America. Many times Protestants had to endure the ridicule and persecution of the priests and their fanatical followers. Therefore, they could not have conceived the idea of having anything to do with the Church which previously had persecuted them. Second, the conservatism of the Presbyterian Church of Brazil led to fears of innovation in the church and of modernism. To complicate the situation, Carl McIntire, from the ICCC (International Council of Christian Churches)—a body formed to oppose the WCC—visited Brazil in 1949 and promoted his fundamentalist agenda. He capitalized on the extreme conservatism of the Presbyterian Church of Northern Brazil and its fears of innovation, and the emerging nationalistic sentiment in the nation.[59] As a result, the leadership of the Presbyterian Church of Brazil decided that they should take a position of non-involvement with both the World Council of Churches and the International Council of Christian Churches. However, the non-involvement policy in ecumenical organizations did not prevent a schism within the Brazilian Presbyterian Church. Israel Gueiros, pastor of Recife's First Church and professor of the seminary of the North, divided the BPC and took with him half of the mem-

58. Pierson, *Younger Church*, 174.
59. Pierson, *Younger Church*, 199–208.

bers of First Church and some congregations with three pastors. They joined Carl McIntire's International Council of Christian Churches and later formed the *Igreja Presbiteriana Fundamentalista* [Fundamentalist Presbyterian Church].[60]

The tensions increased drastically between the Presbyterian Church of Brazil and the Brazilian Presbyterian Youth Movement. The conflict between the Presbyterian youth and the leadership of the Brazilian Presbyterian Church was a conflict between the personal and the institutional. While many pastors wanted to hold their positions of power within the denomination, the youth movement was opening new avenues to power and participation through its organizational qualities and spiritual dynamism. The tension became unbearable when the Presbyterian youth consolidated their power within the denomination. The leaders of the youth movement were efficient workers who constructed networks of contacts throughout the country and internationally through the WSCF. Their constant travels beyond Brazil's borders created some tensions and envy in other national leaders.

The other source of contention was theological. Shaull's missiology urged him to make a decision to follow Jesus Christ in all aspects of human life. Many pastors, presbyters and church members were perturbed by Shaull's teachings of how Christians should be engaged in all processes of human existence. The chief reason for contention was related to the question of how Christians should be engaged in the political processes. By 1960, the leaders of the Brazilian Presbyterian Church dismantled the youth movement, and the last issue of the *Jornal Mocidade* was published that year. Shaull decided to return to Campinas Seminary only to find his teachings being openly opposed by other faculty members. He was transferred to Mackenzie University as academic dean in 1960. His involvement with the Presbyterian Church in Brazil was restricted. By the 1960s, Shaull's missiology was more critical of institutionalized Christianity to the point where he discarded the local church completely in reaction to his treatment and twenty years of failures as he tried to renew the church.

---

60. Ibid., 211; see also João Dias de Araûjo, *Inquisição sim Fogueiras*, 41–47.

*chapter three*

# Towards a Socio-Political Missiology: The Formation of the Sector of Social Responsibility of the Church in Brazil

As an ecumenical leader, Shaull contributed greatly to the development of a Christian social ethics in Latin America. Scholars like Rubem Alves, Paulo de Góes, and Raimundo C. Barreto argued that throughout its history up to the 1950s, Brazilian Presbyterianism had not developed a detailed program of social ethics.[1] Ethical problems were relegated to personal forms of acceptable behavior. Presbyterians had their own way of interpreting the events occurring in the world around them. Rubem Alves summarized Presbyterian Brazilian ethics in the slogan, "let the individual be converted and society will be transformed."[2] Through being confronted with the problems of poverty, injustice, and depriva-tion in Brazilian society, Shaull began to understand that the root of all these problems was structural, and he began in *Somos uma Comunidade Missionaria* to develop a social ethic. He pointed out, "It is necessary not only to give food to the hungry, but also to struggle in favor of eco-nomic systems that could solve the problem; not only to suffer with the exploited peasant, but also to fight in favor of economic agrarian reforms; not only to visit those in the (*favelas*) ghetto, but to make the best effort to change the living conditions of those who live under such misery."[3]

1. Alves, *Protestantism and Repression*, 115.
2. Ibid., 152.
3. Shaull, *Somos uma Comunidade*, 50.

Shaull's position affirmed a new approach to the ethical question in Brazilian Presbyterianism: the root of the socio-economic problem was structural. People were not destined by fate to be poor, but were poor because others were rich in a system that benefited only those in power. Perhaps fatalistic Calvinism encouraged the inaction of its members in a context of hopelessness and despair, while Shaull's missiology of a God involved in the affairs of humanity combined with his North American confidence of turning things around for the best, was a source of inspiration. This chapter traces Shaull's involvement in the construction the Sector of Social Responsibility in Brazil, his missiological constributions to the UCEB (Union of Brazilian Christian Students), and how Reformed theology could contribute to social transformation in Brazil.

## The Sector of Social Responsibility of the Church in Brazil

By 1954, Shaull's fame was growing in ecumenical circles. His ecumenical contacts placed him in a privileged position within the WSCF and the World Council of Churches. In 1954, the WCC celebrated its second meeting in Evanston, Illinois, with the theme of "Christ, the Hope of the World." The conference wanted to give hope to the hopeless situations with which humans were confronted. Shaull was invited by Paul Abrecht, secretary of the World Council of Churches sector of Church and Society, to prepare a report regarding the social responsibility of Christians in Latin America and to contribute to the final report on the "responsible society in a world perspective." Shaull was not thrilled by the first draft of the report because it did not address the political question in relation to the underdeveloped countries. Another criticism that Shaull raised was that the report lacked the specific characteristics of the revolutionary situation in these countries. Shaull perceived that European academics did not understand the social context of the third world, especially the developmental program of industry and modernization as a way of improving the living condition of the poor.

At Evanston, the responsible society was defined and closely related to the idea of Christian hope, not only in eschatological terms but also as a theological category for action toward a better society in history. The Advisory Commission of Evanston stated,

> It is the task of the Church to show how the Lordship of Christ as
> the hope of the world is meaningfully related to every aspect of the
> world situation and the human predicament . . . To the hungry and
> to the poor, to those in bondage and social disorder, the Church
> must be the servant of the Lord who healed all manner of diseases
> and proclaimed liberty to the captives. *As Christians we must sup-*
> *port every effort of peoples and individuals to still their hunger, to*
> *gain the respect of their fellowmen, and to achieve the full stature of*
> *their manhood.*[4]

In the previous Ecumenical Conferences in Stockholm (1925), Oxford
(1937), and Amsterdam (1948), two fundamental points were emphasized: 1) Christians must work for social justice; and 2) no particular
political or economic system can be identified with the will of God or
equated with the Kingdom of God.[5] Evanston followed that same dual
principle. One of the main sections of study was "The Churches and the
Political Upheaval of the Underdeveloped Countries." In this report, the
conception of Western theologians was that underdevelopment would
disappear as more technology and industry came along.

The problems of the standard of living, poverty, inequality, and injustice would be solved if people would make "better and more efficient
use of the land, reorganization of village life, improvement in the means
of transportation and communication, and industrialization."[6] Also, the
increased feelings of national sovereignty as proclaimed by the nationalistic movements and the anti-colonialism of the once subjugated nations
were crucial to understand this period and the missiological responses to
it. The WCC looked at alternatives to totalitarian regimes, arguing that a
responsible society was one in which freedom was the order for all individuals, where the state was responsible for a fair distribution of wealth,
and where the state could be controlled by the electorate.[7]

The World Council of Churches' division of Church and Society
promoted a six-year study program after Evanston on "The Common
Christian Responsibility Towards Areas of Rapid Social Change." Abrecht

4. WCC Advisory Commission on Social Questions, *Christian Hope and the Task of
the Church*, 1.

5. Ibid.

6. Ibid., 42.

7. James W. Kennedy, *Evanston Notebook*, 35.

invited Shaull to lead the study section for Latin America. Because of the anti-ecumenical stance of some sectors of Brazilian Protestantism, Shaull proposed that the program should be "the initiative of an unofficial but representative group of laymen and church leaders in Latin America rather than a suggestion from the Department to the member churches of the WCC."[8] Therefore, in 1955, under the auspices of the Brazilian Evangelical Confederation, the Sector of Social Responsibility in the Church was created in Rio de Janeiro.[9]

In its first meeting, with the participation of forty representatives from eleven evangelical organizations, the Sector of Social Responsibility of the Church addressed the biblical and theological bases for Christian responsibility in politics and society in general.[10] Also, an analysis of the Latin American situation in terms of the best thought about economic problems was discussed in conjunction with an effort to describe the nature of Christian responsibility in society.[11] This first consultation dealt with the social responsibility of the church as a program of study and action. As the first experiment of its kind in Latin America, the first meeting resembled a generic and broad approach to the task of the church in society, whereas by its second meeting in 1957 their program was specific, addressing "The Church and the Rapid Social Changes in Brazil." The studies for the second conference revolved around three areas: industrial, political, and rural. Shaull had indicated in first book, *O Cristianismo e a Revolução Social*, that Latin America was going through a revolutionary process, "the first time that everywhere all institutions of the past seem inadequate and all things appear simultaneously and unprecedentedly out of joint."[12]

The third conference of the Sector of Social Responsibility of the Church took place in 1960. The theme of the conference was "The Presence of the Church in the Evolution of Nationalism." Specialists in the fields of economics and sociology were invited to contribute papers

8. Richard Shaull to Paul Abrecht, October 5, 1954. The Margaret Flory Papers, Yale Divinity School Library, New Haven, Connecticut.

9. Paulo de Góes, *Do Individualismo ao Compromiso Social*, 134.

10. Waldo Cesar, "Church and Society?," 133–48.

11. Richard Shaull to Paul Abrecht, October 5, 1954. The Margaret Flory Papers, Yale Divinity School Library, New Haven, Connecticut.

12. Shaull, *O Cristianismo e a Revolução Social*, 3.

on the rapid social changes occurring in Brazil. The conference was divided into three parts: first, sociologists, politicians, and economists were asked to expound upon the "Brazilian reality." Panelists presented papers on "Rapid Social Transformation and Development in Brazil."[13]

In the second part, theologians and church leaders were commissioned to work on the "presence of the Church in society." Shaull's missiology influenced the discussions on Christian participation in the social, political, and cultural processes that Brazilians were experiencing. For Shaull, theological reflection was missiological in nature, always looking to understand the activity of God's salvific plan for humanity in history. The church was challenged to understand how Marxism as an ideology provided the masses with guidelines for social justice. Therefore, for him, the church was the organization that brought the redemptive work of God in history and helped humans to deal with their despair.[14]

Shaull's study on the biblical and theological foundations for the social responsibility of the church was rooted in the incarnation. Because God was incarnated in Christ, God manifested himself in the world as Lord and Savior. God as the Lord and Savior of the world was also the Lord of history. The participation of God in the world through Jesus Christ was a demonstration of love. Such selfless demonstration of God's love should continue through the ministry of reconciliation granted to the church.[15] Shaull believed that the church was in a special covenant of participation with God to bring to fulfillment the work of Christ. His insistence that the church was called to participate in the events that occurred in Brazilian society testified to his missiological understanding of the actions of God in history. The church was in a privileged position to participate with God in God's mission to the world. For such participation to be effective, Christians have understood, better than everyone else, the context in which they lived. For since the church was related to all the events that occurred around it, it should be the leading voice that gave answers to the problems of poverty, isolation, health care, and urbanization, provoked by the new developmental program.

13. Sector of Social Responsibility of the Church, *Prsença da Igreja na Evolução da Nacionalidade*, 13–27.

14. Ibid., 29–32.

15. Ibid., 33–35.

A progression in themes can be noticed in the conferences of the Sector of Social Responsibility of the Church of the Evangelical Confederation of Brazil from the first gathering under the theme "The Social Responsibility of the Church" (1955), to "The Church and Rapid Social Changes in Brazil" (1957), to "Presence of the Church in the Evolution of Nationalism" (1960). In 1962, the last conference of the Sector of Social Responsibility was celebrated in the Northeast of Brazil. The title of the Conference grasped the political, social, and religious context of Brazil in the 1960s: *Christ and the Revolutionary Process in Brazil.* The Fourth Conference of the Sector of Social Responsibility was the biggest and best prepared of all the conferences. With one hundred sixty-seven delegates from all parts of the world representing sixteen denominations, "the conference was the most daring enterprise in the history of Brazilian Protestantism," said Waldo Cesar.[16] Prominent Brazilian politicians such as Dr. Paulo Guerra, chair of the chamber of deputies; Dr. Luiz Portella, representative of the Major of Recife; the Governor of the State of Pernambuco, Dr. Cid Campaio, and Captain Jorge de Castro of the seventh military region were all present at the inauguration of the event.

Rev. Almir dos Santos, president of the Sector of Social Responsibility, opened the event with the theme "Christ and the Revolutionary Process in Brazil," and explained how Jesus came to evangelize the poor in the Gospel of Luke 4: 16–18. For dos Santos, the good news that Jesus offered was a total social program of liberation for the poor.[17] The presentation of Rev. Joaquim Beato, president of the Presbyterian Seminary of Centenario, centered on the theme "The Prophets in Times of Political and Social Transformations," in which Beato presented the prophets as agents of God's will for the people of Israel and called them to practice political and social justice.[18] The biblical theology movement was influential in how people interpreted the prophets at this time. Biblical theology took the history of Israelite religion and made it the primary source to interpret contemporary events.[19] Rubem Alves, later a leading liberation theologian argued, "while a Greek thinker sought for the explanatory *lo-*

16. Cesar, *Conferência do Nordeste*, 21.

17. Santos, "Cristo," 1–12.

18. Beato, "Prophets," 13–31.

19. Patrick D. Miller, "Biblical Theology," 68.

*gos* of reality as it is, the Hebrew prophet looked for signs indicating the dissolution of existing reality in the name of a new and hoped-for order as yet to be established: the kingdom or reign of God. The Hebrew prophet did not explain; he denounced."[20]

The final major lecture was delivered by Rev. João Dias de Araûjo, Academic Dean of the Presbyterian Seminary of the North, and was entitled "Revolution and the Kingdom of God." Araûjo indicated that the major theme in the ministerial career of Jesus as a preacher and teacher was the kingdom of God. For him, Jesus' representation of the kingdom of God as guided by the sovereignty of God and its relationship to the world provided the seed for a real revolution.[21] Apart from the theological discussions, sociologists, educators, economists, and artists also participated in the conference, and offered the church their best assessment of the Brazilian reality.

## Shaull's Theological Contribution
## to the Brazilian Christian Student Movement

After his doctoral studies, Shaull was invited to attend the First Latin American Conference of the World Student Christian Federation (WSCF) in Sao Paulo, Brazil in 1952. The WSCF was organized on the initiative of John R. Mott, after his attendance at the Scandinavian Christian Student Conference, on August 1895. The major task of the Federation was to recruit Christian students in the universities with the purpose of evangelizing the world.[22] According to Philip Potter, Chairman of the WSCF from 1960 to 1968 and Thomas Wieser, leader of the Swiss and American Student Christian Movement from 1946 to 1960, the agenda of the WSCF in the 1950s was to strengthen the students' understanding of the life and mission of the Church.[23]

The First Conference of the WSCF in Latin America marked a new era in ecumenical, theological, and ecclesiastical relations in the region for the next generation among students. The Bible studies were the re-

20. Alves, *Protestantism and Repression*, 153.
21. Araûjo, "Revolution and the Kingdom of God," 33–57.
22. Potter and Wieser, *Seeking and Serving the Truth*, 1.
23. Ibid., 182–200.

sponsibility of Rudolf Obermüller, pastor of a German Lutheran Church and professor in the Faculty of Theology in Buenos Aires, and Jorge Cesar Mota, General Secretary of the UCEB (Brazilian Student Christian Movement).[24] Shaull was impressed with the conference contributions from the leaders of the WSCF, particularly in the "areas of theological discussion, analysis of social and political issues, and new practices for devotional life," but his biggest satisfaction was the Federation's emphasis on evangelization and its concern for students to participate in the life of the Church.

In this context, both Roman Catholics and Protestants viewed each other with suspicion. Shaull wrote "Evangelism and Proselytism" to show how it was justified for Protestant missionaries to present the gospel of Jesus Christ to Roman Catholic students. In it, Shaull criticized the Roman Catholic Church on four counts: For 1) its lack of a Christocentric position; 2) it kept the Bible as a closed book far from the hands of the masses; 3) the Church's decadence in its spirituality; and 4), the "demonic character of hierarchical power."[25] It is important to understand how progressive ecumenism in Latin America was anti-Roman Catholic, because of the abusive power of the Roman Catholic Church there. Thus for Latin American Protestants, evangelism remained a valid occupation. In this sense, mainline Protestants in Latin America were evangelicals, even liberationist ones.[26] For Shaull, ecumenism was not an excuse to stop evangelizing Roman Catholic students, for they too were in need of the Gospel to orient their lives. In such turbulent times, when students were religiously disoriented, they could all too easily perceive Communism as the most vital alternative for their distress—which was all the more reason for Shaull to bring the message of Jesus Christ and its new orientation to the students.[27]

Guided by his neo-orthodox theology, Shaull kept a dialectical tension between evangelism and proselytism, which at the same time presented Christ as the judge of all churches and Christians. He pointed

24. Ibid., 26–31.

25. Shaull, "Evangelism or Proselytism in Latin America," 14–15.

26. Baez Camargo, "Latin America and the Ecumenical Movement," 5–13; Castro, "Evangelism and Ecumenism in Latin America," 343–52; and Míguez Bonino, "Witness in a de-Christianized Continent," 96–110.

27. Shaull, "Evangelism or Proselytism in Latin America," 16–17.

out, "Our evangelistic task is not that of proselytism but of witnessing to Christ in such a way that men in all churches and outside the Church will be led to an encounter with the living Lord and a personal decision before him."[28] After this initiative was accomplished, and the person being evangelized responded positively to the message, the next step was always to connect the student to a vital community of faith. Evangelism and the church were the two major passions in Shaull's life. He was convinced that once individuals had encountered the gospel, they had no alternative but to follow Christ. They must make their contribution to the work of the kingdom in the world. Shaull pointed out, "To do less than this is to leave our evangelistic task unfinished, to thwart the spiritual growth of such students, and to leave undeveloped their Christian vocation at a moment when this continent needs their services."[29] Therefore Shaull considered evangelism among Roman Catholic students to be a necessity for the future of the nation. The Commission Reports from the Latin American Leaders' Conference, of which Shaull was a member and probably its architect, reiterated this point when it stated, "In presenting this message to them we should not approach them in the spirit of controversy, but studying the Scriptures with them, we must challenge them personally to accept Jesus Christ as Lord and Savior."[30]

Shaull's article for *The Student World* and the Report from the Ecumenical Commission on Evangelism stirred a wave of indignation in European circles, especially in the Anglican and Orthodox communions in England. William Nicholls, an Anglican parish priest of Britain, complained to the Federation about the evangelistic position of Shaull regarding Roman Catholics. He criticized Shaull for not understanding the essence of the Roman Catholic dogma on the Virgin Mary and the Passion of Christ in Latin America."[31] He also accused Shaull of failing to notice that "Whatever may be the effects of popular devotions, they

28. Ibid., 18. Shaull never defined the term "proselytism" in this article. The closest he came was when he said that proselytism was "getting people to join our church or to transfer their membership from one to another." 18.

29. Ibid., 20.

30. Commission Reports from the Latin American Leaders' Conference. Report of the Commission on Ecumenism and Evangelism in Latin America, 36–37.

31. Nicholls, "Letter to the Editor," 257.

cannot nullify the existence of the Mass itself, which is profoundly and inescapably Christological."[32]

Nicholls interpreted Shaull's positions in light of European Catholicism. He pointed out that "it is difficult to take Mr. Shaull's word for the spiritual state of Roman Catholicism in Latin America when he shows such failure to understand the inner meaning of what he sees, and when he repeats charges long proved false in one's own country."[33]

Nicholls cautioned the Federation on this type of evangelistic zeal because European members from the Anglican and Orthodox communions could have serious problems with such evangelistic directions. This was a very old complaint about evangelism in Latin America and one that could be traced back to the Missionary Conference of Edinburgh of 1910 when Latin America was excluded from the evangelistic mission of the Church because it was considered a Christian continent due to the establishment of the Roman Catholic Church. On that occasion, Robert Speer of the Presbyterian Board of Foreign Missions advocated for the inclusion of Latin America as a place where the gospel of Jesus Christ was needed as anywhere else. Together with a group of friends, Speer held a small meeting to discuss plans to establish Protestant work in Latin America. The Committee on Cooperation in Latin America was charged with meeting the challenge of evangelization of those who needed Jesus Christ.[34]

Shaull's response to Nichols resembled that of Speer at the Edinburgh Conference. In his rebuttal to Nicholls, Shaull did not apologize for his evangelistic zeal but argued that if Roman Catholic students assisted at an event promoted by the Federation, they came not as Catholics, but as people desperately seeking assistance in their faith lives. Shaull believed that if Protestants did not act on this opportunity, the students would go to another source that could satisfy their spiritual thirst—which in Brazil at that time might well be Communism.[35]

Shaull was invited to spend the month of September at the Theological Faculty of Buenos Aires. His lectures there on "Christian Responsibility in the Face of Communism" became his first book, *El Cristianismo y la Revolución Social*. In it, Shaull assessed "communism as one of the most

32. Ibid.
33. Ibid.
34. Hogg, *Ecumenical Foundations*, 131–32.
35. Shaull, "Letter to the Editor," 259–62.

vital movements in the world." He mentioned the case of the communist party in Brazil that grew from 4000 members in 1943 to 130,000 in 1944, and an astonishing 800,000 members in 1947. While such theologians as Reinhold Niebuhr considered communism "a political religion which has transmuted the prophets of a utopian faith into tyrannical priest-kings of a vast system of exploitation," Shaull saw it "as the rod of the fury of God to turn a rebel people to obedience."[36] For him, God might be using communism to destroy Christian complacency and awaken the church to strive for justice in the world.[37]

Shaull wanted to understand and interpret for the church what God could be doing in history through communism. He pointed out:

> [W]e will feel obligated to consider and ask, what is the will of God for us who are living in this historical moment? The more we understand that God is working in this crisis, even in communism, to punish our disobedience, destroy our complacency, open our eyes to see God's will and move us to obedience, the more serious would be our interest to understand what God demands of us in this moment.[38]

Shaull believed that Christians were called to testify to Jesus Christ in those areas of social, economic, and political disruption to establish better living conditions for the poor. For Shaull the church of Jesus Christ was also open to any communists who could accept Jesus Christ's demand to follow him. Shaull never stopped being a missionary committed to the evangelization of the world. He expanded the horizons of a new generation of Christian leaders in Brazil who were anxious about the complex situation in which they lived. His missiology was oriented towards God's action in history, transforming the world and opening new opportunities of life for the less privileged.

The Student Christian Movement of Brazil faced constant economic and leadership problems. Shaull commented, "The SCM in Brazil has been very weak, it is composed of a small number of small groups of students, and has not been looked upon too favorably by leaders of the Evangelical

---

36. Niebuhr, "Utilitarian Christianity," 66.
37. Shaull, *Cristianismo y la Revolución Social*, 7–9.
38. Ibid., 72.

Churches."[39] Shaull's first contribution to UCEB was administrative in nature, helping Jorge Mota, General Secretary of UCEB, in the organization of small group of students in the different university faculties. To accomplish this task, Shaull bridged some of the divisions between the UCEB and the local churches. His commitment to the church and its ecumenical vision contributed to this development. Shaull contacted Baptists, Independent Presbyterians, Methodists, Anglicans, Congregationalists, and ethnic Japanese churches to contribute to the formation of university students in their parishes.[40]

However, Shaull soon realized that this was not the answer to what he looked for in the student movement. While the emphasis of the UCEB on church renewal and social responsibility appealed to young people, a number of ecclesiastical authorities were highly critical of it. Students were not attracted to church routines and doctrinal statements that had little relevance to their existence. Nevertheless, Shaull believed that "the Church was called to establish the Christian community in the very center of the natural communities of the world in which they live."[41] Therefore he felt that small group of Christian students should be the *koinonia* of believers within the larger community of students.[42] A new type of church would emerge from their fellowship as they became the church in the midst of the university.

The student fellowships had several objectives such as to provide students with an intimate context in which to study, worship, and to strategize about how to evangelize other students.[43] Shaull's commitment to evangelization and the church was clearly seen in a series of articles published for the new journal *Testimonium* which Jorge Mota had launched as a way to address the problems students faced in the universities of Latin America. Shaull wrote about "The Dynamism of the Christian Religion" which he understood as a gift of God. He felt Christians should trust God and follow God in God's purposes in the world. For this reason, humans should surrender their whole lives to Jesus Christ: "To believe in Jesus

39. Personal Report of Richard Shaull, 1954. The Brazil Mission, The Presbyterian Historical Society, Philadelphia.

40. Ibid.

41. Shaull, "Philosophy of Student Work," 1956.

42. Shaull, "Challenge of Student Work in Brazil," 325.

43. Ibid., 326.

Christ means to recognize the redemptive work on the cross and conse-crate the whole life to his service."[44] The dynamic sources of Christianity, according to Shaull, were a personal relationship with Jesus Christ, Bible study and prayer, and action.[45] It was through these that Shaull believed one could transform society. A spiritual awakening would change society at its core not because of a personal conversion, but because the person who accepted Jesus Christ, who studies the Bible and prays, was called to action; and such action was to serve God in the best possible way in society.

According to Shaull, Christianity had demonstrated throughout the centuries its dynamism and potential to transform the world. Shaull saw that the dynamism of the Christian religion in its historic manifesta-tions was bankrupt. The only dynamic groups that he saw were the sects: Pentecostals, Adventists, and the Jehovah Witnesses.[46] To make things worse, he saw in communism the most dynamic movement in the world. For this reason and because of the inherent dynamism of young students, he felt that the student movement should engage the social problems of Brazil by presenting Jesus Christ as an option around which to reorient the social, cultural, political, and economic aspects of human existence.

He expressed this conviction in the Third National Congress of the Evangelical Youth of Brazil sponsored by the Evangelical Confederation of Brazil gathered in the Adventist School of Rio de Janeiro from June 3 to 9, 1954, and which had as its theme "You are My Witnesses." The Congress was an ecumenical gathering with 129 delegates from the Presbyterians, Independent Presbyterians, Methodists, Baptists, Congregationalists, Lutherans, Holiness, Assemblies of God, and Episcopalians.[47] Shaull was the main speaker. His lecture, "Testemunhas de Cristo num Mundo em Transformação" [Witnesses to Christ in a World in Transformation], con-tinued his theological innovations in the field of Christian discipleship.

Shaull believed that God acts in history through the church, meaning that Christians were people called by God to be witnesses of Jesus Christ. As witnesses of Christ, he felt Christians should have chosen a career in which they could have discerned better the activity of God in the world

44. Ibid., 14.

45. Ibid., 15–16.

46. Shaull, "Dinamismo da Religião Cristã," 12–13.

47. Statistics of the III National Congress of Evangelical Youth of Brazil, 43.

and served humanity through their gifts.[48] This he thought they could do best through a career in the political realm. Christians should understand from the beginning that politics is about the struggle for power. Because the government is the only agency that can bring stability and justice to the inequality between the classes, Christians should be engaged in politics while choosing a party that represents the best possibilities for bringing change.[49] Such change would not come because the believer is a politician, but because the believer is engaged in politics as a disciple of Jesus Christ.

Shaull's advocacy for Christians to engage in political leadership was a significant departure from previous missionaries' teaching that political engagement was a corruption of the human spirit. Arturo Reis, a first generation Brazilian pastor, expressed this sentiment clearly in an article for *O Puritano*, "Politically speaking the influence of Protestantism is nil, and hopefully the Evangelical churches will never think of mobilizing themselves politically. Every church that becomes involved, directly or indirectly, in politics, becomes even more corrupt than the political life itself."[50] Yet now Shaull promoted political life itself as a ministry of testimony to Christ's great love of the world. Shaull considered such work a testimony to the redemptive action of God in Jesus Christ. This demand for Christians to have participated actively in society and specifically in politics was a trademark of Shaull's missiology.

Shaull found in the UCEB an open community that was not bound by the norms and regulations of a church-affiliated organization. Because of its independence from the organized church and thus freedom to engage in the most crucial problems of Brazilian society, the UCEB was the perfect place for him to grow as an established theologian. One of Shaull's duties as advisor and theologian for UCEB was training leaders for the movement.

In 1956, leaders of the UCEB gathered in Curitiba, Brazil. Eighty students from eleven denominations came to hear as Shaull lectured and discussed humanity's distress and alienation from God and one another. In the book that resulted from that encounter, *Alternativa ao Desespêro* [Alternative to Despair], Shaull could be described as a psychiatrist who

48. Shaull, "Testemunhas de Cristo," 32.

49. Ibid., 33.

50. A. Reis, quoted in Pierson, *Younger Church*, 103.

diagnosed his patient and offered help for the stressful situation. He pointed out, "Humans are in a precarious situation, threatened by forces that they neither can understand nor control, victims of a process of disintegration that is express in anxiety and hopelessness; and, many times, in mental instability and suicide."[51]

Christians were not exempt from the difficulties and tragedies of life. They suffered the same maladies as everybody else, the only difference being that Jesus Christ was there to help and transform any adverse situation. In this sense, Jesus was not only the ideal being who taught and did good with an exemplary life, but someone who suffered all the calamities of being human without losing his focus on the major task of his life: to culminate his mission. Shaull pointed out, "The Jesus of the Gospels was convinced that his life constituted the central event in a divine drama of redemption in which God was acting in favor of humans, and insisted that through his coming to the world, this divine drama would reach its climax."[52] For this reason, in Jesus the alienation of humans against God and each other was eradicated and a new era was born through his life, death, and resurrection.

The drama of redemption did not end with Jesus' life, death, and resurrection, but now another new reality came onto the scene: the kingdom of God. Jesus' proclamation of the kingdom of God offered humans a new reality to follow. Shaull stated, "The kingdom of God is this new structure in which Christ, as head, gives his life for men and the world."[53] The new reality of the Kingdom of God needed to be incarnated in the community of believers who had accepted and taken a decision to follow Jesus in a radical life of discipleship. Paul referred to this new reality as the "body of Christ." Shaull said that "our duty is to comprehend and make each time more real our incorporation into that Kingdom, finding in it the foundation for a dynamic missionary life."[54] This new life in Christ helped humans with their relationship with God and the universe, with sin and their comprehension of justification, with the relationship with

---

51. Shaull, *Alernativa ao Desespêro*, 11.

52. Ibid., 27.

53. Ibid.,32.

54. Ibid., 35.

the neighbor in a fellowship-community, and their participation in the work of God in the world.[55]

Shaull argued that there was a bourgeois mentality that captivated Christians into conformity and carelessness. He defined a bourgeois mentality as the space where "human egoism takes a concrete form."[56] It was against this "bourgeois mentality" that Shaull directed his efforts. He wanted to construct a form of Christianity free from such selfishness and egoism and he took the work of God in Christ as a counter-witness to that ideology. When Christians failed to understand this "bourgeois mentality," when they identified their faith with it, catastrophic consequences ensued.[57] Because Christians were supposed to live in the new realm of the Kingdom of God, they were freed from the "bourgeois mentality" to serve God through their lives in the world. Shaull suggested that this witness was revealed in evangelization, through the proclamation of the love of Christ to humans, and service, the proclamation of the love of Christ through acts of mercy, charity, and love.[58] Shaull saw no division between these two actions but rather considered them two aspects of the same reality. Christians were called to serve God through serving the neighbor, and in the midst of such love, they always need to point to the person of Jesus Christ as the only "alternative for despair."

Reformed Theology and the Mission of the Church

From July 28 to August 20, 1959, the WSCF in partnership with the UCEB promoted a study seminar in Brazil. Shaull was the main coordinator of the event that brought students from Asia, Africa, Europe, the United States, and Latin America. The WSCF's five-year plan emphasized the "Life and Mission of the Church." Several events were of particular importance in 1959: the Presbyterian Church in Brazil was celebrating its centennial; the General Council of the World Alliance of Reformed and Presbyterian Churches met in Brazil from July 27 to August 6; and, the

55. Ibid., 39–83.
56. Ibid., 91.
57. Ibid., 93.
58. Ibid., 98.

year 1959 marked four hundred years since the first General Synod of the Reformed Church.[59]

Shaull saw and seized the opportunity of holding the event at the same time that the eighteenth Council of the World Alliance of Reformed and Presbyterian Churches was in session and invited world renowned theologians such as Joseph Hromadka, Czech theologian; John Mackay, President of Princeton Theological Seminary; Paul Lehmann, professor of ethics at Princeton Seminary; and James McCord, President of Austin Presbyterian Seminary, to speak at the event. The theme of the study seminar was "The Reformed Faith and the Mission of the Church in Latin America."

James McCord's first lecture addressed "Some Aspects of Calvinism." McCord emphasized the doctrine of predestination as one of freedom from fate and chance and the psychological threat of damnation.[60] He affirmed that Christianity is a religion of vocation in which the believer was set free for a life of service. In his second lecture on "Predestination," McCord challenged students to consider predestination from a Christological perspective. For him, Jesus Christ was both the elect and electee and brought a new humanity into the world.[61] In "Calvin and the Church," McCord argued that "Calvin used the doctrine of election to give the church the assurance needed for *diaconia*."[62] He read the biblical term *diaconia*—service—as a more primary term than prophet, priest, or king. In this sense, the ministry of *diaconia* or service was given to the church as the ministry of Christ to the world.

Paul Lehmann was another theological giant presenting lectures at the conference, in his case on "Election and Responsibility: A Basis for Christian Action in the World," "What God is Doing in the World," "The Contextual Character of Christian Ethics," and "A Frame of Reference to Christian Responsibility." As the titles suggest, Lehmann analyzed Christian responsibility in the world through reformed lenses.

59. Leaflet of "A Study Seminar in Brazil." Margaret Flory Papers, Yale Divinity School Library, New Haven, Connecticut. Box 11.

60. James McCord, "Some Aspects of Calvinism" Leaflet of "A Study Seminar in Brazil." Margaret Flory Papers, Yale Divinity School Library, New Haven, Connecticut. Box 11.

61. Ibid., 11.

62. Ibid., 12.

In "Election and Responsibility," he stated, "Election means that ultimate issues and motivational issues are decided; I do not need to worry
about the outcome of my behavior nor to worry why I am doing what I
am doing. Christianity gives one power to live as a human being, for in
Christ, God had put one in a context whose direction is given."[63] In this
case, the church was of great importance because it was in the church
that the terms and responsibilities of being Christian were embodied.
Consequently, Christians were called to participate in any activity that
promoted life instead of death, abundance instead of hunger, and hope in
the midst of despair.

Shaull wanted to restore the heritage of the Reformed theologians in
the Brazilian context. At that time, theology in Brazil consisted of com-
mentaries on the theologies of Luther and Calvin by Charles Hodge, Josiah
Strong, and Louis Berkhof who collectively represented the right-wing of
ultra-Calvinism. There were not many primary sources in the Campinas
library and the sense of a dynamic Reformed theology that should always
be in the process of reforming itself was absent from the Presbyterian seminaries. In a general sense, Calvinism was identified more with the rigid
scholastic approach of the seventeenth century than with Calvin's own
thought in the sixteenth century. Galasso Faria, a Brazilian theologian,
argued that "Brazilian evangelicals had learned that Calvinism had to do
with the teachings of total depravity of human beings and the doctrine of
double predestination, in which God, from creation, had elected some for
salvation and others to eternal damnation."[64] Yet from childhood, Shaull
had understood the Christian faith as a drama of redemption in which
God always made God's way for the benefit of humanity. He pointed out,
"I find that I respond to events around me as a Calvinist. That heritage has
come to shape decisively my attitude toward the world and my sense of
what is important in my life."[65]

For Shaull, the retrieval of the Reformed heritage was of utmost importance for the development of new ways of interpreting God that could
serve for the renewal of the church. In his first lecture, "Some Aspects of
the Human Situation in the Sixteenth Century," Shaull described the six-

63. Leaflet of "A Study Seminar in Brazil." Margaret Flory Papers, Yale Divinity School
Library, New Haven, Connecticut. Box 24.

64. Faria, *Fé e Compromiso*, 189.

65. Shaull, *Heralds of a New Reformation*, 8.

teenth century as having gone through rapid social changes; specifically he highlighted the rural areas where feudalism as a social system collapsed because the guarantees that the peasants once had were no longer available; the emergence of cities where new centers of trade and commerce created a new class-- the bourgeoisie; and in conjunction with the cities, new centers of economic power arose. Shaull argued, "As a result, practically all the categories by which people tried to understand their responsibility in medieval society were shattered and new categories did not yet exist."[66]

The church was not equipped to deal with these social changes. According to Shaull, all the philosophical and theological structures of the past which were formerly based on a true understanding of ultimate reality through the senses were crumbling in the face of doubt and uncertainty. In this context of complete disintegration of the old social, political, and religious structures, Luther's message of justification by faith had become the way of restructuring human existence with a certainty of a forgiving God who justifies freely the sins of believers.

In the "Reformation and the Sixteenth Century World," Shaull analyzed the correlation between religion and the concrete human situation where it was lived. The Reformation was of course primarily a religious movement. As a religious movement it gave hope to thousands of human beings who were in despair. Nevertheless, that hope not only had a spiritual dimension, but also social, political, and economic repercussions. There was an interrelationship between the Reformation as a religious movement and the Reformation as a socio-political event. Shaull pointed out, "The reason why we must think this way is that the same God who has acted to save us in Jesus Christ is the sovereign Lord of men and of the world. The same Jesus Christ who died on the cross is the agent of creation and of providence, working to unite all things in Himself."[67]

Shaull contrasted the human situation of the fourth century with the twentieth century in "Twentieth Century Human Situation," and said that human beings were confronted with rapid social changes that they could not control. The structures of society were inadequate to understand the

---

66. Ibid.

67. Shaull, "Reformation and the Sixteenth Century World," *The Reformed Faith and the Mission of the Church in Latin America* (A Study Seminar in Brazil), 1–2. The Margaret Flory Papers, Yale Divinity School, New Haven, Connecticut.

contemporary facts of social, personal, and political disintegration and insecurity of the masses. Shaull saw a solution to this crisis in Augustine's doctrine of the Trinity, specifically in

> the affirmation that in the midst of change and decay, of conflict and chaos, there is one supreme reality which is the foundation of everything that exists. This reality is that of a personal God who has a purpose for the world and for human life. He is active in the world to fulfill this purpose. His presence and activity constitutes the supreme reality of the world.[68]

The sovereignty of God juxtaposed to God's activity in the world created in human beings a sense of purpose for existence. Therefore, humans knew that all events in history moved toward the particular goal of the final consummation in Christ. Trust in the divine activity was therefore the basis for the actions of Christians in the world because God made all things new at every moment.

Shaull wanted to relate the Calvinistic understanding of Christianity to the contemporary situation of Brazil and do so in terms of the mission of the church. He thought that the contemporary Presbyterian Church was not free to respond effectively to the social transformation occurring in the Brazilian context—much like Roman Catholicism had been in the sixteenth century, without adequate ways to respond to the problems of society.[69] Shaull pointed out, "The renewal of the Church is not only a question of rediscovering the Gospel. It is also the discovery of adequate forms by which the Gospel becomes incarnate in the Church and in the world."[70] As Calvin communicated and made the Gospel relevant to the conditions of the sixteenth century in new ways, the Brazilian Church was called to incarnate the gospel for its own needs.

Shaull was developing his missiology from a long history of public theology as attested to by the Reformers. This tradition of public theology began with Luther's theology of the "two kingdoms," especially, his 1523

68. Ibid., 2. The next chapter examines more thoroughly how Augustine's *City of God* became a primary source for Shaull's theology of history and social change as well as for Gustavo Gutiérrez's construction of a theology of liberation.

69. Shaull, "The Mission of Calvinism in Brazil Today," *The Reformed Faith and the Mission of the Church in Latin America* (A Study Seminar in Brazil): 1. The Margaret Flory Papers, Yale Divinity School, New Haven, Connecticut.

70. Ibid.

tract, *Temporal Authority: To What Extent It Should Be Obeyed,*" which argued that the world could be divided into the Christian kingdom and the non-Christian kingdom. He stated:

> We must divide the children of Adam and all mankind into two classes, the first belonging to the kingdom of God, the second to the kingdom of the world . . . All who are not Christians belong to the kingdom of the world and are under the law. There are few true believers, and still fewer who live a Christian life, who do not resist evil and indeed themselves do no evil. For this reason God has provided for them a different government beyond the Christian estate and kingdom of God.[71]

Luther's political theology was based on a dialectic theory of law and gospel, in which two kingdoms were centered. The two doctrines were closely connected to each other, focusing on his pivotal proclamation, "salvation by faith alone." For Luther, salvation was not dependent on the law, but on God's grace as the core of the gospel. Nevertheless, he could not abandon the law. The law taught one to love God and neighbors and to live morally. In the secular kingdom, the law prevailed and in the spiritual kingdom, the gospel did. Luther's two governments were distinct from each other in their functions and roles. However, the two were under God's governance. The two kingdoms were complementary and dialectical to each other. The reciprocal action between the two as well as their own functions was none other than the service to God and neighbor for the sake of Christ. In the spiritual government, people could be "righteous" Christians through the leading of the Holy Spirit under the grace of Christ. In the temporal government, the wicked and non-Christians should be restrained by the government to protect people from chaos. However, since the law contained nothing that would lead individuals toward the fullness of life found in the Gospels, the state should be a separate entity led by natural reason.[72]

Calvin developed this point further, insisting that because Christ was the creator of the law, Christ was also the Lord of the secular kingdom. Because Christ was the Lord of the secular kingdom, the state assumed a more positive role in the theology of Calvin. He encouraged King Francis I,

71. Luther, *Luther's Works, Vol. 27,* 90.
72. Couenhoven, "Law and Gospel, or the Law of the Gospel?" 184.

> Your first duty as a monarch is to found your kingdom on jus-
> tice—but if you take no interest in the religious question and al-
> low yourself to be deceived by the slanders of those who called
> evangelical Christian revolutionaries in order to avoid the embar-
> rassing questions with which they confront them, you are making
> yourself an accessory of injustice, and your reign is then no more
> than common banditry! So do not deceive yourself. The greatest
> politician, however proud of his successes and showered with
> honors, deceived himself completely if he imagines that he is going
> to establish a prosperous regime without concerning himself with
> the truth that is in Christ.[73]

The church became a watchman over the state as it pointed to divine justice as a way of righteousness on earth. When Calvin settled in Geneva
in 1536, he brought a religious and social reform in worship, morals, and
doctrine. According to Swiss theologian and economist André Biéler, in
Calvin's *Articles of Church Government*, "one sees the spiritual demands
expressing [Calvin's] idea of a society built up and organized in accor-
dance with the standards of the Word of God."[74] Calvin proposed a total
reformation in worship, morals, and doctrine.

Shaull also appealed to the teachings of the radical Reformers who
concluded that the church's ministry could not tolerate subjection to politics and opted for a total separation between church and state. This group
of Christians considered that the church should not be confused with
the rest of society or the state, that it should in fact remain differentiated
from society. These particular Christians, known as Anabaptists, insisted
that the only way to be free from Christendom was through a rebaptism
of adults and the rejection of infant baptism.[75] The vital faith of these
Christians led them to nonconformity and their contrast between church
and civil society was a subversive force in society that eventually led them
to be persecuted by both Roman Catholics and Protestants. So Shaull was
retrieving a long established tradition of social transformation and public
theology based in the Reformation principle of the priesthood of all believers and their responsibility as Christians for the world.

73. Calvin, *Institute of the Christian Religion I*, 69.

74. Ibid., 77.

75. González, *Story of Christianity*, 56.

Shaull challenged the Presbyterian Church of Brazil to retrieve its Reformed heritage, not as a copycat of scholars' interpretations of Calvinistic theology, but rather by incarnating the Gospel so that it could take form in the world and give guidance to the problems human beings faced. Therefore, the rediscovery of the church was a rediscovery of incarnational forms as well as the Gospel. Shaull suggested four areas in which new forms of Church life were needed: 1) new theological structures; 2) a new form of Christian life; 3) new structures of Christian community, and 4) a new form of Christian witness in the world.[76]

In this sense, Shaull was in tune with broader missiological currents that understood mission as the participation of the local church in the ongoing work of God in the world and with the larger Reformed tradition of public theology. The Calvinistic emphasis on the sovereignty of God who was always directing the world to redemption was for Shaull the principal hermeneutical tool to renew the church and its mission in the world. Shaull stated, "The Christian is free to live on any frontier in which God has placed him because he knows that God is in control of the world and of the Church, despite the seeming indications to the contrary."[77] This assertion of the God who acts on behalf of humans became the major missiological and eschatological motif in Shaull's theology which was always geared to the transformation of society.

76. Shaull, "The Mission of Calvinism in Brazil Today," 3.
77. Ibid., 5.

*chapter four*

# Richard Shaull's Missiology of Revolution as Forerunner of Latin American Liberation Theology

The ministry of Richard Shaull in Brazil reveals the struggles of a young theologian trying to interpret the Gospel of Jesus Christ to a new generation of students, pastors, and lay Christians who wanted new ethical and theological paradigms by which to make sense of their lives. Throughout his ministries as seminary professor, theological advisor for the Presbyterian youth, ecumenist for the WSCF and the WCC, and theologian for the Sector of Social Responsibility of the Church, Shaull was like a prophet who interpreted the oracles of the God active in history, and brought a new theological formulation to the oppressive context of Brazil.[1] This chapter presents Shaull's missiology of revolution as a forerunner to Latin American liberation theology which developed in the late 1960s and early 1970s.

## Shaull's Missiological Contribution to Iglesia y Sociedad en América Latina as a Forerunner to Latin American Liberation Theology

Shaull had been in contact with the ecumenical movement for almost a decade now while he served as missionary in Brazil from 1952 to 1962. Together with Waldo Cesar, they organized the Sector of Social Responsibility of the Church. This organization gave a Christian re-

1. Leão Neto, "Richard Shaul," 83–110.

sponse to the social transformations that occurred in Brazil during the 1950s and 1960s. The World Council of Churches had developed similar programs to that of the Sector of Social Responsibility of the Church in Brazil throughout Latin America, especially in Montevideo, Uruguay and in Buenos Aires, Argentina. In Uruguay the program was built up under the leadership of Luis Odell, a Methodist lay leader. In Argentina, José Míguez Bonino, a Methodist theologian, was in charge of coordinating the movement. In this way, the work of the WCC in Latin America expanded to a continental movement dedicated to understanding, assessing, and interpreting the social, political, cultural, and economic reality of the continent.[2]

## Shaull's Contribution to Latin American Ecclesiology: Huampaní, Perú, 1961

The first time that all members of the different Sectors of Social Responsibility of the Church met together was in Huampaní, Perú, from July 23 to 27 of 1961. The general purpose of the meeting was to respond to the increasing preoccupation of Latin American Protestantism with the rapid social transformations occurring in the continent, and how to be witnesses of Jesus Christ in that context.[3] The major theme of the conference resembled that of the first meeting celebrated in Brazil in 1955: The Social Responsibility of the Church in Rapid Social Change. Forty delegates from fourteen denominations attended, representing seventeen countries of Latin America and the Caribbean. José Míguez Bonino opened the event with an exposition of the biblical and theological foundations of the social responsibility of the Church.[4] The conference was divided into three major study sections: 1) Christian Responsibility in the

2. Shaull, *Surpreendido*, 184–87. There are very few studies about ISAL, most of them in Spanish. For example, Julio de Santa Ana, "ISAL, Un Movimiento en Marcha," 49–57; Mortimer Arias, "El Itinerario Protestante," 49–59; and Carmelo Alvarez, "Iglesia en Diáspora de Ricardo Shaull," 43–53; Alan Neely, *Protestant Antecedents of the Latin American Theology of Liberation*, 165–208. For critiques against ISAL see C. Peter Wagner, *Latin American Theology*; C. Rene Padilla, "Iglesia y Sociedad en América Latina," 119–47; Samuel Escobar, *La Fe Evangélica y las Teologías de la Liberación*, 67–83; and Emilio A. Nuñez, *Teología de la Liberación*, 49–78.

3. *Encuentro y Desafío*, 12.

4. Ibid., 19–26.

Face of Rapid Social and Cultural Change; 2) Prophetic Influence of the Christian on Political Life in Latin America; and 3) Christian Concern for Economic Development and Progress.[5] Shaull participated and drafted the conclusions of the "Prophetic Influence of the Christian on Political Life in Latin America" and wrote a study paper on "The Present Life and Structure of the Church in Relation to Her Witness in Latin American Society."[6]

Shaull believed that God was working for the redemption of humanity at the frontiers, or leading edges of human life. This definition of frontier was not exclusive to Shaull as it was used by leaders of the ecumenical movement and the Student Christian Movements. For example, Newbigin argued that the new missionary frontier was not geographical but rather ideological, while Margaret Flory, leader of the Student Volunteer Movement and the WSCF, used it as the main theme of the 18th Quadrennial Meeting of the Student Volunteer Movement held in Athens, Ohio, in 1959. In that conference nine "frontiers" were addressed: 1) technological mayhem; 2) racial tensions; 3) nationalism; 4) non-Christian faiths; 5) modern secularism; 6) responsibility for statesmanship; 7) the university world; 8) displaced, rejected, and uprooted people; and 9) communism.[7]

Shaull participated in this event with a paper on "New Patterns of Obedience in Mission." On that occasion, Shaull emphasized the Lordship of Jesus Christ in the world and indicated that the "same God of Jesus Christ is at work leading all human life and all human history toward the goal he has set for it."[8] Because the Lordship of Jesus Christ was real in the world, even though the world was going through all kind of racial, political, social, and cultural tensions, "life becomes mission, for in every situation we find ourselves, we live to witness."[9] Thus, Shaull proposed that the "frontiers" of missionary engagement were in the university, the

5. Ibid.

6. Shaull, "Vida y Estructura de la Iglesia," 2–8.

7. Roche, "Initiating and Sustaining Ecumenical Ministries," 95–96.

8. Shaull, "New Patterns of Obedience in Mission" lecture given at the 18th Quadrennial Conference on the Christian World Mission at Athens, Ohio, December, 1959. The Richard Shaull Papers, Special Collections, Speer Library, Princeton Theological Seminary, Princeton.

9. Ibid., 3.

professional sphere, and in the local church. He quoted Philippe Maury's book, *Politics and Evangelism*, and emphasized that one of the new frontiers was the political realm.

At the Huampaní Conference of ISAL in 1961, Shaull drew on an established ecumenical line of thought concerned with God's redemptive activity and Jesus' Lordship in the world. Using the prophets of Israel as examples of the way God acted in history, the document turned to the theological doctrine of the incarnation. When Christians recognized the love of God in Jesus Christ and his lordship over everything, they had to understand that Christ as event was present in the "here and now" of the historical process.[10] Shaull reminded his hearers that the church as the body of Christ should be in a constant state of discernment to understand where God was active in history. He insisted that everything that transpired in the world, be it social, economic, cultural, or religious, was intrinsically connected to politics. The church was called to function as a prophetic witness that contributed to the renewal of those structures that had deviated from its original purpose of serving human beings.

The document exposed such structures in need of renewal as the agrarian system in the rural areas, the brutal spread of corruption in the political process, and the disintegration of cultural life. But how, it asked, was the church going to renew these structures? Should the church as an institution be involved in the struggle? Or, should individual Christians participate as citizens in the political process? The answer was that individual Christians should be the ones involved in the struggle to bring renewal to the oppressive structures. The report concluded that the church should not be involved as an institution in the political process because that could compromise its witness.[11]

In the section on the "spheres of Christian action in Latin American politics," the Huampaní report was strategic, leading Christians to act according to the supreme calling of Jesus Christ of bringing social justice to the world. It stated,

> In the biblical concept, social justice is the action of God demolishing everything which oppresses and enslaves man, making way for a new society in which human dignity shall be fully recognized. The purpose of Christian social justice is to grant man adequate

10. Ibid., 40–41.

11. Ibid., 44.

> means for a true life in Jesus Christ, and this is also the justifica-
> tion for the efforts devoted to this cause. It also means that true
> social justice is impossible without true freedom.[12]

Because individual Christians must work within the established socio-political structures, their actions could be tainted already by sin, but they should strive to create conditions that witness to the actions of God in history through a constant discernment in prayer and guidance by the Holy Spirit.[13] In this sense, Christian social justice was directed against systemic evil as represented in everything that was against life. This understanding of social justice guided Shaull's missiology; because God was already breaking all the oppressive structures through the process of revolution in history, Christians should participate in the revolutionary process as agents of a new world order with the conviction that they were making it possible to keep "human life human."[14]

Apart from clarifying the relationship between ideology and politics in Latin American Christianity, Shaull's other contribution to ISAL was the formulation of a new ecclesiology emerging from the need to incarnate the Gospel in Latin America. The criticisms of Johannes Hoekendijk against the missionary movement for having a bogus church-centric approach to mission became the norm in ecumenical circles in the 1960s. After Hoekendijk's address in the Teaching Conference at Strasbourg, France, in 1960, where he proposed that the world and not the church should provide the agenda for the missionary movement, ecumenical missiology turned to the world as the crucial *locus* for mission.[15]

After Strasbourg the Commission on World Mission and Evangelism, a newly formed organization after the integration of the World Council of Churches and the International Missionary Council in the third assembly of the WCC in New Delhi, 1961, held its first meeting in December, 1963, in Mexico City, with the theme "Witness in Six Continents," which took the world as the principal place for the drama of redemption.[16] The

12. Ibid., 48.

13. Ibid., 49.

14. Paul Lehmann, *Ethics in a Christian Context*. Shaull included this phrase in his theological vocabulary that eventually led to his missiology of humanization that influence ISAL.

15. Bosch, *Transforming Mission*, 382.

16. Orchard, *Witness in Six Continents*.

study project, "The Missionary Structure of the Congregation," which culminated in its two reports: *The Church for Others* and *The Church for the World*, emphasized the world as the place where God was at work.[17] And the Geneva Conference on Church and Society in 1966 addressed the revolutionary mood of the times as the place where God was actively redeeming society. In all these events, Shaull was a proponent of the idea that God was active in the historical process redeeming human beings through secular channels. The message that Hoekendijk proclaimed at Strasbourg about the world providing the agenda for missionary service changed the missionary impulse of the 1960s.[18] Shaull took Hoekendijk's criticisms very seriously and followed his lead but continued to endorse the church as the channel through which God's purposes could appropriately be done on earth.

Shaull's first ecclesiological breakthrough came with the preparation of a study article for a national conference in Huampaní in 1961. His study paper on "The Present Life and Structures of the Church in Relation to Its Witness in Latin American Society" criticized the missionary movement's imposition of foreign church structures on the "younger churches."[19] He suggested that by imposing the old structures of church life on a new context, the church lost its capacity for renewal, thereby becoming a static institution whose purpose became the continuation of the existing structure. Instead, he urged the church to find new structures of life in order to be an effective witness to Jesus Christ in the world. Shaull grounded his ecclesiology on two principles: 1) the need to indigenize the gospel to make it relevant to the contemporary world, and 2) the need to discover new forms of individual and community life.[20]

Shaull's missiology was rooted in the sovereignty of God who manifested himself in the incarnation of Jesus of Nazareth and continued to be revealed to humanity through the church. In this concrete understanding of the incarnation where God took human form in Jesus, the church was called to incarnate the same reality in its daily struggle. Shaull pointed out, "In the work of evangelism we are faced with a new, revolutionary and

17. Department of Studies on Evangelism, *The Church for Others and The Church for the World.*

18. Hoekendijk, "Christ and the World in the Modern Age," 75–82.

19. Shaull, "Vida y Estructura de la Iglesia," 2.

20. Ibid., 4–6.

secular mentality, and we are called to present the message of Christ to people whose lives are disintegrating under the impact of contemporary social forces."[21] Shaull's evangelistic zeal was not lost in his unconsciousness, but it was always present with new force as he tried to interpret the gospel to revolutionaries and secularists.

The need to incarnate the gospel in the Latin American reality called for new ways of understanding the church. As all the previous structures of the Presbyterian Church in Latin America were struggling for survival, Shaull proposed new patterns for community life based on a radical understanding of Jesus' demands of discipleship: the church as *koinonia* of believers. For Shaull, life in community was the major evangelistic tool the church could offer in sharing the Gospel. Shaull proposed the formation of small Christian communities within the natural communities in which Christians were involved already. He pointed out, "It is necessary to form small communities of Christians in the natural, precarious and diverse communities of modern society—in neighborhoods and apartment buildings, among students, workers and professional groups."[22] In this sense, the local congregation continued to exist only as a home base of preparation and support for the believers who were engaged in evangelism in their respective natural communities. This ecclesiological model implied that Shaull was going to be free from the scrutiny of local congregations or missionary agencies. In his model for a public theology, in which context was becoming more intertwined with the stories of the Bible, Shaull declared plainly that God was actively redeeming humanity and transforming the world to God's own likeness.

The desire to contextualize the Gospel of Jesus Christ to the developing situation into the social, political, cultural, and religious panorama of Latin America persuaded him that only individual Christians committed to such a principle could transform the structures of the church. As the institutional church became more rigid and irrelevant, he proposed new ways of being the church in the world. Shaull was invited by members of the commission on evangelism of the WCC to write the preparatory study for the Mexico City Conference of 1963 on "The Witness of the Congregation in Its Neighborhood." As stated previously, the Commission on World Mission and Evangelism came into being after the integration

21. Ibid., 5.
22. Ibid., 6.

of the World Council of Churches and the International Missionary Council. The Commission of World Mission and Evangelism became the successor of the International Missionary Council in the World Council of Churches.[23]

In the study paper, Shaull continued to challenge and defend the ministry of the local congregation in its task to evangelize the world. He pointed out, "The missionary expansion of the church as well as the witness of the Christian in his daily life in the world flow naturally out of the life of a vital Christian community. For this reason, the greatest hindrance, at present, to the witness of the congregation in its neighborhood is the breakdown of congregational life and the unauthentic forms it has taken."[24] Surprisingly, Shaull's first quotation of the meaning of the congregation came from Karl Barth. He quoted from Barth's *Church Dogmatics,*

> The Holy Spirit is the awakening power in which Jesus Christ has formed and continually renews His body, i.e., His own earthly-historical form of existence . . . The work of the Holy Spirit to which (the church) owes its existence is something which is produced concretely and historically in this world. It is the awakening power of the Word made flesh, of the Son of God, who himself entered the lowliness of an historical existence in the world.[25]

Thus, the historicity of God's activity in the world came from Shaull's interpretation of Barth and not from Marxism, even though Marx helped him to see how structures of power affected the historical process. For Shaull, God was active in history in the reality of the incarnation of God in Jesus of Nazareth, Jesus' resurrection from the dead, and the redemptive activity of the Holy Spirit on earth. For that reason, those who had been confronted and taken by the reality of God's self-revelation in history were supposed to be drawn "inescapably to the concrete realities of hu-

---

23. Yates, *Christian Mission*, 155–58.

24. Shaull, "The Witness of the Congregation in Its Neighborhood" A Study paper presented to Section III The Witness of the Congregation in Its Neighborhood of the Commission on World Mission and Evangelism of the World Council of Churches, 1. The Richard Shaull Papers, Special Collections, Speer Library, Princeton Theological Seminary, Princeton.

25. Barth, *Church Dogmatics*, 642, 652; quoted in Richard Shaull, "The Witness of the Congregation," 1.

man existence in our time, to the new world around us with all its change and excitement, its promises and threats."[26] Shaull understood that the Christian congregation as the embodiment of Jesus Christ should take center stage in the human struggles for humanization and give new life in Christ to those in need. Therefore, the world would be the place where mission was directed and communicated. Shaull stated, "If the congregation is not deeply involved in the real life of the world, its worship and sacramental life can hardly portray the meaning of God's grace and love for daily life."[27]

In the México City Conference of 1963 a new understanding began to emerge of mission being to all six continents. This concept eliminated the geographical presupposition of missionary activity going from north to south or west to east. Also, mission began to be understood as the place where God was active in the world. However, the way God was active in the world through secular agencies apart from the church was something the participants of Section III, "The Witness of the Congregation in Its Neighborhood" could not solve nor come to an agreement on as to its true meaning. For example, they debated again and again the relationship between God's action in and through the church and everything God was doing in the world independent of the Christian community. The following questions were raised: Can a distinction be drawn between God's providential action and God's redeeming action? If the restoration and reconciliation of human life is being achieved by the action of God through secular agencies, what is the place and significance of faith? If the church is to be wholly involved in the world and its history, what is the true nature of its separateness?[28]

Even though the participants could not agree on answers to these questions, several significant understandings emerged: a) the congregations should constantly ask themselves: where was God present and at work in the world? b) Christians should take the incarnation seriously and be Christ to the neighbor by serving and suffering through solidarity in the arenas of the world's struggle not only as individuals but also as congregations; and c) Christians should by word and deed interpret for

26. Shaull, "The Witness of the Congregation," 2.
27. Ibid., 7.
28. Section III, "The Witness of the Congregation," 157.

the world the Savior-hood as well as the Lordship of Christ in the events of the time.[29]

The report offered three forms that the congregation should take in the modern world: 1) small cell communities that would meet in the particular neighborhood such as residential communities, trade unions, political life, the university, and the professional world of business; 2) congregational forms of transformation that could transcend the cultural, racial, and social lines of separation among humans, and 3) forms of church life in the midst of the most basic and deep human problems of society. Lesslie Newbigin pointed out that "Mexico must be regarded as especially significant for the fact that it conceived the missionary task in the context of what God is doing in the secular events of our time."[30] As demonstrated, Shaull was part of a larger group of missiologists involved in the ecumenical movement who were trying to understand and respond to the challenges of secularism and rapid social change in the world. As such, he was an interpreter and advocate of ecumenical missiology to Latin America.

Shaull's major ecclesiological contribution in Latin America came with the publication in 1963 of the article "La Forma de la Iglesia en la Nueva Diáspora" [The Form of the Church in the Modern Diaspora].[31] Julio de Santa Ana, a leading Latin American theologian, and Carmelo Alvarez, professor of World Christianity at Christian Theological Seminary, recognized the enduring contribution of Shaull's article to the ecclesiology developed in Latin America by ISAL.[32] Shaull's ecclesiology was central in his missiology. The church as a missionary community was called to incarnate its message in the world, thereby bringing about change in the structures of society. Shaull understood that as Christianity became accommodated to the cultural and social structures of society, its ability to be critical and relevant to the needs of humans could diminish.

29. Ibid., 158.

30. Newbigin, "Mission in Six Continents," 194.

31. Shaull, "Forma de la Iglesia," 3–17. This was first prepared for the installation address of Richard Shaull in accepting the chair of Ecumenics at Princeton on December 9th, 1963, but it did not have any major impact in the life of the Church of the United States. Instead, the article was a major influence in the ecclesiological development of ISAL in Latin America.

32. Santa Ana, "ISAL," 49–57; and Carmelo Alvarez, "Iglesia en Diáspora de Ricardo Shaull," 43–53.

In this sense, Shaull challenged the notion of Christendom in the modern world, pointing out that God was bringing the church to a modern form of Diaspora.[33] The new Diaspora manifested for Shaull many new realities which were juxtaposed to his missiology and the contexts he perceived.

The new Diaspora was based on a biblical understanding of Israel as the people of God scattered throughout the world. After receiving the benefits of liberation from slavery and a new land, Israel lost its identity as a nation when everything they knew crumbled in front of them. The events marking the disintegration of Israel as a nation, according to Shaull, could be correlated to the church that has lived in Christendom since the Middle Ages.[34] For him, it was time that God began a scattered activity that would place the church in the midst of the modern world. The tension of judgment and grace were implied in Shaull's conception of the modern Diaspora because the Jewish dispersion came as a consequence of God's judgment on Israel, but at the same time such judgment was a calling to be a unique people, to be the light of the nations.

For Shaull the new dispersion meant a new opportunity to incarnate the message of salvation in solidarity with the world that was crying as if in birth pangs for its redemption. To accomplish this purpose, new forms of church life needed to emerge to confront the new situations people confront daily in society. Shaull proposed three approaches:

> The nuclear Christian community (congregation) should now take form within the diverse precarious communities in which Christians are dispersed. In the modern dispersion, the service of the Church to the world should take the form of solidarity with man in his struggle to make and keep human life human. The understanding of the Church in the modern Diaspora as a fellowship of believers close to the one developed at the time of the Reformation.[35]

Shaull had struggled with the tension between the theological affirmation of the church as the Body of Christ and the sociological affirmation of the church as an institution throughout his whole ministerial career as a missionary in Latin America. Shaull finished his article with a provocative question, "Should we not, in the modern Diaspora, place less emphasis

---

33. Shaull, "The Form of the Church," 5.

34. Ibid., 6–7.

35. Ibid., 11–18.

upon the gathering of *professed believers* into a religious community, and concentrate more on the formation of *smaller communities* of *witnesses,* dedicated to this task of witnessing to the reality of God's grace in the world and calling men to receive it and live by it?[36]

When Shaull described the essence of the Church, it included the institutional forms it took, and such forms were representative of the nature of the Church.[37] Nevertheless, Shaull's ecclesiology became a source of inspiration to a new generation of Latin American theologians who were eager to serve as witnesses of Jesus Christ in the concrete historical circumstances developing in the continent.[38]

El Tabo, Chile, 1966: Shaull's Understanding of History

Shaull's missiology of God's actions in history directed the theological vision of ISAL. The report of the II Conference of Church and Society in Latin America in El Tabo, Chile, recognized Shaull's contribution, noting how he gave form to the movement through his writings, his leadership role in the study groups, and through his lectures in regional conferences. He was one of the most quoted and influential ecumenical leaders in Latin America. In this sense, he helped to create for the first time in the history of Protestantism in Latin American a theological stream that made the social, political, economic, and cultural context of the continent the basis of its vision.

In the five years following the Huampaní Conference, ISAL's development was astonishing. The movement's publications, social action projects, and leadership training focused on three areas: 1) the study of ideology and history as theological categories, 2) the responsibility of Christians amidst rapid social change, and 3) the role of revolution in Latin America. The range of these ISAL publications is worth mentioning. The journal *Cristianismo y Sociedad* began its circulation in 1963 as a quarterly publication. *Cristianismo y Sociedad* served to propagate the

36. Shaull, "The Form of the Church," 17.

37. Ibid., 14–16.

38. Many Latin American theologians followed Shaull in their construction for new forms of the Church in Latin America. Hieber Contreris reformulated the work of the Church using three central themes: the church as evangelizer, prophet, and servant. "Presencia Cristiana en la Sociedad Secular," 255–69.

ideas of the group not only in Latin America and the Caribbean, but also throughout Europe, as the journal was first financed by the WCC.

The themes of the articles presented there had a wide variety of subjects such as: Christianity and Marxism, issues of church and state, the social responsibility of Christians, social ethics in a revolutionary context, and the social reality of Latin America. Articles by European and North American theologians were also translated and circulated in the journal. Shaull contributed several articles during the first years of the journal's circulation. In the second issue of the journal he contributed an article entitled "Recientes Estudios sobre el Desarrollo Politico en Asia, Africa, y America Latina," which elucidated the predominant socio-economic model of development of the early 1960s.

According to Shaull's analysis, the process of development in Latin America was conditioned by the structural changes people wanted to implement in the continent through the political process. Shaull saw Marxism as being the only ideology capable of directing the future of the continent, but warned that Marxism should not be equated with Russian communism. As Latin America was more suspicious of North American capitalism than it was of communism, Shaull reminded readers that one form of oppression could be as bad as the other. He proposed a middle way between Marxism and capitalism for Latin America. He pointed out, "The result of all this is a certain type of humanistic socialism that repudiates some of the central theses of Marx, and certain aspects of the dehumanizing tendencies of capitalism."[39] However, Shaull was not convinced that the revolutionary process of bringing new political and social structures in some parts of Latin America was going to be possible because of the influence of the United States in some of these countries.[40] By this time, Shaull had changed his perception of the United States as the

39. Shaull, "Recientes Estudios sobre el Desarrollo Politico en Asia, África, y América Latina," 43–50.

40. Ibid., 50. The case of Guatemala was an example of U.S. intervention in Latin America. President Jacobo Arbenz wanted to make agrarian reforms and expropriated several thousand acres of the U.S. United Fruit Company (the biggest landowner in Guatemala). In 1954, Eisenhower supported the CIA-planned invasion to "liberate" Guatemala from communism. The fact is that from 1954 to 1986 all the country's rulers were military men who defended the oligarchy and the business class by means of repression and violence. See Berryman, *Stubborn Hope*; and Klaiber, *The Church, Dictatorships, and Democracy in Latin America*.

savior of the world to the U.S. as being one of the causes for the unrest of the masses in Latin America.[41]

ISAL translated from English to Spanish several important books related to the Latin American context, books like Egbert de Vrie's *Men in Rapid Social Changes* (1962), Paul Abrecht's *The Church and Rapid Social Changes* (1962), and Philippe Maury's *Christianity and Politics* (1964).[42] Alan Neely, professor of mission at Princeton Seminary stated, "Of the books published by ISAL, none had the impact among Protestant Christian youth in Latin America that Maury's *Cristianismo y Politica* did."[43]

In 1965 ISAL compiled another book of essays by distinguished Latin American thinkers entitled *Hombre, Ideología y Revolución*. Shaull's essay in the book "Una Perspectiva Cristiana del Desarollo Historico y Social" [A Christian Perspective about Historical and Social Development] argued for a theological dialogue with the social sciences and especially sociology in order to understand the present process of 'development' in Latin America and how Christians should be part of such process. This theme of offering a Christian answer to the political and ideological context of Latin America was not new for Shaull. For example, he was one of the main speakers in the Presbyterian Continental Study Congress on "The Nature of the Church and Its Mission in Latin America" where he presented a paper on "The Church and the Political-Ideological Situation in Latin America."[44] Present at this event was Lesslie Newbigin, Bishop of the Church of South India; John A. Mackay, retired president of Princeton Seminary and adjunct professor at the American University in Washington, D.C.; Thomas Liggett, president of the Evangelical Seminary of Puerto Rico; and Orlando Fals-Borda, dean of the faculty of sociology of the National University of Colombia, Bogotá.

To Shaull's mind, average Latin American Christians were not prepared to guide humanity in the process of national development because

41. This theme of Shaull's change of perception of his country of origin will be developed more thoroughly in the next section of the chapter which describes Shaull as a severe critic of U.S. foreign policy in Latin America.

42. de Vries, *El Hombre en los Rápidos Cambios Sociales*; Paul Abrecht, *Las Iglesias y los Rápidos Cambios Sociales*; and Maury, *Cristianismo y Política*.

43. Neely, *Protestant Antecedents*, 173.

44. Shaull, "La Iglesia y la Situación Politico-Ideologica de America Latina," 154–65.

they had relinquished their social responsibility and preferred to engage in a spirituality that ignored the daily struggles of the masses of powerless and oppressed humanity.[45] Christians were supposed to be key players in this process of development because it was in the Bible—particularly in the Exodus story and the liberating ministry of Jesus of Nazareth—that people found the deep roots for revolutionary processes. Following Augustine, Shaull understood that the starting point for doing theology was not an esoteric truth that should be imposed on an alienated world, but rather in the concrete revelation of God amidst human struggle. For that reason, Shaull suggested,

> the duty of Christians is not to impose certain values, but rather to recognize and follow those values that are prevalent in the world; it is not to give meaning to life, but rather to find the meaning of life in a world that participates in the divine redemption; it is not to establish a new order in the universe, but rather to participate in the new order of the things that are taking shape through social transformations.[46]

This attitude allowed Christians to be engaged in the social revolution taking place in Latin America with a certainty that, even though they did not possess all the answers, they were nonetheless called to participate and contribute to the process of revolution in a spirit of prayer and discernment of how the will of God could be interpreted in each particular situation.

Shaull criticized Marxism for its naïve over-confidence in human reason's ability to order the historical process. Likewise he questioned existentialism and secularism because they failed to see in history a sphere of progressive realization for conditions of humanization. Instead, Shaull conceived Christian theology as best equipped to see the historical process as the sphere where the "Providence of God is active or the place of action of a Sovereign who is present in history and at the same time transcends history."[47] In this sense, history is the place where the grace of God was manifested more concretely, and where Christians, through a process

---

45. Shaull, "Una Perspectiva Cristiana del Desarrollo Histórico y Social," 78–79.

46. Ibid., 79.

47. Ibid., 81.

of discernment, could work for the humanization of society through their collaboration in the creation of a new order.

Shaull's optimism about a God who acts in history came from his conviction of the Lordship of Jesus Christ in the world which, at the same time, became the intersection between his thought and the ecumenical movement. For example, Lesslie Newbigin argued for the present Christ and the coming Christ.[48] The Christ who has come and lived among humans was a one-time event in history. He took the world's sin upon himself at the crucifixion and destroyed the power of death through his resurrection. This was the assurance Christians receive from God, that Jesus Christ saved us through his life and death on the cross. But the understanding of the Christ event could not be relegated to the past as a remote piece of history because Christ is a real presence for Christians. In other words, Christ was present in the experiences of his people, and through those experiences of grace, the Lordship of Christ was perceptible in the life of believers.[49] However, there was an eschatological expectation that Christ would make all things new. Human beings were still suffering from sickness, egoistic and selfish rulers, wars, and chaos. The Lordship of Christ sometimes seemed elusive and fragile. Newbigin pointed out that, "The very reason for which the full unveiling of His victory is delayed is that He wills to give time to all men everywhere to acknowledge Him and to accept freely His will. The time that is given to us is a time in which His victory is to be proclaimed and acknowledged in every corner of the earth and in every sphere of human life."[50]

The participation of Christians in helping to construct a new world order did not meant that by changing the established structures of society the true meaning of being human would be accomplished. The danger of the new order becoming worse than its antecedent was clearly seen in Russia and more recently in China and Cuba. For that reason, Shaull never placed his trust in any political or ideological movement, even though he encouraged Christians to participate in the political process and the ideological groups battling for power. He suggested that Christians should be present in the political process and be dialogue partners with ideologies such as nationalism and Marxism, because Christians brought a critical

48. Newbigin, "The Present Christ and the Coming Christ," 119.

49. Ibid., 120.

50. Ibid., 121.

orientation to the process, an orientation rooted in the God who wanted to redeem humanity. Shaull pointed out, "Jesus Christ is the incarnation of God in this present and real situation of men in the world, and his message—the Kingdom of God—has a political character. The new man—the new creation—is the result of this concrete encounter in the daily life of men in society...in the Christian perspective, what is to be essentially human is the result of the encounter of man with the historical reality that transcends him."[51] Thus, the Lordship of Christ and the sovereignty of God were crucial theological motifs in Shaull's missiology. He took those conceptions and interpreted them with the conviction that God was going to do something meaningful through the witness of Christians in the world.

Shaull's presentation at El Tabo proposed a complete actualization of the Christian faith. As the traditional theological formulations of the past were inadequate to guide the new generation of Christians in Latin America, new forms of expression were considered vital to the continuance of the Christian witness in the continent. For Shaull, all theological terms needed a revaluation, taking into consideration that the metaphysical language of the past constructed reality in a transcendental mode and made it impossible for a true understanding of the temporal realm and ways of changing it.[52] The theology of history that he proposed was based on a correlation of the Christian faith and the world. To accomplish this task, Shaull recommended that a serious dialogue take place between theology and the social sciences. As a forerunner of Latin American Liberation Theology, Shaull anticipated the hermeneutical process of interpreting reality as one of constant change in which "the quest for truth becomes a perpetual movement of partial success, failure, and renewal."[53] In this sense, reworking the previous conceptions of reality was an ongoing exercise that should orient the Christian community in their historical process of solidarity with society.

Shaull's vision of interpreting the humanizing activity of God in the world was to understand that "the biblical message describes the way

51. Ibid., 90.

52. Shaull, "Y un Dios que Actúa y Transforma la Historia," 58.

53. Ibid., 60. For a description of the hermeneutical circle as used by liberation theologians see Segundo, *Liberación de la Teología*, 11–14.

which God acts to grant and sustain the 'human' condition of man."[54] This is explicitly expressed in the Bible through the Exodus story of slavery and liberation and through the Prophets who spoke the oracles of God in political terms. For him, this activity of God to liberate humanity was the central message of the Bible. He summarized it in two premises: 1) "the affirmation that man has the possibility of realizing his humanity, because his life forms part of a sovereign or autonomous situation. Life is basically response, acceptance of the gift of what man could not attain on his own"; and 2) "this ultimate reality that transcends us is revealed to us by grace."[55] For this reason, the basic task of Christians was to be active participants in the frontiers where the basic struggles for human dignity were taking form. It was in this frontier of ideological and political engagement that the new theological language should emerge.

Shaull developed a theology that took the actions of God in history as revelatory of God's desires to redeem humanity. In the new theological approach, history was perceived as the place where God acts, but also as the place where Christians were involved daily in their struggles of life in cooperation with God. The old separation of church from society was overcome: ISAL began to understand that the church was part of society and could not be separated from the contradictions that every human being in Latin America was experiencing in the political, social, cultural, and religious realms. In this sense, it was not enough just to understand the rapid social changes occurring in the continent: Christians had to participate in those changes. Julio de Santa Ana argued, "The emphasis is placed on the ethical aspect rather than revelational. In this new perspective, man is both the subject and the provisional object of history."[56] As history becomes the place of God's actions in the world, Christians were encouraged to discern where the Spirit of God was bringing liberation. Because of this conception of history as the place where God acts, ideology and revolution became concepts used by theologians of ISAL to decipher the humanizing activity of God in the world. Therefore, this perspective was epitomized in Shaull's presentation in El Tabo when he talked of a "God who acts and transforms history."[57]

54. Ibid., 61.
55. Ibid., 62.
56. Santa Ana, "ISAL, Un Movimiento," 52.
57. Shaull, "Y un Dios que Actúa y Transforma la Historia," 57–70.

Already at UCEB, Shaull had introduced the study of ideology to Brazilian students in an attempt to understand better the situation which that country was going through politically. For Shaull, revolution was a fact. The whole continent was on the verge of erupting at any moment due to the unrest of the masses pressing for a better life. Julio de Santa Ana argued that the root of this problem lay in the social differences in the continent and the injustices that derived from it.[58] The dissatisfaction of the masses arose from many things: hunger, insufficient housing and health care, and illiteracy. But for Shaull, the biggest problem of all was the revolution that had happened in the soul of humans. The revolt against anything that had to do with religion or the moral bonds of the past produced a mentality that saw no need to seek a spiritual path.[59] The social condition of the poor who were abused and exploited by the rich for their benefit and profit was the major outcome of the extreme poverty of the masses. In this situation of constant death, the fate of the poor was not that hopeful. Since his early ministry in Colombia, Shaull understood the need for industrial workers to organize in unions, and the collaboration of Christianity with the government to bring about changes that would benefit the masses. After twenty years as missionary in Latin America, he was more convinced than ever that the political arena was the best channel through which to bring systemic changes.

For those involved in the process of social revolution who wanted to bring changes to the structures of power within the political realm, the use of the concept of *ideology* occupied a central place in Latin America. In a booklet for UCEB written in 1962, Shaull presented the relationships among ideology, faith, and social revolution. He began by introducing Karl Marx's concept of ideology. Then Shaull expounded Lenin's positive use of ideology as a powerful weapon in the hands of the proletariat to dismantle the forces of power within the structures of society constructed by those who wanted to perpetuate the status quo for their own benefit.[60] In Latin America both definitions of ideology were used to understand and interpret reality in an attempt to hold power or change the structures.

Shaull advised that Latin Americans should make critical use of both the negative and positive meanings of the term *ideology* as they struggled

58. Santa Ana, "La Insatisfacción," 26–35.

59. Shaull, *Encounter with Revolution*, 16–18.

60. Shaull, *Ideology, Faith and Social Revolution*, 1–2.

for the implementation of a better society. He pointed out, "the question must be raised whether all ideologies, as rational constructs, do not tend inevitably to violate reality."[61] For him, humans should understand that any rational construction should be perceived as limited and not the last expression of reality because any reality is much broader and deeper than the formulation of it. For this reason, any ideology that was absolutized as a weapon of social change was in grave danger of becoming totalitarian, ignoring the principle of humanization to which it was committed.[62] It was here, in the process of humanization, that Christianity could engage in critical dialogue with the ideologies because they were all supposed to be searching for the same result: total humanization.

Throughout his writings, Shaull never gave a complete definition of humanization, but always related it to the possibility of an encounter between the redeemer God of Jesus Christ and human beings. He stated, "It is a way of understanding *our history* in light of the specific history of Israel and of Jesus Christ. It is a description of humanity and of the possibilities of humanization revealed in Jesus of Nazareth."[63] By contrast, for Marxists, humanization was related to creating economic, political, cultural, psychological, and social conditions that made possible an equal and productive existence for every human being. According to Julio Barreiro, a Marxist Brazilian sociologist, "man in Marx was a being that in the course of history produces himself. Man had the ability to develop himself and transform himself constantly. Therefore, history is only the history of his self-realization through the means of work and production."[64] Of course this conception was very limited in its total description of anthropology, but one thing that it pointed out was the historicity of humanity or humanity's immanence in the world. For this reason, history became central in the missiology of Shaull because human beings had the capability to change society if they had a humanizing encounter with the humanizing God of Jesus Christ.

Shaull believed that as Christians live the present in faith, looking always to the future eschatological manifestation of Jesus Christ in the world, they should find meaning and purpose through participation in

61. Ibid., 3.
62. Ibid., 4.
63. Shaull, "Y un Dios que Actúa y Transforma la Historia," 60.
64. Barreiro, "La Naturaleza del Hombre en Marx," 19–20.

God's redemptive work of humanization in the world. Shaull understood that Christians had to live their lives in the midst of those political institutions that were in crisis; for it was there that the judgment and grace of God could be seen most clearly. This meant that Christians should not flee from their responsibility to engage Marxist groups in dialogue and search for authentic solutions to the problems facing the continent.[65]

Shaull's ecumenism broadened in this period, and called for a mutual cooperation with those movements that were committed to the total transformation of the political forces that dehumanized society. It was not that Christians should accept all the propositions of Marxism, but rather that they should engage critically with any members of any ideology who wanted to absolutize their position. Shaull's missiology of social involvement was directed towards the transformation of society; but rather than being a means to Christianize the revolution or the political realm it was a testimony to the humanizing activity of God's redeeming power in history. In this sense, to evangelize was to be engaged in social justice.

## Shaull's New Ecumenical Vision: Protestants, Roman Catholics, and Marxists Together

Shaull's final years in Brazil from 1960 to 1962 were a time of struggle, testing, and radicalization in his ecclesiastical and theological endeavors. He was forced to resign in 1959 from Campinas Seminary after he experienced continual pressure from some of its students, faculty, and administrators.[66] His work with the Brazilian Presbyterian Youth Movement was also coming to an end after a new fundamentalist leadership emerged in the Presbyterian Church of Brazil both quenched the youth movement, reorganized its structure under the leadership of ordained pastors, and canceled the *Jornal Mocidade*.[67] In the early years of his ministry in Brazil, Shaull's missiological positions were oriented to the transformation of society through the intervention of the church as a community of believers in Jesus Christ. Through this community, God was acting in history by bringing the redemption of humanity closer to its final consummation.

65. Shaull, "La Iglesia y la Situación Político-Ideológica de América Latina," 164.

66. Pierson, *A Church of Need of Renewal*, 223.

67. João Dias de Araûjo, *Inquisition without Burnings*, 22–29.

Nevertheless, the social implications of Shaull's message of a missionary God directing the community of believers to help in the struggles of society was received with antagonism by the older generation of national leaders. Not only this, but for the ecclesiastical authorities, Shaull's insistence on a new theological language that could respond to the concrete circumstances of Brazil was too threatening.

By 1961, the situation in Brazil was turning increasingly revolutionary as Jânio Quadros resigned the presidency and João Goulart became the new president. Politics were increasingly polarized, with some seeking radical reforms and others wanting to maintain the status quo. Interestingly enough, these same positions were taken by groups within the Church. Members of the UCEB (Brazilian Christian Youth Movement) began a process of radicalization, proclaiming that "the contemporaneity of Christianity was on the Left" while others opted for clericalism and authoritarianism.[68] Nationalism was increasing, with protests against foreign investments and capital from the United States. According to Paul Abrecht, chair of the Commission on Church and Society of the WCC, there was a radical nationalism in many undeveloped countries that was committed to a total ending of ties with the colonial powers.[69] Because of the tremendous industrialization of Brazil, thousands of rural workers moved to the cities looking for a better life. The internal migrations from the rural areas to the cities created a huge problem as human beings were forced to live in cramped *favelas* without necessities such as potable water and sewage systems, which created a health hazard for thousands. With the country going through a revolutionary process, Shaull's missiology took a more radical form.

As Shaull tried to confront the issues he was facing as a missionary in the disintegration of Brazilian society, his most basic theological assumptions collapsed before him. The new generation of students entering the universities was more conscious than ever of the social and economic problems of the country. After President Quadros' resignation, university students were the first ones to react; in this context a widespread radicalization began to emerge in the UCEB. The UCEB declared that it would be a movement "on the side of those working for radical changes in basic structures of society as the essential condition for the humaniza-

68. Barbara Hall and Edir Cardoso, "SCM Odyssey," 7.

69. Paul Abrecht, *The Churches and Rapid Social Change* 102.

tion of Brazilian life; that is, we took the position of the Left. The now-famous phrase that signaled our conviction was, The contemporaneity of Christianity is on the Left."[70] The revolutionary process in UCEB was intensified by students who saw no need for theology, biblical studies, nor wanted any association with the church, if the church would not "accept our radical commitment to the humanization of Brazilian life through revolutionary political action."[71]

One of the things that changed in this period was the students' understanding of Marxism. During the first years of his ministry Shaull aspired—as would any other Protestant missionary of the time—to work for the conversion of Roman Catholics and Marxists. Now Shaull had to step back and reflect on Marxism as the only political force that gave direction to students in Brazil. Hall and Cardozo argued, "We were exposed to all the vigor of the Marxist interpretation, which seemed for a while to be the only one which made sense of what was happening."[72] In a time of total disintegration and chaos, a time in which religion was used to hold together a complete social-political system, the attraction of Marxist thought needed to be reexamined. Shaull argued that if Christians were to think about their own vision of a more just and human society, they would recognize that the Marxists' vision of society was close to their own.[73] For Shaull, that implied that Christians and Marxists should enter into a new agreement and try to understand each other and work for the same goal of humanization. Not only were Marxists influential at that time, but some sectors of the Roman Catholic Church were also starting to emerge with a new vision of liberation.

In the first articles Shaull wrote for the *Student World* in 1952, he had advocated for the right of Protestants to evangelize Roman Catholics and present to them the demands of Jesus Christ. Ten years later, Shaull was forced to recognize that Roman Catholics who were struggling in the same cause of making better conditions for those dehumanized by society were his companions in the cause. Shaull's first cordial and ecumenical contact with a member of the Roman Catholic Church was with Paulo Denis, a Dominican friar who lived in the convent of São Paulo

70. Barbara Hall and Edir Cardozo, "SCM Odyssey," 7.

71. Ibid., 8.

72. Ibid., 9.

73. Richard Shaull, "Entre Jesus e Marx," 202.

and wanted to participate in the Bible studies of the UCEB.[74] After some weeks of Bible studies together and commenting on how the Bible could be related to the Brazilian reality, Shaull was invited to the Convent to start conversations on the developments in French Catholic thought by the Dominican friars. Carlos Josaphat, one of the Dominicans who participated in those events remembered Shaull as one of the first Protestant missionaries ever to participate in such dialogues.[75] This ecumenical initiative caused an uproar in the Presbyterian Church of Brazil, which saw the new openness to Roman Catholics as a betrayal of the cause of Jesus Christ. The editorial of the journal *O Puritano* reported:

> Those pastors and believers who trust in the attitude of the Roman Catholic Church (which is sympathetic at times), even to the point of foreseeing ecumenical collaboration with the figure of the woman of the Apocalypse, the Church of the Pope, deceived themselves . . . Ecumenism, collaboration, union, with those who believe in the inspiration of the Bible, but not with those who burn it in public squares. Against those, struggle to the death.[76]

However, several valuable projects did develop as a result of the cooperation between Protestants and Roman Catholics. The first collaboration was the result of a grant the group received from the United States to initiate a joint publication. The Centro Ecuménico de Documentação e Informação (CEDI) grew out of those first encounters, as did a new journal. The first issue of the journal *Paz e Terra* was published in July 1966 and presented articles by theologians, social scientists, and Marxists, all trying to give an accurate solution to the problems of the nation.[77] This context began to lead Shaull's missiology down a radical new path, one in which he increasingly recognized the oppressive character of social structures. These structures were the ones dominating society and serving the interests and the perpetuation of the status quo. During this part of his life, Shaull began to construct a theology of structures that used eschatology as a framework.

---

74. Ibid., 205.

75. Frei Carlos Josaphat, "Uma Figura Humana e Evangélica," 60–61.

76. Editorial, *O Puritano*, 201.

77. Waldo Cesar, "Do Individualismo á Comunidade," 46–47.

*chapter five*

# A North American Revolutionary?
# The Ministry of a Returned Missionary

The period from 1962 to 1966 marked a new era in Shaull's life as he began a new ministerial career as professor of ecumenics at Princeton Seminary. One of Shaull's biggest tasks back home was to inform North Americans of the dreadful living conditions of Latin Americans—something he had been doing since the beginning of his days as a missionary in Latin America. The first time that Shaull raised North American students' awareness about this was at the Seventeenth Quadrennial Conference of the Student Volunteer Movement held in Athens, Ohio, from December 27, 1955 to January 1, 1956, when he described the living conditions of people in Latin America as going through a process of revolution.[1]

Under the leadership of Margaret Flory, the event was one of the biggest student conferences in the history of the United States.[2] The theme of the Conference was "Revolution and Reconciliation." An estimated three thousand five hundred students from around the world attended the SVM Conference at the University of Ohio and approximately one thousand of those students were from the non-Western world.[3] Women had a great representation at the conference, and showed they were particularly committed to the missionary cause of the church and to the min-

1. Shaull, *Encounter with Revolution*, 3–19.

2. Roche, "Initiating and Sustaining Ecumenical Ministries," 90–95.

3. "Annual Report of the Office of Student Work" n.p., n.d. Richard Shaull Papers, Special Collections, Speer Library, Princeton Theological Seminary, Princeton. mimeograph.

istry of reconciliation. Japanese and Korean students attested to the mood of reconciliation when they celebrated a service together in the chapel, letting go of their mutual hatred generated by the Japanese occupation of Korea.[4] Ruth M. Harris, a distinguished Methodist worker with the Board of Global Ministries for more than thirty years and with strong connections with the Philippine human rights movement, remembered Shaull's presentation in Athens as crucial to shaping her passion and development as a missionary and a women's advocate.[5] After Beatriz Couch, then a student at Princeton Seminary and later the first woman professor of theology at ISEDET in Buenos Aires, Argentina, heard Shaull speak, she went back to Princeton Seminary and organized a group of eight students to travel all around Mexico preaching the gospel in every single town she visited.[6]

This chapter describes Shaull's arrival back to the United States as a returned missionary, his radicalization about the missionary enterprise, and his resignation as a professor of Princeton Seminary. First, the chapter describes Shaull's activities while a professor at Princeton Seminary. In his first years as professor, Shaull worked with Margaret Flory and Charles West on several projects such as the Frontier Internship in Mission Program, which sent students for two years to study in universities in the non-western world, and the Inter-American Affairs Project, which concentrated its efforts on developing U.S. relations with Latin America.

Second, Shaull was one of the main speakers at the Conference of Church and Society of the WCC in Geneva in 1966. This meeting was of the utmost importance because it was an earnest attempt by the WCC to understand the revolutionary realities which shaped the modern world. Shaull challenged the ethical paradigm of the responsible society as elaborated previously by the ecumenical movement, and proposed a contextual ethics of revolution based on the actions of God in history. In this part of the chapter, his missiology will be the principal motif through which to understand the development of his approach to social ethics. Finally, his missiology as a radical returned missionary was developed in the context of his participation in the New Left with radical students, the formation

---

4. Roche, "Initiating and Sustaining Ecumenical Ministries," 92.

5. Harris, "Ruth Harris," 15–16.

6. Roche, "Initiating and Sustaining Ecumenical Ministries," 93.

of NACLA (North American Congress for Latin America), and the establishment of an alternative Christian community in Philadelphia.

## The Inter-American Affairs Project

Based on his experience with seminary and university students in Latin America, Shaull was convinced that the university could become one of the most influential forces in shaping the process of humanization. In an effort to understand this process, through Shaull's initiative and in collaboration with Margaret Flory and the WSCF, Princeton Seminary brought together twenty-five university teachers, students, and pastors from the non-western world during the first semester of 1963.[7] The focus of their time together was to understand the role of the university in the process of national development and how the Christian community could be part of it. Therefore, in the midst of social disintegration and chaos, the university was called to be a place of orientation and hope. Shaull pointed out, "We are called to concern ourselves with the task of giving form to the Christian community on the frontiers of humanization in the university."[8] This evidenced a slight change in Shaull's understanding of the church. Earlier he had conceived the church as being a "fellowship of believers—a *koinonia*, now he wanted to present the church as a "community called to serve." He pointed out,

> If we take seriously what we profess about the Lordship of Christ over the world and the presence of grace and of the Spirit in the center of life and of history, what is called for is a community which points to these realities and makes them visible in human relationships. This community comes into existence as those who are willing to share the suffering of Jesus Christ as the man for others—be they 'believers' or 'unbelievers'—do so in interrelatedness at some concrete point in the university.[9]

In this new conception of the church, anyone who was contributing to the process of humanization was considered to be part of it. As Johannes Verkuyl said, "whenever love for God and one's neighbor is

7. Shaull, "Community and Humanity in the University," 307–23.

8. Ibid., 315.

9. Ibid., 320–21.

blooming, there God is engaged, and the signs of the messianic kingdom become visible . . . Everything directed toward welfare, liberation, and the unshackling of the fetters of injustice—in short, everything 'salvation oriented'—has to do with the *missio Dei* and is within the perspective of the messianic kingdom."[10] Thus, Shaull envisaged the university as a "form of the church in the modern Diaspora" in that it could open new possibilities in the process of humanization. Also, he overcame the tension of the theological and sociological understanding of the church, basing his missiology in an understanding of the church as a community of people called to serve—*diakonia*. He recognized that as these new communities were called to serve humanity in the university, they might feel out of place in the institutional church. Shaull pointed out, "I personally believe that our obedience in the university requires us to move ahead toward the formation of this type of Christian community, even if this leads to great tension, perhaps open conflict in some cases, with the church organization."[11] After experiencing many traumas within the institutional church as a missionary, Shaull was convinced that the institutional church had no future in the "new missionary frontier." Yet Shaull really never spelled out what these Christian communities would look like because he trusted that the shape of the communities would emerge in a process of trial and error.

While in Brazil, Shaull contributed to the five-year study program on "The Life and Mission of the Church" sponsored by the WSCF. However, the missiology of the WSCF had moved from that stage of finding meaning in the life and mission of the church to the concept of "Christian presence." The central concern now was not the church but the world, and because the WSCF was at the center of educational institutions the university became the church within a church. The concept of Christian presence as developed in the WSCF was not limited to a passive role but rather included "involvement, engagement, and responsibility in and for the world."[12] Shaull was attracted to the concept of Christian presence because it gave him space to continue his missiological thinking about a God who was active in history, specifically in the revolutionary process.

10. Verkuyl, *Contemporary Missiology*, 4–5.

11. Shaull, "Community and Humanity in the University," 323.

12. Potter and Wieser, *Seeking and Serving the Truth*, 209.

As the process of secularization increased in the world, theological categories which were valid in the past lost their vitality. Shaull pointed out, "The process of secularization has swept away our two-storied, metaphysical conception of reality. With it has gone the assumption of the existence of an eternal rational order which man could know and from which truth, values, and an ideal order of society could be deduced… Secularization has also meant the lost of a total worldview in which all knowledge might be integrated and all areas of life and society related to each other in any comprehensive way."[13] The world, according to Shaull, was in a stage of revolution.[14] Shaull adhered to the missiology of Christian presence, but opted to develop a missiology of revolution in the 1960s. For example, Shaull participated in the United Presbyterian Consultation on an Ecumenical Approach to Christian Presence in the Universities Abroad held at Krisheim House, Philadelphia in January 1965. He pointed out three factors that contributed to the shift in language from that of "mission" and "witness" to "presence." First, he attributed the change of perspective to the disintegration of present structures and the collapse of a metaphysical worldview. Second, the impact of secularization upon all aspects of human existence was something that challenged the church to seek for new alternatives to describe the mission of the church. Finally, "presence" was a sign of hope in a situation where Christians had little to say because they had not caught up with the developments in the modern world.

For Shaull, the old theological paradigm of a metaphysical understanding of reality and the assumption about "truth" and a rational order of the cosmos had run its course. The process of secularization and the technological revolution were now the two major realms for the new missionary enterprise.[15] For Shaull, the concept of Christian presence probably was too passive to be implemented in the revolutionary context of Latin America where Christians were called to active, positive, and critical engagement in the revolution.[16]

13. Shaull, "Community and Humanity in the University," 308.

14. Shaull, "New Revolutionary Mood in Latin America," 44–48.

15. Shaull, "The Christian World Mission in a Technological Era," 212.

16. Shaull, "Fe, Ideología, y Revolución Social," 41–47; and "Hacia una Perspectiva Cristiana de la Revolución Social," 6–15.

We find a new concept that helped Shaull in his missiological career in the early 1960s in the publication of Arend Th. Van Leeuwen's book *Christianity in World History.*[17] In this book, Van Leeuwen depicted the nature of God's action in history as happening in two concrete stages: First, he reviewed the religions and cultures of the East and indicated that they produced a way of life "ontocratic" in nature—meaning that in those cultures a total order of harmony existed between the eternal and the temporal, the divine and the human. The divine order was identified with nature and society as the embodiment of a cosmic totality. Thus, all representatives with authority in society were divinely elected to preserve an established divine pattern that could not be changed or challenged.[18] Second, compared to this "ontocratic" understanding, the people of Israel had a theocratic understanding of reality: God had destroyed all static patterns of society and created something new in their place.[19] The eschatological undertones of this conception of a theocratic understanding of reality paralleled Shaull's conception of God who acts and transforms history. If Christians were living in the present as in the future, they should be able to discern where God was desacralizing the established ontocratic patterns of modern society. Therefore, the frontier on which God was working became in Shaull's missiology a place of disruption and new creation.

This idea is particularly well depicted in one of Shaull's favorite Bible passages—Jeremiah 1:10 "See, I have set you this day over nations and over kingdoms, to pluck up and to break down, to destroy and to overthrow, to build and to plant."[20] To Shaull this meant that as God destroyed old structures that dehumanized individuals, the church needed to create new structures whose goal was the total humanization of society.

Shaull had exhibited a pattern of messianism since his missionary assignment in Colombia where he described himself as a missionary "maverick." Other missionaries complained to the Board of Foreign Missions accusing the Board of favoritism toward Shaull, who to their mind did not follow the procedures to communicate to the Board and imposed his projects upon the mission. Shaull did not go through the established

17. Van Leeuwen, *Christianity in World History.*
18. Shaull, "The Van Leeuwen Thesis," 68–71.
19. Ibid., 69.
20. Shaull, "The New Challenge before the Younger Churches," 201.

channels of communication in the "mission field." Where as missionaries were supposed to present their case first to the Field Representative, Shaull typically skipped that process and sought approval for his projects directly from the Board.

In Brazil, Shaull clashed with the fundamentalist faction of the Presbyterian Church and was pressured to resign from his teaching position at Campinas Seminary in 1958. His ecumenical initiatives with Roman Catholics and Marxists went beyond the teachings of previous missionaries regarding the proper relationship with those bodies. Shaull's insistence on constructing his missiology based on the political, social, and economic context was another reason for the increasing rift between Shaull and the larger Presbyterian Church in Brazil, while his missiology of social transformation through God's redemptive activity in history and the revolutionary process placed Shaull as a liberal missionary in a conservative context. Not surprisingly, Shaull's work as a constructive theologian flourished the most through his involvement in the broader ecumenical movement, especially through the Sector of Social Responsibility of the Church and the Brazilian Christian Movement (UCEB). Should Shaull be blamed for his messianic vision or his prophetic stand? Did his messianism prevent him from compromising with those who held more conservative political and theological views?

By 1964, Shaull was an established missiologist in a privileged academic institution in the United States. He continued to see the world going through a revolutionary process, but to claim revolution in Brazil at that moment was like a death sentence for the military repression was too strong and an insurgency would simply result in more blood-shed. Circumstances had moved beyond Shaull's called to revolution. A more moderate theological language was in the making in Latin American Roman Catholicism and ISAL: a language of liberation.[21]

Shaull continued his work with the Inter-American Program. In 1966 he was the principal speaker at several conferences in the United States. For example, in the Latin American Affairs Seminar, sponsored by the United Campus Christian Fellowship and the National Student Christian Federation, held at the University of Pittsburg on February 16–18, 1966,

---

21. Gutiérrez, "Toward a Theology of Liberation," 62–76; and Alves, *Toward a Theology of Liberation.*

he presented a paper on "God's Present Action in Latin America."[22] In it, Shaull described the revolutionary mood in Latin America and explored the contrast between the industrial revolution and the lack of social development. For Shaull, the economic situation in Latin America, complicated by the uneven distribution of land and capital, outdated methods of farming, dependence on foreign trade, and the political crisis were all examined in light of the church's responsibility to act in solidarity with the revolutionary forces of change.[23]

The National Student Christian Federation of North America organized a Consultation on Latin America at Stony Point, New York on June 25-26, 1966. Twenty representatives of different student movements, professors of theology, and social scientists were present at that event, among them Margaret Flory, secretary for the National Christian Federation; Feliciano Cariño, leader of the Philippines student movement; Barbara Hall, fraternal worker in Brazil; Richard Graham, professor at Cornell University, and Richard Shaull. Most of the conference dealt with understanding the revolutionary process in Latin America. Luis Alberto de Souza, a Brazilian Roman Catholic theologian, expressed the situation in Latin America as being composed of two contradictory ideas: first, radical revolution in Latin America was a reality; and second, radical revolution was an impossibility.[24] The tension between the reality of revolution as represented by the exploited masses and the impossibility of attaining the revolutionary goal of constructing a new society led Shaull to take more radical stances in his missiology. However, after Shaull was targeted as an enemy of Colombia and Brazil and expelled from those countries by conservative regimes which had evolved into dictatorial powers, and after the invasion of Santo Domingo by the United States which disrupted a democratic process and deposed its leader, Shaull entered into a stage of fatalism. He pointed out, "No clear strategy with which to bring change seems to make sense. In Brazil, April 1964, proved that revolution and enthusiasm is impossible. Santo Domingo showed that even popular up-

22. Leaflet on The Latin American Affairs Seminar: A Brief Report. The Margaret Flory Papers, Special Collections, Yale Divinity School Library, New Haven.

23. Ibid.

24. Luis Alberto de Souza, "Report on the Consultation on Latin American Concerns," The Margaret Flory Papers, Special Collections, Yale Divinity School, New Haven.

risings are futile, and Dominican elections, that democratic process will not do it."[25]

One clear example of Shaull's shifting position was on the matter of pacifism. His years at Elizabethtown College with the Moravian Brethren introduced him to pacifism and non-violence, but twenty years of missionary work in a context of brutal exploitation aroused in him doubts about his stance. Alberto de Souza challenged the conference participants' views of pacifism, saying "Pacifism is on the side of the revolutionary forces in the United States. It is akin to those who are engaged in humanizing existing society. But Latin America requires change, and in this context those who hate violence and think non-violence is moral are part of the established order. In a situation, then, in which non-violence is useful to the status quo, is aggression and violence out?"[26] These words certainly struck a cord in Shaull's consciousness. The issue of violence as a possibility became real for him because he was convinced that God was on the side of the poor and oppressed and against the oppressor. Shaull later acquiesced to the idea of violence against the structures of oppression.

Contextual Ethics of Revolution at Geneva, 1966

In contributing to the formulation of a relevant Christian social ethics in the midst of rapid social transformations, the 1966 Geneva Conference of the department of Church and Society followed the tradition of the Ecumenical Movement at the Stockholm Conference of Life and Work in 1925 and the Oxford Conference in 1937 and the Conferences sponsored by the World Council of Churches in Amsterdam, 1948, Evanston, 1954, and New Delhi, 1961. The Geneva Conference was the WCC's most serious attempt to understand the current revolutionary situation in the modern world. Present at Geneva were more than 420 participants, including thirty-five observers and eighteen guests, who ha come from eighty nations and 164 churches.[27] Two of the most notable aspects of the

25. Shaull, "Report on the Consultation on Latin American Concerns." The Margaret Flory Papers, Special Collections, Yale Divinity School, New Haven.

26. Luis Alberto de Souza, "Report on the Consultation on Latin American Concerns" The Margaret Flory Papers, Special Collections, Yale Divinity School, New Haven.

27. Thomas and Abrecht, *Christians in the Technical and Social Revolutions of Our Time*, 6.

Conference were first, the high percentage of lay leaders who were economists, politicians, and social scientists, and second, the high proportion
of delegates from Asia, Africa, and Latin America.[28] The purpose of the
Conference was to gather representatives of the social sciences and theologians to examine contemporary problems in the world and explore what
might be the implications of those problems for human relationships:

> The accelerating technological development of our time; the lib-
> eration of peoples from various kinds of dominance together with
> their new expectations of a fuller life; the growing division between
> the rich and the poor countries; the conflicting interests and con-
> sequent power struggles of the nations in an increasingly interde-
> pendent world. To recognize the way in which these revolutionary
> changes have affected and continue to affect Christian discipleship
> in the modern world. To consider, in light of such recognition, the
> bearing of the Christian Gospel on social thought and action: to
> formulate, for consideration by the Churches, proposals for the
> strengthening and renewal of their ministry by society; to help
> the WCC in formulating policies which will give expression to a
> Christian concern for human solidarity, justice and freedom in a
> world of revolutionary change.[29]

The opening days of the Conference were dedicated to its main four
themes: the potential of the scientific and technological revolutions; the
political and economic dynamics of the new nations; the search for a new
ethos for new societies; and finally, the challenge and relevance of theology to the social revolutions. Shaull, together with H.D. Wendland, former rector of the University of Munster, and Vitali Vorovoy, professor of
Church history at Orthodox Theological Academy in Leningrad were the
main speakers for the plenary session on "The Challenge and Relevance
of Theology to the Social Revolution of Our Time."

Since the first meeting of the World Council of Churches in
Amsterdam in 1948, the theory of the "responsible society" had guided
the social ethics of the World Council of Churches. The ethics of the "responsible society was defined as a society where the state is responsible
for a just distribution of wealth, where the individual is guaranteed freedom, and where the state is responsible to and can be controlled by the

28. Abrecht, "Development of Ecumenical Thought and Action," 251.
29. Ibid., 8–9.

electorate."[30] The freedom that the "responsible society" promoted was in opposition to the totalitarian and fascist political regimes that violated the principle of freedom. As the Amsterdam Conference assembled right after World War II when communism as a political alternative was spreading throughout Asia and Africa, the Christians gathered at that Conference decided that they should criticize and oppose communism as well as laissez-faire capitalism.[31]

Walter George Muelder, dean and professor of social ethics at Boston University, pointed out eight principles that could be derived from this ideal as applied to contemporary culture and society:

> 1) The role of religious norms in the just and free society; 2) the conception of man, his dignity, rights and self-realization in community with others; 3) the nature, authority, and scope of the modern state and its function in relation to the community; 4) the interpretation of the political, economic, and social spheres of society; 5) the dialectic of such ideals as equality, freedom, and justice within the notion of responsible living; 6) the responsibility of persons to domestic and international orders of freedom and justice; 7) the accountability of power groups within nations; and 8) the responsibilities of nations to one another and to the future of responsible international order.[32]

Muelder emphasized the religious component of the idea of the responsible society and recognized that ultimately the church's responsibility was to God and from there ethical principles should emerge based on justice, freedom, equality, and solidarity.[33] Therefore, what the responsible society wanted to create was a third way or an alternative to communism and capitalism, a way that could secure a persons' full freedom with respect to justice, equality, and religion. Maulder's alternative emphasized the importance of the individual person, which made his notion of a responsible society different from Marxism.

---

30. *The Message and Reports of the First Assembly of the World Council of Churches*, 51.

31. Grenholm, "Christian Social Ethics in a Revolutionary Age," 34–36; and Walter G. Muelder, *Idea of the Responsible Society*, 8–9.

32. Muelder, *Idea of the Responsible Society*, 8–10.

33. Ibid., 11.

One basic presupposition of the ethics of the responsible society was that economic development could be achieved through the process of modernization and industrialization. Yet as the goal of freedom was intrinsically connected to justice and equality, the logical assumption was that through the process of industrialization and technological improvements the underdeveloped nations would keep pace and attain the same degree of prosperity and development. Muelder pointed out, "The more socially concrete expressions of the responsible society relate to land reform, planning for production, and raising the standard of living with the assistance of technical 'know how' and capital from abroad."[34] A couple of years before the Geneva Conference, Shaull had had the same confidence that technology and development would change the lot of the poor in Asia, Africa, and Latin America. But Shaull's conception of development was intrinsically connected with a change in political and social structures.

The 1950s saw the emergence of the development programs instituted by the colonial powers to help the former colonies advance their economic programs. Lesslie Newbigin pointed out, "As the sense of a single global community grew stronger, so also did the sense that an obligation rested upon the wealthy nations to help the poorer to raise their standard of living."[35] The assumption that the underdeveloped nations just needed monetary and industrial help from the developed ones in order to advance their economic and social lot turned out to be a false hope. When the development dreams of the 1950s did not materialize but instead aggravated the lot of the poor, a new wave of criticisms and a total rupture with those assumptions emerged in the 1960s. Comblin argued that by the 1960s Latin Americans understood that "underdevelopment is [was] not belated development at all; on the contrary, it is [was] nothing less than a secondary effect of the development of the developed nations."[36] What became clear was that the relationship between the developed nations and the underdeveloped ones was one of domination. The more technology and financial aid was given to the underdeveloped nations, the more economic benefits the developed nations obtained through high interest loans and subsidies. Shaull challenged the ethical paradigm of the responsible society and the developmental program, and proposed an

34. Ibid., 25.
35. Newbigin, "Mission in Six Continents," 174.
36. Comblin, *Church and the National Security State,* 33.

option for a contextual ethics of revolution based on the actions of God in history.

Previous scholarship has claimed Richard Shaull to be the "theologian of revolution" because of his participation in the Geneva Conference of the WCC in 1966.[37] In fact, however, the central elements of a theology of revolution had been present in Shaull since his first encounter with poverty in Latin America in 1942. Therefore, the major problem with these studies is that they do not place Shaull in his previous historical context as a missionary in Colombia and Brazil and the missiology he developed from those experiences. They only address Shaull's contribution after his missionary experience and do not take into consideration that his formation as a missionary in situations of oppression was in fact what led to his revolutionary ideals. The other major problem of the two principal studies (*Christian Social Ethics in a Revolutionary Age* and *An Analysis and Critique of the Theory of Revolution in the Theology of M. Richard Shaull*) is that they take the word "revolution" as the *locus* to understand Shaull, when in reality he is better understood through his missiology of the *kononia*—a community of witnesses-servants.

Shaull contributed to two preparatory studies for the Geneva Conference. First, at the invitation of the Christian Church Disciples of Christ he collaborated in preparing the study guide for that denomination entitled *Revolution and Renewal.* Second, in the preparatory volume for the Conference, *Christian Social Ethics in a Changing World* edited by John Bennett, Shaull wrote the article "Revolutionary Change in Theological Perspective."

In "Revolutionary Change in Theological Perspective," Shaull continued to use technology as a starting point for formulating his missiology. For him technology represented the new frontier in which the destiny of human beings could either be improved or dehumanized. But as with the structures in Latin America that were dominated by a small minority who held all the economic and political power, technology in the West was dominated by an elite group of wealthy people who were "willing to go to

---

37. Grenholm, *Christian Social Ethics in a Revolutionary Age*; Mark O'Keefe, *An Analysis and Critique of the Theory of Revolution in the Theology of M. Richard Shaull*; Jose Comblin, *The Church and the National Security State*; and Hugo Assmann, *Theology for a Nomad Church.*

almost any length to preserve" their hold on it.[38] The context of development put pressure on the issue: for the more technology and financial
aid the developed nations sent to Latin America, the more they gained
economically by doing so. While the developed nations (in this case the
United States) presented a façade of being a good neighbor by providing
technological and financial aid to Latin America, in reality their behavior caused the underdeveloped nations to dig their own "dependency"
graves. Shaull rightly perceived the ambiguous character of the technological era as bringing both positive and negative consequences to the
processes of industrialization, urbanization, and economic development
in Latin America.

Along with all the good aspects of the technological revolution,
Shaull also recognized the downside of the process: "This technological progress has often tended to increase the misery and insecurity of
the poor, provide even greater opportunities for the few to profit, and
leave the masses in greater insecurity than before."[39] Here, Shaull was
departing from the notion of the ethics of the "responsible society" that
through responsible economic incentives and technological development
the underdeveloped nation would attain the same degree of prosperity as
the developed nations in the West. The clear division between the ones
who had the benefits of technology and the ones who were the victims
of it, between the rich and the poor, set the stage for social revolution.
Shaull concluded that all the major issues related to such humanization
or dehumanization would be decided on the frontier of the revolutionary
process.

Shaull's theological standpoint on revolution was guided by his understanding of God as the creator and ruler of the cosmos. His Calvinist
heritage regarding the sovereignty of God allowed Shaull to construct a
theological position in which God as Creator and ruler of the cosmos
was also ruler and Lord of history. His eschatological emphasis on God
acting in history with the goal of redeeming humanity was central to his
missiological affirmation of the justification for Christians to participate
in such redemptive activities in society. Shaull thought that the best way
to achieve this ideal was through an understanding of "the revolutionary

38. Richard Shaull, "Revolutionary Change in Theological Perspective," 24.
39. Ibid.

character of biblical messianism."[40] It was in the dynamic historical character of God's action that Shaull saw the future restoration of all things through God's transformative grace. His own messianic vision and interpretation of the prophets gave him a sense of eschatological expectation that God would intervene in the revolutionary affairs of the world and at the same time gave him the boldness to face the present as if living in the future eschatological era where God would be completely manifested in God's reign of mercy, justice, and righteousness. But this same conviction of his election to accomplish a special task on earth would be his downfall in many projects to come and his later frustration and distancing from the missionary cause.

Drawing on the Augustinian view of social change attested to in the *City of God*, Shaull proposed a Trinitarian way of understanding the activity of God in history as being foundational. He pointed out, "Convinced that the Logos of Christ, revealed in Scripture, was the ultimate reality in human life and history, he [Augustine] could think and act in the conviction that each and every occurrence in the manifold of events bears witness to the activity of God."[41] Robert Dodaro offers a groundbreaking study abut Augustine's political and ethical thought in relation to his theology. In answering how Augustine constructed a just society, Dodaro invites his readers to reconsider not just fragments of Augustine's political or ethical thought, but rather to bring together various areas of his thought such as "Christ, human knowledge, the church, and scriptural hermeneutics."[42]

For Dodaro, Augustine constructed his thought of a "just society" in objection to Cicero's claim that "Rome has ceased to be a commonwealth when it abandoned justice."[43] Because civil virtues were never part of Rome, Dodaro argues that Augustine saw this as a way to question the nature of secular virtues while claiming Christ as the best example of a true statesman because of his conduct and eloquence. Because Christ was the best example of conduct and eloquence, Christ was the only being that could heal human beings of their ignorance and weaknesses. True

40. Ibid.,28.

41. Ibid., 29.

42. Robert Dodaro, *Christ and the Just Society in the Thought of Augustine* (Cambridge: Cambridge University Press, 2004), 1.

43. Ibid., 2.

virtue and the establishment of a "just society" come to human beings only through the mediation of such virtue through Christ as testified in scriptures. Dodaro points out that "Augustine concludes that its [just society] capacity to achieve true justice depends on the extend to which it follows [just society] the example of Christ and the saints in praying, 'forgive us our sins as we forgive those who sin against us" (MT 6:12).[44]

In this sense, Augustine wanted believers to recognize their own sinfulness and the false assumption that individuals could produce their own true virtue. True virtue was a mystery hidden from reason but revealed in Christ's mediation of true virtue to humanity through his examples of "spiritual arts of penitence—self-examination, confession, prayer for pardon, and forgiveness of others, especially of enemies."[45]

No matter how chaotic human beings perceived certain historical moments to be, Christians were called to recognize that there, in the midst of chaos, God was directing history to its final consummation of the Kingdom. Shaull stated, "Historical events were seen as occurring along a line set by the dynamic reality of God's Providence, his bringing in of his Kingdom, the work of the Holy Spirit in the world and the movement of history toward its final goal."[46] For this reason, Christians should be prepared to engage in the revolutionary process, and understand that in order to live, they must first go through the process of dying. To die to the abusive structures of oppression and fight for their eradication was to live the new life attested to in Christ. The major challenge for Christians in this process was to understand how to be agents of humanization and not participate in the silence of promoting the status quo. To follow Christ demanded from Christians a total engagement in the revolutionary process because theologically revolution was God's way of humanization.

One of the most drastic changes in Shaull's missiology occurred at this same intersection between the role of the Christian in the revolution and the role of the church. An ambiguous tension between the church as institution and the church as people of God was always present in his arguments. By the late 1960s, the church as institution had completely disappeared from Shaull's missiological language, replaced by *koinonia*-- the witnesses and agents of God called to be on the frontlines of God's

44. Ibid., 201.
45. Ibid., 218.
46. Ibid., 30.

redeeming activities of humanization. So was Shaull called a theologian of revolution because he took that term as a theological category or because of his complete break with the institutional Church as a means to bring social change? Shaull was definitely one of the first theologians to appropriate the term "revolution" and use it as a theological category, but his break with the institutional church could also be considered to be a sign of his frustration with the ineffective structures of church life.

Shaull envisioned for Christians an orientation for ethical decisions rooted in a contextual ethic, using as *locus* the theology of messianism as advocated by his mentor Paul Lehmann.[47] Paul Lehmann was best known for his contextual ethics. In contextual ethics, moral decision-making in the context of actions took precedence over their laws or consequences. Lehmann stated, "Christian ethics as a theological discipline is the reflection upon the question, and its answer: What am I, as a believer of Jesus Christ and as a member of his church, to do?"[48] Contextual ethics placed God at the center of the historical situation and asked what God was doing in such specific event. In general, the response was that God was active and present doing God's will in the formation of a better world; but such activity was best discerned by the members of the *koinonia*. Lehmann points out, "Christian ethics is *koinonia ethics*. This meant that it is from, and in, the *koinonia* that Christians get the answer to the question: what am I, as a believer in Jesus Christ and as a member of his church, to do?"[49]

In the *koinonia* the will of God became "a concrete matter of politics."[50] By politics, Lehmann was referring to the Aristotelian notion of politics which suggested that the goal of an action was to establish social fellowship, a context in which a truly human life could be possible for everyone. Thus, politics was an "activity, and reflection upon activity, which aims at and analyzes what it takes to make and to keep human life human in the world." The biblical answer to that axiom was that only through Jesus Christ can human life in the world find its true meaning.[51]

47. Ibid., 40.
48. Lehmann, *Ethics in a Christian Context*, 25.
49. Ibid., 47.
50. Ibid., 82.
51. Ibid., 85.

To accomplish such a task, the *koinonia* needed a theology of messianism—what Lehmann said was that "a theology of messianism is a theology with the accent upon the politics of God, that is, upon what God has done and is doing in the world to keep human life human."[52] Lehmann helped Shaull to understand theology as a powerful transformational force that could be used to interpret and analyze the current social changes of the times and how to participate in them as a Christian. Shaull stated, "For him (Lehmann) the Bible offers a messianic vision of a world in transformation. Therefore, theology must be done vis-à-vis the coming of God's kingdom."[53] Shaull never equated the social revolution with the Kingdom of God but argued that the Kingdom transcended all political and social improvements anyone could achieve on earth. At the same time, the immanence of God through the historical event of the incarnation was a crucial motivation to strive for social justice in the world. Therefore, the Christian contribution to the revolutionary goals was to guide and orient the revolution in the process of humanization in a way that included the Christian actions of forgiveness, justice, and reconciliation.

One of the most radical criticisms against the contextual ethics of Shaull in the preparatory study came from ethicist Paul Ramsey. He argued that "the theology of the conference was a Christological-eschatological dynamic monism" and attributed the elevation of this position to Shaull's essay "Revolutionary Change in Theological Perspective." He criticized John Bennett, editor of the volume, for placing Shaull's chapter in the most prominent position at the beginning of the study guide which he felt indicated that all the ethical and theological reflection should follow Shaull's contextual ethics of revolution.[54] Ramsey accused Shaull of a truncated Barthianism as theological paradigm while "stressing Christ and the revolutionary situation, lopping off Barth's own prolongation of his Christocentric ethics into a doctrine of man and of creation."[55] The preparatory study guide became an issue for many traditional ethicists such as Paul Ramsey because Shaull advocated a departure from neo-orthodoxy and previous ethical stands of the ecumenical movement.

---

52. Ibid., 105.

53. Shaull, "Entre Jesus e Marx," 188.

54. Ramsey, *Who Speaks for the Church?* 76.

55. Ibid., 77.

Though Shaull was indeed not an ethicist but a missionary, he believed that for the Christian ethical action and evangelistic witness were fundamentally the same. For that reason, his ethics revealed more his convictions as a missionary than his scholastic training in ethics.

Since his encounter with students in the UCEB in the early 1960s, Shaull had known that a metaphysical understanding of reality was no longer capable of orienting and guiding the reality in which people were living in Latin America. As the metaphysical worldview collapsed, he searched for new categories, which he found in the theological messianism of Lehmann. Therefore, Shaull's theology was not a truncated Barthianism, as Ramsey argued, but rather a contextual missiology rooted in the historical developments taking place in Latin America. The eschatological orientation of God's final consummation of all things was present in Shaull's dictum of a God who acts and transforms history in the form of justice, freedom, and equality. In this sense, revolution became a theological category of Christian interaction with those forces that were striving to create a society based on those principles of justice, freedom, and equality.

With this in mind, we can better understand why Richard Shaull's address at the Geneva Conference of Church and Society was entitled "The Revolutionary Challenge to Church and Theology." In it, Shaull continued his missiological interpretation of the God who acts redemptively in history by calling the *koinonia* of witnesses to work for the transformation of society.[56] Shaull invited the participants of the Geneva Conference to make a methodological change in their theological interpretations. He pointed out, "All of our encouraging theological reflections will not be of much help to the new revolutionaries unless they are set within this concrete revolutionary situation and related to the questions arising there. Our first theological task is to take that step."[57] Shaull was inviting the participants of the Geneva Conference to enter into the world of the other, in this case of the poor and oppressed masses of society who lacked basic human necessities. Since the time of his ministry in Colombia, Shaull had been calling for a new style of doing theology. The new approach to theological reflection was rooted in the concrete social, political, economic,

---

56. Shaull, "The Revolutionary Challenge to Church and Theology," 25.

57. Ibid., 26.

and cultural contexts of everyone interested in the work of evangelization or humanization.

Shaull proceeded to delineate how this new theological expression could be achieved and took as an example his own experience with revolutionary students in Brazil. As technology became a total system of social domination and an ethos that offered unlimited possibilities to those who already held power and the impulse to keep it by all means possible, the new revolutionaries were sure that only through a process of structural change could a new humanity emerge. At this point, Shaull was influenced by the New Left theoretician, Herbert Marcuse and his book *One Dimensional Man.* Shaull described Marcuse's central thesis which argued that "technology, together with an ideological ethos accompanying it, is producing a system which tends to be totalitarian."[58] As the established system supplied some of the basic needs to some of its adherents and empowered others with great wealth, an ethos of secularity entered the scene and created a static way of life without any challenge from any sector of the population. In this one-dimensional existence, the only remedy was revolutionary action. But how should revolutionary action be accomplished?

Shaull proposed that the best way to accomplish revolutionary action was through the creation of small guerilla units which would concentrate on carrying out surprise attacks on the systemic structures of oppression that functioned in society. To him, such units could be an effective political strategy. Shaull pointed out, "In fact, the formation of such guerilla units, with a clear sense of self-identity, a vision of a new social order, and a commitment to constant struggle for change, inside or outside certain social structures, may offer one interesting prospect to build a new society."[59] Interestingly enough, the guerilla units to which Shaull referred had a similar function and description as the Christian *koinonia* of witnesses or cell groups. Another new development in Shaull's social ethics was that he now considered the use of violence as a viable means to achieve social transformation. He stated, "We would not go as far as professor Wendland and Philip to urge exclusive reliance on non-violent action, or insist that the Christian should have no participation in the

58. Ibid., 26.
59. Ibid., 28.

use of violence. There may, in fact, be some situations, in which only the threat or use of violence can set the process of change in motion."[60]

Until this conference, Shaull had never expressed any proclivity to violent action in his missiology. Yet he had been challenged on this by Luis Alberto de Souza at the Consultation on Latin American Concerns held at Stony Point, New York, in June 25-26, 1966, and maybe it was there that he developed this position. Was his frustration the result of the bitter experience of trying to bring renewal to the church in Latin America without achieving his goals? Was he thinking of the political turmoil created in Brazil after the military coup? Was he thinking of the United States and its problems with racism and its exploitation of developing nations? What was going on in his mind for him to endorse some type of violence? One thing was clear to Shaull: theology could advance the revolutionary process by helping tear down old structures of oppression.[61] He pointed out, "The new revolutionary needs those resources of transcendence and transgression which free him to break the bonds of the secular, empirical ethos, dream new dreams about the future of man, and cultivate the creative imagination so as to be capable of thinking about new problems in new ways, and defining new goals and models for a new society."[62]

Shaull was sure that a process of theological contextualization based on the redeeming activity of God in history was the first step to creating a new tomorrow today. In such historical process, the abstract principle of the "responsible society" would be of little or no help in the process of creating a new theological language: "Ethical orientation can be provided only as values are translated into specific social goals, specific human needs, and specific technical possibilities and priorities."[63] Only through participation in the historical revolution could theologians find that new language needed for the new missionary frontier of technology and secularization. The new theological language would come only as a result of that incarnational engagement as a witness of God's redeeming activity in the world.

60. Ibid.
61. Ibid., 29.
62. Ibid.
63. Ibid., 31.

Shaull's article caused an uproar in many theological circles around the world. He was criticized by theologians of the WCC, Roman Catholic theologians, and North American ethicists. Paul Ramsey, we have seen, accused Shaull of a truncated Barthianism. He pointed out, "A reason for the truncation was that the conference began with "man's disorder" (or man's revolutionary prospectus) rather than with God's design; and of necessity one cannot go very far in prolonging that into theological ethics even if he is accustomed to disciplined reflection."[64] Other criticisms from Latin America and Europe were more positive regarding some aspects of his theology. For example, Juan Luis Segundo praised Shaull for his concrete approach to revolution in Geneva, but criticized Shaull for not going far enough in the translation of his language from the historical process to theological discourse.

Segundo illustrated the ambiguity of Shaull's theological translation by quoting a section of the preparatory study "Revolutionary Change in Theological Perspective." "The kingdom of God always stands over against every social and political order, thus exposing its dehumanizing elements and judging it. At the same time, the Kingdom is a dynamic reality; it is 'coming' through the work of him who is restoring the nations and in whose good time the kingdom of this world shall become the kingdom of our Lord and Christ."[65] Segundo argued that for Christians seeking a historical orientation the first phrase would disconcert them because of its static character. Then Shaull presented the second phrase as dynamic and argued that the Kingdom was *coming,* but again asking by whom the Kingdom is coming? Segundo stated that when the time came for action, Christians seeking a concrete historical orientation in Latin America could not find anyone who could help them strategize options for political and social change because God is the only one restoring the nations.[66] Therefore, he asked, where is the historical concreteness in Shaull's theology of revolution? Maybe because similar criticisms had earlier been raised against him, Shaull concretized the historical process using the idea of guerilla warfare for social and political action in his address at the Geneva Conference.

64. Ramsey, *Who Speaks for the Church?* 77.

65. Shaull, "Revolutionary Change in Theological Perspective," 36. Segundo, *Liberación de la Teología,* 168.

66. Segundo, *Liberación de la Teología,* 169.

Another big critic of Shaull's contextual ethics of revolution was Arthur Rich, professor of theology at the University of Zurich, who wrote "Revolution as a Theological Problem" after the Geneva Conference.[67] Rich's paper was circulated for study and discussion in ecumenical circles promoted by the Department of Church and Society of the WCC. Rich's main question was how to discern the positive aspects of revolution and how an ethical principle should be applied. Should it be based on established norms? Or did Christians know the process from a contextual ethics and needed no norms to guide them? As the Geneva Conference assumed a contextual ethics, theologians who were against such an approach perceived it as causing serious theological problems.[68]

The main question that contextual ethics raised in Rich's theology was how the will of God was revealed, "*out of* the concrete revolutionary situation, or *in relation* to it?"[69] Rich argued that if contextual ethics developed *out of* the revolutionary process, they were similar to the conservative social ethics. Rich argued, "For both the will of God becomes transparent in the process of history." If this was the case, Rich advised that contextual ethics would be entering into the old structure of theological positivism, and revolution would become revolutionary conservatism.[70] He insisted that the will of God in revolutionary action be examined in relation to the Word of God and not deduced primarily from the concrete situation. Drawing on Karl Barth's thought, he argued that "God's commandment will have to be constitutive, as a substance of the Gospel, which authorizes the believer amid a revolutionary world to lead a revolutionary life whose aim is change."[71]

However, Shaull opposed exactly this type of argumentation because of its metaphysical tendency to impose a set of rules and regulations, even if they were derived from the Bible. He would reply that because of the contextual character of the revolutionary process in Latin America, theologians from the West would need to submerge themselves completely in the world of the poor and oppressed in those countries in order to articulate a new messianic language about God instead of relying on previous

67. Rich, "Revolution as a Theological Problem," 1–8.
68. Rich, "Revolution as a Theological Problem," 6.
69. Ibid.
70. Ibid., 7.
71. Ibid., 7.

theological formulations. Shaull would reject any Barthian interpretation of the events taking place around him and would strive to wrestle with the problems in new and creative ways. In this scenario, his own experience as a missionary in a revolutionary context became the chief criterion he used to formulate a contextual missiology. After the Geneva Conference of Church and Society, Shuall became the theologian of revolution with a message of disruption and breaking with the structures of the past. This messianism of breaking with all established norms and structures would lead him to many personal and ministerial failures.

## North American Congress for Latin America

After the Conferences of El Tabo, Chile, and Geneva in 1966, Shaull's contact with theologians and leaders in Latin America diminished. The initial arrangement of spending one semester in Princeton and the rest of the time in Latin America became a burden that he could no longer bear. The amount of work was too much for him to keep up with, given all the things he needed to accomplish in his missiological career.

Understandably then when Shaull disconnected himself from Latin America, he experienced a loss of identity. He discovered he was no longer just a North American, but rather a North American with a Latin American heart. This sense of loss of vocation, identity, and broken dreams led him to engage causes of freedom, justice, and equality in the United States. Interpreting the context of the mid 1960s in North America, Shaull was involved in the Civil Rights Movement, the New Left, and the North American Congress for Latin America (NACLA). This section presents Shaull's missiological radicalization and his involvement in NACLA, and his theological initiatives with students from the non-western world.

Shaull's persistence in his desire for systemic change in social structures correlated with those of the New Left in North America. He was certain that neither the old liberalism nor any form of political conservatism in North American would improve the lot of the poor. The New Left was a movement that stimulated much of the intellectual ferment in the 1960s in North American universities. One characteristic of many members of the New Left was their sense of historicism; they felt that if they understood the past they could shape the future.[72] Apart from this, what most attracted Shaull about the movement was its commitment to creating a better world based on freedom, justice, and equality. Already at the Geneva Conference, Shaull had drawn on Herbert Marcuse's argument of technology as a totalitarian system of domination which produced a one-dimensional man in a society without oppositions. Marcuse was considered by many to be the intellectual guru of the New Left, even though he rejected that characterization.[73] When *One Dimensional-Man* was published, North America was going through a severe racial crisis with the intensification of the civil rights movement and the antiwar coalition against the Vietnam War. The book helped a new generation of students and radicals, like Shaull, to dream of the construction of a new society by showing the inconsistencies of the present political structure in the United States.

While at Princeton Seminary, Shaull came into contact with the Students for a Democratic Society (SDS). Now firmly established in North American soil, Shaull was convinced that the same revolutionary principles once operating in Brazil were also thriving in North America through the civil rights movement, the anti-Vietnam war movement and the New Left. His previous experience in Brazil with radical students in the UCEB had prepared him for this type of ministry. When the U.S. invaded the Dominican Republic in April, 1965, sending 22,000 soldiers to secure its interests in that Island by overthrowing President Juan Bosch, a social Democrat with leftist ideals, Fred Goff, son of Presbyterian missionaries in Colombia, was called by a prominent liberal politician named Allard Lowenstein to form a group to monitor the upcoming election in the Dominican Republic.[74] Lowenstein organized a group called Commission for Free Elections in the Dominican Republic. While in Colombia, Goff's and Shaull's paths had crossed due to Shaull's friendship with Fred's parents. Fred invited Shaull to participate in the Commission for Free Elections as a Protestant representative in the upcoming election in the Dominican Republic.[75]

72. O'Neill, *The New Left*, x.

73. Marcuse, *The New Left and the 1960s*.

74. Rosen, "NACLA," 14.

75. Ibid., 13.

The elections were a disaster, with electoral districts reporting coercive tactics against Bosch's supporters. The popular uprising that sought to restore the constitutional government of Bosch was crushed by the U.S. marines. It was obvious that the United States would not tolerate a government with friendly ties to Fidel Castro's Cuban regime.[76] As in Brazil a year earlier, the United States proved that it would go to any lengths to consolidate its power in the region by backing rightist military regimes that agreed with U.S. policies. This event convinced Shaull that the U.S. would crush any revolutionary movement that tried to bring about social change.

Yet for Shaull, the way ahead was revolution, a counter discourse in opposition to the existing political order. Shaull became a prominent figure in the University Christian Movement (UCM) and the SDS. Fred Rosen, an economist and director of NACLA argued, "the UCM formed a Latin American Concerns Committee with a mandate to work for changes in U.S. Latin America policy, to participate in the formation of study groups and dialogue groups in Latin America and to start a publication."[77] Shaull hosted a symposium at Princeton Seminary with UCM members and participated in a second meeting in Chicago. In that meeting, the North American Congress for Latin America (NACLA) was formed as a distinct group whose purpose was to present empirical documentation of U.S. involvement in Latin America. The first official meeting of NACLA was in New York at the Interchurch Center which headquarters mainline church and mission boards. Through Shaull, NACLA was given free office space for the first year in the Presbyterian offices in the Interchurch building. The goal of the empirical research being done at the center was to reveal the internal inconsistencies of U.S. foreign policy in Latin America in order to change it. NACLA still today continues its mission of exposing U.S. domination in Latin America.

In February of 1966, Shaull was invited to participate in a symposium at Union Theological Seminary in New York. The other presenter for the occasion was Carl Oglesby, President of the Students for a Democratic Society, the largest affiliate of the New Left. The discussions provoked by that encounter resulted in an ongoing dialogue between Oglesby and Shaull and led to their co-authoring a book entitled *Containment and*

76. Tyson, "El Sistema Interamericano despues de Santo Domingo," 44–46.
77. Ibid., 15.

*Change.* In the first part of the book, Oglesby evaluated U.S. involvement in Vietnam and the meaning of the Cold War in that context. In the second part, "Revolution: Heritage and Contemporary Option," Shaull proposed several tactics and strategies for the new revolutionaries emerging in the United States.

Chief among these tactics and strategies was Shaull's broad goal of strengthening previous ideas of God's action in history, the justification of ideology as a theological tool, a new theological interpretation of the old symbols and signs presented in the Bible, and how the revolutionary was called to a ministry of transgression against the status quo. In particular, Shaull proposed, first, a search for a new sense of solidarity among humans to create a lifestyle with a "deep moral passion" in a world dominated by technology.[78] For Shaull, this meant that society needed to be more involved in the control of the economic order and to create new models for the ordering of economic life. He promoted a new form of personal existence in which individuals could achieve their potential by using revolution as the channel for change. Second, Shaull revisited the concept of ideology and used it as a theological source. Shaull pointed out,

> For ideology is the product of thought about the concreteness of man's life in the world in the context of his wider historical and human experience; it offers the possibility of explaining something of the latent meaning in the history that is to be made. It represents an attempt to look at particular social developments in the light of the past as well as the future; a search for understanding in order to define goals and work for change.[79]

Shaull insisted that theologians needed to be involved in the ideological process of searching for definite goals for the transformation of society. He was convinced that Christianity offered a variety of concepts, symbols, and signs through specific experiences in the Bible that could help interpret contemporary reality by giving Christians the possibility of a positive contribution in the new age that was emerging. To him, the church had lost the ability to create new meanings through the biblical symbols and images because it had acculturated itself to a position

78. Shaull, "Revolution: Heritage and the Contemporary Option," 185.
79. Ibid., 212.

of privilege and power in society through its self-understanding as the *corpus Christianum.* So in response, Shaull tried in particular to retrieve those biblical symbols found in the Exodus narrative that demonstrated the process of moving from slavery to freedom, and the New Testament story of Jesus of Nazareth who suffered death on the cross in order to be resurrected to a new life. Shaull understood Christians to partake of divine revelation when they took possession of those symbols, giving them central meaning through a correlation of what happened in the Bible and their own stories.

A Theological Community

While still teaching at Princeton Seminary, Shaull embarked on another project based on his experience in Colombia and Brazil. In both of these countries, Shaull had initiated communities of theological and social activism. In the midst of the turmoil of the late 1960s in the United States, Shaull and eight theological students formed what they called "A Theological Community." The Community was an experiment in theological education and patterns for changing lifestyles. It was designed as a two-year internship for students who wanted an orientation toward relating theological methodology to their involvement in specific social contexts. For Shaull, this venture was part of his missionary vocation: "My concern for the Christian mission today becomes more and more a concern for the discovery of new theological methodologies by which the resources of our heritage can once again become operative in shaping experience and society."[80] Shaull presented a proposal to President McCord that delineated all the details of the project from its rationale, objectives, implementation, and context to its evaluation and budget.

Most of the time McCord consented to Shaull's ideas and experiments, and this time was no exception. He granted Shaull the budget for the first two years of operations. Charles West remembered that Shaull was highly regarded by McCord and that basically Shaull did whatever he wanted in the Seminary.[81] The first class of the new Theological Community in-

80. Richard Shaull to James McCord, January 14, 1970. The Richard Shaull Papers, Speer Library, Princeton Theological Seminary, Princeton.

81. Interview with Charles West at Princeton Theological Seminary, January 18, 2007.

cluded Bruce and Sandy Boston with their three children; Bruce was a Ph.D. student at Princeton Seminary while Sandy was a housewife; also Barbara Hall, ex missionary to Brazil and writing a dissertation at the time on New Testament studies at Princeton Seminary; Joan Romero, a Roman Catholic ex-nun writing at the moment a Ph. D. dissertation at Harvard University; Gil Romero, married to Joan and writing a dissertation on Old Testament apocalyptic literature at Princeton Seminary; Vicky Wingert, an Anabaptist psychiatric social worker and her husband; Vern Wingert, a children's caseworker for the City of Brotherly Love, and of course Shaull himself. Even though the theological community was supposed to be on the margins of society, they were all elite students finishing their doctoral programs in prestigious seminaries and universities in the United States. One criticism against the theological community was that even though they were living with the poor, they thought and talked *for* the poor and not *with* the poor. In other words, the poor were objects of investigation by a think-tank group of well-intentioned people who however did not take the words of the poor and oppressed as the starting point of their theological work.

The plan for this theological community was to work on vocational, economical, educational, life-style, and theological alternatives. It was a deviant community in the sense that it broke with the norms established by society to create its own worldview based on mutual respect and love. Because most of the participants were writing dissertations while they were involved in the theological community, vocational alternatives surfaced in their struggles to define their profession. For example, they rejected the competitive nature of the academic world in hiring faculty members. The community was not anti-intellectual, but rather "not committed to beating each other's brains out to get a job, get published, get promoted, get tenured, get on the lecture circuit, or get a prestige post at a prestige school. That, for us, is a demonic reward system."[82] Thus, the vocational alternatives of the theological community were formed in the collegiality of brotherhood/sisterhood while they tried to partake of a common livelihood based on their common economic gains.

The educational alternatives that the theological community engaged were based on the insights emerging from the Brazilian educator

82. Boston, "Report from A Theological Community," 36.

Paulo Freire and his method of conscientization. For the group, education could never be a neutral endeavor but worked either to liberate or to enslave. Bruce Boston, a member of the community, pointed out, "education functions simultaneously either to liberate persons to create their own world by opening options in closed situations, or to close those options by demanding that persons function within the limits laid down by the given intellectual, political, social, and cultural universe of discourse in which education occurs."[83] The theological community was transcending the educational norm of the transmission of information from one generation to the next and opted for a process of critical reflection in the midst of everyday life concerns.

During this period, Shaull continued to struggle theologically to formulate a new way to speak about God. His missiology was directed to those symbols of the biblical heritage that could serve as means of social transformation. However, language about the institutional church disappeared from his vocabulary and instead he spoke of the true church as taking shape in the small theological community. Shaull produced several essays while at the theological community which revealed the messianic expectations of his missiology and his conviction that God was actively transforming the world.

Shaull understood the people of Israel to have an expectation of an event that would bring the intervention of a Messiah, a ruler whose appearance would mean the establishment of a new order. Shaull took this messianic expectation and related it to the historical process as the embodiment of Jesus Christ on earth who brought new life for humanity: "In the messianic perspective, new possibilities for human life appear in history after all human possibilities have been played out."[84] Even though history was moving toward the goal of a new heaven and a new earth, the creation of a new humanity, and the possibility of human fulfillment in a new society, Shaull understood that history does move forward, but "it does not move upward in spirals because of the fact that time and again God's action for the liberation of man runs into difficulties."[85]

Shaull understood forces, powers, and principalities that were out of the control of humans as being responsible for what goes wrong in the

83. Ibid., 37.
84. Ibid., 217.
85. Shaull, "A Theological Perspective in Human Liberation," 511.

world. The powers were not necessarily personal beings or fallen angels. Nor did they possess or inhibit people to accomplish their wicked acts. According to Shaull, the demonic could be described as the deviation of institutions or agencies from their original purpose of serving humanity.[86] To Shaull, the clearest expression of this struggle was the crucifixion of Jesus, an event in which the state and religion joined forces to erase the problem of someone who was questioning the status quo.[87] So, for example, Jesus was sentenced to death on a cross, and though most would understand him by that death to have been defeated by the powers, in fact for Jesus and his followers the cross itself epitomized the victory of death over life. For through Jesus, this event was transformed. As Paul stated in the letter to the Colossians, "And having disarmed the powers and authorities, he made a public spectacle out of them, triumphing over them by the cross" (Colossians 2:15). This event, according to Shaull, represented a "matrix out of which a revolutionary view of history could eventually emerge."[88]

For Shaull, there was a political significance in parabolic action. The parable was one of the literary genres most used by Jesus of Nazareth, a story genre which provided new insights into some aspect of everyday life. Parables revealed the hidden realities that were used to oppress and exploit certain events or groups of people. Shaull perceived that parabolic action could shed some light on the problem of the relationship between stability and change, and the role of violence in social transformation.[89] The only way that change and stability would occur was if they could "take shape on the other side of change."[90] The powers and principalities tended to make ultimate claims upon society, and retained a sense of ultimate meaning that was changeless. Because the parables made this reality transparent, humanity was challenged to take a stand. Therefore, in the U.S. political context, a parabolic act "is an act which attempts to expose the real situation in which this country [U.S.] is trapped, at this moment in history...the one thing that makes sense in such a world is the affirmation of our freedom to live and to create a new possibility over

86. Shaull, "Revolution: Heritage and Contemporary Option," 217–20.
87. Ibid., 219.
88. Ibid.
89. Ibid., 223; Shaull, "Political Significance of Parabolic Action," 27–29.
90. Ibid., 223.

against the present system."[91] As change and stability could come only after the present social structures were transformed or eradicated, the use of violence became an ethical crossroad.

Yet already at the Geneva Conference, Shaull had suggested that in some circumstances only the use of violence could set the process of change in motion. For him the use of violence was something inherited in the struggle as some people would use violence to maintain the status quo and others would use violence to overthrow a system that dehumanizes life. Referring to the use of violence in the U.S. in the context of the late 1960s, Shaull pointed out, "We are free to admit the possibility that acts of violence may have their place in the struggle of the dispossessed people in our urban ghettos and in the underdeveloped world."[92] In a lecture delivered at the University of California, Irvine, on May 7, 1968, Shaull argued that there were only three alternatives or solutions to social structures: death, fascism, or violent revolution.[93] For him, the best or most viable way a society could change its course was through revolution. In this lecture, Shaull identified abuse of power as the underlying source of such institutional violence. When established orders of society did not let go or share their power, violence ensued.[94] According to Shaull, Christians should approach the use of force in a different light--namely, they were free to participate in the revolutionary process because they were looking at the current events eschatologically, seeing the present reality of chaos and destruction as the context in which the redeeming activity of God could be operative and in need of interpretation:

> The coming Kingdom of God is the focus of our attention. This means that our vision of the type of society for which we struggle is not determined primarily by certain principles deduced from metaphysical worldview, not by a theory of natural law, but rather by the biblical and theological descriptions of the shape of the new humanity: the picture of the new man within a transformed social order. In eschatological perspective, we not only believe that a new future is possible; we are convinced that now that future is taking shape in our midst. In this context, the future becomes an explo-

91. Shaull, "Political Significance of Parabolic Action," 28.
92. Shaull, "Revolution: Heritage and Contemporary Option," 225.
93. Shaull, "Revolutionary Violence in Social Reconstruction," 5.
94. Ibid., 17–18.

sive force in every present; the coming Kingdom of God stands in judgment over every status quo.[95]

The eschatological expectation of a new humanity within a transformed social order was a guiding principle for Shaull. Thus, violence could be the only solution to ending a dehumanizing society. Shaull supported civil disobedience and resistance to legal authority because in themselves these had parabolic action and served to expose the irrationality of the present system of oppression. Therefore, ideology needed to be rehabilitated as a Christian strategy of transcendence and transgression.

According to Shaull, the "type of transcendence we find in the Bible is more eschatological than metaphysical; it refers not so much to an Eternal Order above man as it does to the Future which transgresses against and transcends the present."[96] Even though revolution was still central in Shaull's missiology in the late 1960s, liberation was emerging as a new theological term in his eschatological messianism. For Shaull, the context of personal liberation was centered in the life, death, and resurrection of Jesus Christ.[97] Shaull insisted that as Christians learned to be free under the sovereignty of God in history, they could discover the possibilities and potential of helping to create a new humanity.[98] Shaull envisioned this new humanity as one freed from the past in order to interpret the present in light of the future.

Final Years at Princeton Theological Seminary

After the Geneva Conference of Church and Society of the WCC, Shaull entered a new stage in his life. The experience of being excluded and marginalized from the life of the Presbyterian Church of Brazil had been a traumatic experience. Charles West, who arrived at Princeton Seminary at the same time as Shaull, remembered the first four years after their arrival when they team-taught a class on "Christian Witness in the Contemporary World." How Shaull progressively took over the course can be seen in the syllabi for the classes from 1963 to 1965. In 1963, the class was dominated

95. Shaull, "Confronting the Power Structures" 1–2.
96. Shaull, "Revolution: Heritage and Contemporary Option," 233.
97. Shaull, "A Theological Perspective on Human Liberation," 514.
98. Ibid., 514; and Shaull, "The New Humanity in a Technological Age," 10–11.

by a neo-orthodox orientation which gave prominence to the ethics of Karl Barth with Charles West teaching the bulk of the course. In 1964, Barth's ethics in *Church Dogmatics* became merely suggested reading and was replaced by Dietrich Bonhoeffer's *Ethics*. By 1965, both Barth and Bonhoeffer had been replaced by the Paul Lehmann's *Contextual Ethics* and Arend Th. Van Leeuwen's *Christianity in World History* with Shaull teaching most of the course.[99] In 1966, West took a sabbatical leave, and when he returned felt he could no longer continue to teach with Shaull because Shaull now held such a startlingly radical position regarding the mission of the church.[100]

In the winter of 1967, *Theological Education* published a symposium on the future of theology in the United States. On that occasion, John C. Bennett, President of Union Seminary in New York, was the main panelist and Shaull was invited to be the respondent. Even Bennett, who was President of one of the most progressive seminaries in the U.S., had a difficult time with Shaull's proposals. Bennett positioned revolution as an ideological weapon and not as a concrete reality when he declared, "I am thinking of revolution as a conscious effort to direct historical change in the interests of social justice rather than as the reality of rapid social change itself."[101]

Shaull's response was based on the differences between their interpretations of social revolution. Bennett's definition did not take into consideration the context in which the social revolutions were taking place while Shaull made the context of such revolutions the center of his theological program. For Shaull, the social revolution of the times was connected with the process of secularization in the West, and the terrible living conditions of the marginalized and oppressed (such as Latin Americans and Blacks in the U.S.) Shaull further made a proposal about theological education in the U.S., particularly regarding the relationship between the nature of teaching and learning. He proposed a student-oriented learning with problem-posing as a process instead of the old

99. Syllabi for the course Christian Witness in the Secular World" 1963, 1964, and 1965. I appreciate greatly the help of Charles West who provided the syllabi for these courses from his personal papers.

100. Interview with Charles West at Princeton Theological Seminary, January 18, 2007.

101. Bennett, "Theological Education and Social Revolution," 283.

and repetitive approaches of memorizing information. He pointed out, "In fact, we may discover that a professor can make his most effective contribution to the learning and teaching process when he works on a problem with a group of students and is there to help them when they find it necessary." Thus, theological education should be done in the context of the dynamic historical process in which God was at work. Shaull was proposing a contextualized education which took as *locus theologicus* the concrete contemporary situation.[102] The biggest problem with this approach was its elitism and individualism because the "contextual expert" was the one capable enough of guiding the process of discernment about where God was active in history.

It was his experience as a missionary that led Shaull to understand theological reflection in a new manner. For him theology should be a living conversation between the believer and the social, political, cultural, and religious context in which the believer participated. After returning to the United States, he perceived that his theology differed greatly from the one taught at Princeton Seminary. Princeton Seminary had become the center of neo-orthodox theology in the United States. Shaull faced the tension between his theological reflections lived in the midst of revolution and those of his North American peers who stood securely in the comfort of an intact structure in the church and the academy. Shaull's starting point for theological reflection was his involvement in the struggle for life against death, justice against injustice, freedom against slavery.

In discussing the contextual nature of theological reflection and how revolution was central to understanding and formulating a new theological language with his North American colleagues, Shaull understood that his theology was more radical than what he had first imagined. His debates with European and North American theologians convinced him that there was a huge gap separating them. The more his critics wanted to prove him wrong, the more Shaull went in the opposite direction. For example, the same principles of the urgency for experimentation and development of new forms of theological education and the necessity for

102. Shaull, "Response to President Bennett," 291. It is important to notice the influence of Paulo Freire's *Pedagogy of the Oppressed* on Shaull. In 1966, while Shaull was at a conference in Boston, Paulo Freire gave him a manuscript for him to translate, find a publisher, and write the introduction. That manuscript was *Pedagogy of the Oppressed*, which was first published in English thanks to Shaull. Interview with Luis Rivera-Pagan at Princeton Theological Seminary, January 18, 2007.

those exploring new theological methods to be interacting constantly with the concrete situations around them, was viewed with suspicion by the whole department of theology at the Seminary.

Shaull had directed several doctoral dissertations like Rubem Alves' *Toward a Theology of Liberation*, 1969 and Jong Bock Kim's *Historical Transformation, People's Movement and Messianic Koinonia: A Study of the Relationship of Christian and Tonghak Religious Communities to the March First Independence Movement in Korea*, 1976. Both of these dissertations were groundbreaking theological works, and both of the authors became theological celebrities in Latin America and Asia. However, Shaull was accused by the chair of the dissertations' committee, Seward Hiltner, of incompetence in directing doctoral students.[103] The issue was that according to Hiltner, Shaull had polarized the arguments of one of his students between "adventurous dealing with new material and competent scholarship about the background."[104] It seemed that in Shaull's attempt to guide students to enter into a conversation between the Christian tradition and the contemporary context, the contemporary context was not described and analyzed according to the requirements of academic scholarship. But for Shaull, Western theological formulations and methodologies were bankrupt because of its metaphysical worldview on which they were predicated. Shaull pointed out, "I am open to critical evaluation of my own competence in working with doctoral students, but I think it is only fair to insist on one condition: that those who make such criticisms be at least willing to give some serious consideration to what I am trying to do."[105]

Perturbed by the whole incident, Shaull wrote to President McCord, insisting that he was being misunderstood by his peers for what he was doing in theological methodology. He pointed out, "If this is at all indicative of the general climate of the Doctoral Studies program, I am not at all convinced that I should encourage the type of students that I am interested in to come here, or try to work with those who do."[106] The struggle did

103. Seward Hiltner to Richard Shaull, May 12, 1969. The Richard Shaull Papers, Special Collections, Speer Library, Princeton Theological Seminary, Princeton.

104. Ibid.

105. Richard Shaull to Seward Hiltner, June 2, 1969. The Richard Shaull Papers, Speer Library, Princeton.

106. Richard Shaull to James McCord, June 2, 1969. The Richard Shaull Papers, Speer Library, Princeton.

not end there, but continued for more than a decade. As Shaull continued to work with students from the non-western world, and as their process of liberating themselves from Western philosophy and culture developed, the situation became increasingly complicated for those students. Shaull was evaluating and working with the students in identifying areas of importance to them, while the doctoral program was evaluating the same students according to a quite different set of expectations. Shaull pointed out, "I see no alternative but disengaging myself from the Ph.D. program as it is presently operating, and finding other ways to pursue what is compelling for me."[107] In 1977, Shaull resigned from the Ph.D. Committee and withdrew from all the other committees he was serving. Shaull was frustrated with the whole atmosphere at the Seminary and began to build a strategic plan for his future.

Shaull was clear about his basic commitment and consuming passion for social transformation. His ministerial duties were directed towards the transformation of society. But he began to question how this vision fit with the academic ethos of Princeton Seminary. On February 9, 1977, Shaull addressed the Seminary's community at Miller Chapel. The title of his address was "A Time for Decision." In a bold manner, Shaull pointed out his struggles with the doctoral program and the whole educational system for its ineffectiveness and its oppressive character, then went on to address the political crisis he perceived in the nation, and the crisis of the church.

First, Shaull said he regretted having helped to maintain a doctoral program which had been a burden rather than an adventure in theological reflection. He pointed out, "We perpetuate uncritically a theological language arising out of the intense struggles of men and women in other times and places, but which had largely lost its transformative power."[108] He considered the whole educational paradigm to be in need of re-construction. He continued to insist that the starting point for theological reflection should be the lived experience of a new reality. In other words,

107. Richard Shaull to James McCord, November 8, 1977. The Richard Shaull Papers, Speer Library, Princeton.

108. Shaull, "A Time for Decision" Address delivered at Miller Chapel, February 9, 1977. The Richard Shaull Papers, Speer Library, Princeton.

"Theology should be done in the context of praxis, in the midst of our contemporary struggles for human liberation."[109]

Second, he continued to see the United States as a superpower in a quest for world domination. He stated, "To the extent that I think and live in the light of the coming Kingdom, I am more acutely aware of the depth of the crisis we now face as a nation. I perceive it as a crisis caused by an economic system spreading increased injustice, exploitation and repression at home and abroad; by sterile and sclerotic institutions and structures which are becoming more destructive by the erosion of a system of values which no longer offers us a rewarding or fulfilling life."[110] His anguish in witnessing a political system that was becoming more totalitarian and repressive, both at home and abroad, gave him the courage to continue his denunciations against such system for the rest of his life.

Finally, his vision of the church as a community of witnesses in service of God to restore society continued to inspire him to challenge its institutionalization.[111] The time was coming for Shaull to decide what would be his future in a place in which he saw no possibilities for what he wanted to accomplish in life. On March 6, 1979 Shaull wrote a letter of resignation to President McCord, expressing his hope for a new future. He stated, "You have frequently mentioned the fact that I am above all a missionary. This is true. I would like to spend whatever time I may still have at my disposal working at several tasks which are now compelling me. One of these is a greater involvement with people engaged in theological work in several Third World situations."[112] After seventeen years of being a professor at Princeton, Shaull came to the conclusion that he needed to be free from all structures to live fully his calling to ministry. As he died to the present order, he knew that "the power of Christ in [his] life and the world as the presence and power of a New Future, already breaking into the dehumanizing structures around [him],"[113] would guide him to new adventures in faith.

109. Ibid.

110. Ibid.

111. Ibid.

112. Richard Shaull to James McCord, March 6, 1979. The Richard Shaull Papers, Speer Library, Princeton.

113. Shaull, "A Time for Decision" Address delivered at Miller Chapel, February 9, 1977. The Richard Shaull Papers, Speer Library, Princeton.

*chapter six*

# The Homecoming of a Returned Missionary: From Savior of the World to Devouring Dragon: 1980–1988

After his resignation as professor at Princeton Seminary on March 6, 1979, Shaull began a new missionary career as a volunteer fraternal worker on many projects in Latin America and the United States. As he entered into retirement, he struggled with the concept that the aging process was a time of inevitable decline.[1] At age 60, Shaull was in charge of the Task Force on Aging of the Presbyterian Church USA and so was greatly involved in discussions on aging. He did not want to be labeled as an "unproductive and dependent person."[2] Age would not stop Shaull from working tirelessly for the kingdom of God through the transformation of society.

In the 1980s, when Shaull came back to North America after some years of spending half of each year in Latin America, he was an evangelist to many Presbyterian Churches, seminaries, and universities and served again as a cultural and political bridge between the two Americas. This chapter explores Shaull's last years as a missionary. There are two ongoing themes or motifs in Shaull's missiology during this period. First, Shaull worked as a fraternal worker to Latin America. In this task, Shaull rediscovered a paradigm for constructing theology based on the experience

1. Shaull, "The Inclusive Christian Promise of New Life," 40–41.

2. Shaull, "The Vocation of the Chronologically Old in an Aging Society" A paper presented at the Task Force on Ministries with Aging Persons at the General Assembly of the United Presbyterian Church, May 28, 1980.

of the poor. Second, because of his contact with Latin America, Shaull was more than ever convinced that new foreign policy alternatives were needed desperately in the United States. Through books, sermons, and articles, he strove to raise North American Protestant consciousness of the terrible conditions the Reagan administration was creating through its foreign policy toward Latin America.

## Fraternal Worker with the International Subsystem Service of the United Presbyterian Church in the USA

Shaull worked as fraternal worker for the International Subsistence Program of the Presbyterian Church U.S.A., which for six months a year sponsored him and his new wife, Nancy Johns, to work in a Latin American country.[3] Nancy Johns is a psychologist who had worked in Latin America in several programs related to education. She worked as a missionary in Brazil with the Presbyterian Church at the same time Shaull was there, but their paths never crossed as they were in different regions. They met for the fist time in 1953 when Johns was the national moderator of the Presbyterian youth movement preparing for the 1955 World Student Christian Federation's meeting in Athens, Ohio. They reconnected in 1980 in a missionary meeting at Stony Point, New York, sponsored by the Presbyterian National Student Movement and chaired by Margaret Flory. In 1981 they married and began a missionary career together. She was an integral part of his ministry in Shaull's last years.

With energy and vision, Shaull returned to Latin America for a collaborative project with the International Subsistence Service Program of the Presbyterian Church USA (PC USA), today known as the Mission Volunteer International Program, and *Comúnidad Teologíca Evangélica*

3. Shaull left his wife in the late sixties to live in Philadelphia in an intentional community. Shaull struggled for several years with the idea of a divorce. After thirty-one years of marriage to Mildred, Shaull finalized his divorce in 1978. One important deduction from this painful experience was that Shaull never saw Mildred as being capable of being an equal partner in mission. For example, Mildred said: "Dick always thought it was a good idea for me not to express myself on political or religious matters." Letter of Mildred Shaull to Angel Santiago-Vendrell, May 4, 2004. Personal files of the author. Also, Shaull barely mentioned his two daughters Wendy and Madelyn throughout his life. Shaull was the example of a man who wanted to save the world yet neglected his own family.

*de Chile* and *Comisión Evangélica de Educación Cristiana* (CELADEC). In the 1960s, mission and unity were seeing as integral parts of the church in ecumenical circles. The idea of mission and unity in six continents shaped the way mission agencies worked out its mission policies. In 1973, the United Presbyterian Church USA formed one single unit, the Program Agency, to address the theological and practical understanding of the emerging ecumenical paradigm.[4] In 1983, the UPCUSA welcomed into its body the Presbyterian Church in the United States, which split from the main national body in 1861 at the start of the Civil War. The new denomination adopted the name Presbyterian Church (USA). Now, what was called the Program Agency was renamed the Mission Volunteer International Program.

The Mission Volunteer International Program offered opportunities for adults who were willing to share their gifts and live at a subsistence level. The appointment for any particular placement from the Mission Volunteer International Program was two years. Shaull's project goal was to create an ecumenical dialogue between Christians in Latin America and the United States. The idea was for the Shaulls to spend six months of each year in Latin America in close association with base communities, other grassroots groups, and theological seminaries, while the other six months of the year would be dedicated to working in urban centers, churches, and academic institutions in North America. The main purpose was to provide an opportunity for North Americans to understand and appreciate the new theological and ecclesiastical developments in Latin America and to describe U.S. intervention in the region.[5]

The first assignment of the Shaulls was to the *Comunidad Teológica Evangélica* of Chile during the second semester of 1983. Shaull taught a course entitled "The Poor, the Church, and the Gospel." Shaull argued that because biblical faith was concerned primarily with the poor, liberation should be integrated into three distinct elements in the salvific process: a) liberation of the poor from oppressive economic, social, and political conditions; b) the ongoing historical process of the creation of new human beings and a new society; and c) Christ's liberation of each person

---

4. Karla Ann Koll, "Presbyterians, the United States, and Central America," 87–102.

5. Shaull and Nancy Johns, Proposal for Missionary Work in Latin America, October 6, 1982. The Richard Shaull Papers, Speer Library, Princeton Theological Seminary, Princeton.

from sin, the ultimate root of injustice and oppression.[6] He pointed out, "I am forced to conclude that the struggle between those who have and those who have not is often a struggle between those forces moving toward death and those forces moving towards life."[7]

The classroom was crowded with eighty students from ten different Protestant denominations in attendance. Various Roman Catholic students and theologians attended the seminar and opened new terrain in interdenominational relations. Hellmut Gnadt, president of the Evangelical Theological Community, assessed the event as "unique in the history of the C.T.E." because it was the first time that Roman Catholics had attended the institution.[8] Shaull invited well known and respected Roman Catholic liberation theologians such as Sergio Torres, Ronaldo Muñoz, and Fernando Castillo to attend the seminar and talk about the new theological developments of the progressive Roman Catholic Church. As in the past, Shaull was an ecumenical bridge figure trying to convey the best of liberation theology to his Protestant audience and vice-versa. Through liberation theology and its deep commitment to social transformation, Shaull was trying to overcome centuries of mistrust and enmity between the two main religious groups in Latin America.

The effect of the Second Vatican Council, the Medellín Conference of Latin American Bishops in 1968, and the Puebla Conference in 1979, was that many Roman Catholic priests, nuns, and lay leaders moved into solidarity toward the poor and began to read the Bible and rethink their faith in dialogue with them. On January 25, 1959, Pope John XXIII called an ecumenical council to update (*aggiornamento*) the church and seek greater Christian unity. Pope John XXIII died in 1963, but the work continued under his successor, Pope Paul IV.[9] The Second Vatican Council was a turning point in the history of the Roman Catholic Church with significant contributions to the field of missiology; indeed, William B.

---

6. Shaull, "The Poor, the Church, and the Gospel" lecture delivered at Comunidad Teologíca Evangélica de Chile, Spring 1982. The Richard Shaull Papers, Special Collections, Speer Library, Princeton Theological Seminary, Princeton.

7. Richard Shaull, "The Latin Phoenix," 9.

8. Hellmut Gnadt to Benjamin Gutierrez, "Evaluation of Richard Shaull's Time at C.T.E." September 24, 1982. The Richard Shaull Papers, Special Collections, Princeton Theological Seminary, Princeton.

9. Cunningham, "Vatican II," 532.

Frazier, a Maryknoll priest, argued that since Vatican II "we can identify no less than nine missiological breakthroughs between 1965 and 2000" in the Roman Catholic Church:

> From unrefined to unmistakable articulation of the universal availability of salvation; from mission as a function of the church to the church as missionary in its very nature, from exclusion to inclusion of the local church in full missionary responsibility; from mission-sending churches and mission-receiving churches to mutuality in mission; from minimal to full participation of the laity in the missionary vocation of the church; from functional to organic bonding between priesthood and mission; from one to five components in evangelism or from proclamation to presence and witness, human development and liberation, liturgical life, prayer and contemplation, interreligious dialogue, and proclamation and catechesis; from culture-dismissive to culture-intensive evangelization; and, from long-term neglect toward emerging regard for foundational missiology.[10]

The opening of Vatican II to the needs of the world and its calling to "scrutinize the signs of the times" was taken and applied by CELAM, The Episcopal Council of Latin America, which was established in 1955 during the International Eucharist Congress at Rio de Janeiro. As stated in the previous chapter, The Second General Episcopal Conference (Latin American Conference of Bishops) met at Medellín, Colombia to apply the results of the Second Vatican Council to the churches in Latin America. In this conference, the reality of poverty of millions of Latin Americans was taken as the basis of pastoral and missionary work. As this was also the time when the military regimes began to control many countries in Latin America, the Bishops in Medellín came into solidarity with the poor, denouncing those regimes opposed to the well-being of poor Latin Americans.

In 1973, Gustavo Gutiérrez's seminal work, *Teología de la Liberación: Perspectivas*, was translated into English. With this publication, Latin American liberation theology became a phenomenon in theological circles around the English-speaking world. Gutiérrez challenged the theological world by proposing a new methodology in theological inquiry and a new missiology in the practice of the church. For Gutiérrez,

10. Frazier, "Nine Breakthroughs in Catholic Missiology," 9–14.

Christian life was centered in love and faith and on a commitment to God and neighbor: "This is the foundation of the *praxis* of the Christian, of his active presence in history."[11] Thus, Gutiérrez challenged the theological establishment by proposing a new theological methodology based on the involvement of Christians in the world. Theology was a critical reflection on Christian *praxis* in light of the Word of God.[12] This theology did not stop at reflecting in the world, but rather tried to be an active part in the transformation of the history of humankind.[13]

Missiologically, Gutiérrez tried to answer the question about the relation between salvation and the historical process of human liberation. For Gutiérrez the problem was the program of development. The assumption that the underdeveloped nations just needed monetary and industrial help from the developed ones in order to advance their economic and social lot turned out to be a false hope. Gutiérrez pointed out, "It has become ever clearer that underdevelopment is the end result of a process. Therefore, it must be studied from a historical perspective, that is, in relationship to the development and expansion of the great capitalist countries. The underdevelopment of the poor countries, as an overall social fact, appears in its true light: as a historical by-product of the development of other countries."[14] Thus, missionary action had to be involvement in the salvific plan of God who saved human beings in and through history. Specifically, Gutiérrez pointed out, "Salvation is not something otherworldly, in regard to which the present life is merely a test. Salvation is something which embraces all reality, transforms it, and leads in to its fullness in Christ."[15]

The implication of this view was that there were not two histories, one sacred and the other profane, but rather that history should be conceived as one. Salvation and creation were in essence one interrelated event. Gutiérrez stated, "Biblical faith is, above all, faith in a God who reveals himself through historical events, a God who saves in history. Creation is presented in the Bible, not as a stage previous to salvation, but as part of the salvific process . . . It is the work of a God who saves and acts

11. Gutiérrez, *A Theology of Liberation*, 7.
12. Ibid.,11.
13. Ibid., 15.
14. Ibid., 84.
15. Ibid., 151.

in history; since humankind is the center of creation, it is integrated into the history which is being built by human efforts."[16]

Gutiérrez followed the ecclesiological perspectives delineated in the Second Vatican Council which conceived the Church as a sign and sacrament of salvation. The Church was described as God's sacrament in the world, "an efficacious sign of grace" through which an authentic encounter between God and humanity took place, and the unity of all humankind was revealed.[17] In this new understanding, the Church was missionary by its very nature.

Latin American liberation theology was the most significant and influential theological movement in the Catholic Church since Vatican II. Suddenly, after Gutiérrez's *A Theology of Liberation*, the theme of liberation as a theological category was adopted worldwide. For example, Feliciano Cariño, the new General Secretary of the WSCF elected in 1972, drafted a paper by the working group on "Liberation and Theology" during their executive meeting in Buenos Aires, Argentina in September of 1974. The paper, "Christian Witness in the Struggle for Liberation," argued that "No theological thinking can take place faithfully outside of the political question. It is our conviction that the locus for theological thinking in our time is in the political struggle of peoples for liberation."[18] Liberation theology was also adopted as a focus by the World Council of Churches.

The Fifth Assembly of the World Council of Churches met at Nairobi, Kenya, from November 23 to December 10, 1975, on the "Jesus Christ

16. Ibid., 154. The language and theology of history of Gutiérrez seems identical to that of Richard Shaull. Gutiérrez's point of commonality with Shaull was in their interpretation of Augustine's theology of history in *The City of God*. Gutiérrez pointed out, "The function of theology as critical reflection on praxis has gradually become more clearly defined in recent years, but it has its roots in the first centuries of the Church's life. The Augustinian theology of history which we find in *The City of God*, for example, is based on a true analysis of the signs of the times and the demands with which they challenge the Christian community." 6. Shaull, on the other hand, saw in Augustine's *City of God* a view of social change based in a Trinitarian way of understanding the activity of God in history as foundational. He pointed out, "Historical events were seen as occurring along a line set by the dynamic reality of God's providence, his bringing in of the Kingdom, the work of the Holy Spirit in the world and the movement of history towards its final destination." Shaull, "Revolutionary Challenge in Theological Perspective," 29–30.

17. Gutiérrez, *A Theology of Liberation*, 255–85.

18. Cariño, "Christian Witness in the Struggle for Liberation," 1.

Frees and Unites." The Report of Section V was entitled "Structures of Injustice and Struggles for Liberation." The Report focused on patterns of domination against marginal groups in the world such as women, ethnic minorities and racially oppressed people, the poor and underprivileged, victims of human rights violations, political prisoners, and the unemployed. It also considered the extent to which national and international military-economic systems created and perpetuated their domination.[19]

In 1976, Pittsburgh Theological Seminary invited Richard Shaull and Gustavo Gutiérrez to deliver together the Schaff lectures on the theme "Theology and Revolution." Gutiérrez's essay "Freedom and Salvation: A Political Problem" addressed the long Dominican theological tradition of Bartolomé de Las Casas' equation of justice and salvation. For Las Casas, Christ was present in the Indian, and so to harm the native occupants was to harm God. From there came the cry of Las Casas: "Christ has been crucified a thousand times in the Americas."[20] Therefore, to do theology in Latin America, according to Gutiérrez, was to ask the question of "how to announce God as *Father* in a non-human world?" Theology today could only be done in solidarity with those who suffered: the poor, the exploited, and the non-person.[21] Theology for Gutiérrez was an understanding of faith—a rereading of the Word of God as it is lived by the Christian community in history. It was a "second act marked by the experiences of the people and the categories the poor and exploited used to transform history."[22] Theology became a critical reflection on the historical praxis of the Christian community that was looking for its own liberation. Taking the historical context of exploitation and poverty in Latin America meant that the church needed to take a stand and rethink radically its mission in the world. For Gutiérrez, "This will be achieved for the theology by placing the political commitment of liberation in the perspective of the free gift of total liberation through Christ."[23]

Shaull's resulting essay "The Death and Resurrection of the American Dream" was therefore a critique of North American power and influence in the world. For Shaull, "the American dream has turned into a night-

19. Hill, "Structures of Injustice and Struggles for Liberation," 1.
20. Gutiérrez, "Freedom and Salvation, 65–67.
21. Ibid., 79.
22. Ibid., 184.
23. Ibid., 84.

mare for many within the country, as well as for the Third World."[24] Only a revolution of human consciousness would save North America, said Shaull. So Shaull called for the judgment of North America, urged for a transformation of values, hoped for a new society, and questioned all the foundations of the establishment.[25]

He never left the idea of small groups of Christians gathered together to create a counter-cultural stand against the established social and political structures and always thought that the political question was religious in nature.[26] After this meeting with Gutierrez at Pittsburgh Theological Seminary, Shaull adopted and became an interpreter of liberation theology.

Shaull's second assignment as fraternal worker was to Nicaragua. His first request was to Brazil due to his history with the church in that country, but because of his previous difficulties with the Brazilian government in the 1960s, it was impossible for him to procure an entry visa at that time.[27] The other possibility presented to Shaull was Nicaragua due to the revolutionary situation which the country was going through as a result of the Sandinista uprising. The idea of Nicaragua seemed perfect for the type of work Shaull was interested in and he and Nancy Johns agreed to immerse themselves in the Nicaraguan reality. Beginning on January 15, 1984, Shaull started a new assignment as a fraternal worker to Nicaragua.

When the Sandinistas seized power in 1979 from the Somoza dictatorship, other Central American countries such as Guatemala and El Salvador were also on the verge of revolution. The Somoza regime was a family affair that lasted from 1936 until 1979 when the dictatorship was overthrown by the Sandinista National Liberation Front (SNLF). During World War II and the Cold War, the Somoza regime was loyal to Washington, and this won the regime economic and military concessions. In 1956, Anastacio Somoza was killed by the poet Rigoberto Lopez Perez. Somoza was succeeded by his older son Luis A. Somoza Debayle who governed until 1963, when the U.S. government placed pressure on him

24. Shaull, "The Death and Resurrection of the American Dream," 99.

25. Ibid., 99–119.

26. Ibid., 146–54.

27. Shaull to Benjamin Gutiérrez, June 25, 1984. The Richard Shaull Papers, Speer Library, Princeton Theological Seminary.

to hand over power. He died the same year his younger brother, Anastacio (Tachito) Somoza Debayle became president as the result of massive fraud. He was as repressive as his father and brother, but according to Jeffrey Klaiber, a Jesuit priest and professor at the Catholic Pontifical University of Peru, "not as prudent." Under his regime, the Nicaraguan people experienced new levels of corruption, repression, torture, and death.[28] By 1979, the constituents who had legitimized the regime i.e., the middle and upper classes and the Roman Catholic Church, were distancing themselves from Anastacio Somoza Debayle.[29] The Somoza dictatorship came to an end after two important events: the aftermath of the earthquake of 1972 during which Somoza appropriated the humanitarian and reconstruction aid packages for himself and his cronies, and the assassination of Pedro Joaquim Chamorro, editor of *La Prensa*, a paper critical of the Somoza regime.[30]

The Sandinista National Liberation Front began its operations in the early 1960s. One of the most important characteristics of the SNLF was that devout Christians were involved in the struggle to liberate Nicaragua from the repressive Somoza regime. For the Christians who participated in the revolution there was no contradiction between the teachings of Jesus and their struggle for liberation through the revolution. When the revolution was victorious in Nicaragua on July 19, 1979, the new government declared its willingness for the church to be part of rebuilding the nation. The SNLF appointed four priests to high positions in the government: Miguel d'Escoto was appointed as foreign minister; Ernesto Cardenal as minister of culture, and Fernando Cardenal as the national vice-coordinator of the Sandinista youth movement.[31] Apart from these well known priests, many other lay Christians were active government officials, among them Roberto Argüello, President of the Supreme Court; Carlos Tunnermann, Minister of Education; and Maria del Socorro Gutiérrrez de Barreto, General Secretary of the Ministry of Housing among others.[32] However, not everyone shared the enthusiasm in legiti-

28. Klaiber, *The Church, Dictatorships, and Democracy in Latin America*, 195–96.
29. Ibid., 198.
30. Diederich, *Somoza*, 93–105.
31. Cabestrero, *Ministers of God Ministers of the People*, 4.
32. Cabestrero, *Revolutionaries for the Gospel*, 1986.

mizing a revolutionary government with Marxist tendencies, especially the United States.

When Shaull arrived in Nicaragua in 1984, the revolutionary government had been in power for five years. He was to collaborate with the Centro Antonio Valdevieso, an ecumenical study center named after a sixteenth-century Nicaraguan bishop who was killed while defending the local people. The Centro Valdevieso was directed by Father Úriel Molina, a Franciscan biblical scholar who was a pioneer in the formation of ecclesial base communities.[33] In his first five months, Shaull traveled all over Nicaragua trying to understand the revolution as Christians saw it. Not only was Shaull in contact with the Centro Antonio Valdevieso, he also lived with a poor family in an ecclesial base community in Managua. Apart from these activities, Shaull taught two courses in the Presbyterian Seminary of Managua on the Protestant Reformation, and gave a number of workshops for the Roman Catholic Delegates of the Word who were lay people trained and authorized to lead worship in the absence of a priest. Shaull also traveled to the interior of the country and saw the economic devastation of the rural areas.[34]

Another important event during his five months in Nicaragua was his participation in the Conference of Evangelical Reflection on the Elections. Present at the event was Commander Carlos Nuñez, President of the Council of the State. Shaull presented a paper on "A Biblical Perspective on Democracy." As in Brazil, his missiology continued to be rooted in the sovereignty of God in history which was always on behalf of humans. Shaull traced this biblical theme of liberation from oppression from the Exodus story to the Sandinista revolution.[35] He considered the Sandinistas to be representatives of the liberating power of God who was creating a new world through the revolution. His dream for a revolutionary movement that would transform society was very much alive in the Sandinistas. In other words, the Nicaraguan revolution validated Shaull's early missiology of a God who was actively transforming the world in history.

Shaull praised the revolutionaries because they were trying to open a new chapter in human history by organizing a new economy to serve the

33. Ibid., 26.

34. Shaull and Nancy Johns, *Responding to the Cry of the Poor*, 1–4.

35. Shaull, "Una Perspectiva Biblica sobre la Democracia," 4–6.

needs of the majority, the poor. Not only were the Sandinistas organizing a better economic system, they were extending power to the poor to participate in the government. For him a biblical perspective on democracy needed to include three crucial elements: 1) a preferential option for the poor; 2) a guarantee of human rights, the most important being the right to live, and 3) freedom.[36] Liberation and democracy were understood by Shaull as existing only if the revolutionary process continued in the formation of new structures of power in society. After Shaull's experience with the ecclesial base communities and the struggle of the people of Nicaragua to become subjects of their own existence, he was sure that the U.S. intervention in conducting a civil war against a sovereign nation was wrong and needed to be exposed in North America. He became a missionary to the United States with a clear message of God's preferential option for the poor, and the church's role in changing U.S. foreign policy.

Missiologically, Shaull abstained from generic conversations on Christian unity or interreligious dialogue going on in ecumenical circles in the 1980s, and concentrated on his experience with the poor as the way ahead. Timothy Yates described the missiological developments during the decade from 1980 to 1990 as concerned with issues of unity in mission, pluralism and the enlightenment's legacy.[37] Christians became aware that the previous formulations to engage the religious other needed to be reevaluated, and so in Christian circles the theme of unity became central and more desirable.[38] Together the Roman Catholic Church and the World Council of Churches created a document entitled *Common Witness*. The document emphasized the renewal of a common witness centered in Christ which called Christian believers to "a new obedience and a new way of life which is itself a witnessing communion."[39] The document continued, "Christian witness receives its incarnation and force out of calling of the People of God to be a pilgrim people giving witness to Christ our Lord in communion with the cloud of witnesses...As the Church is one body of many members, Christian witness is by its nature communitarian."[40] The practical aspects of common witness were delin-

---

36. Ibid., 7.

37. Yates, *Christian Mission in the Twentieth Century*, 224–51.

38. Ibid., 225–27.

39. WCC, *Common Witness*, 11.

40. Ibid., 14–15.

eated as witness in *diakonia/koinonia*, in the promotion of human rights, through Bible research, through theological discussion, and in religious education.[41]

Another important document produced by the World Council of Churches was *Mission and Evangelism: an ecumenical affirmation.* Following the fifth assembly of the WCC in Nairobi, 1975, the Commission of World Mission and Evangelism was asked to prepare a document containing the basic beliefs of the ecumenical movement.[42] The document was approved in 1982 by the central committee of the WCC. The ecumenical affirmation could be regarded as the most important document on mission and evangelism produced in the twentieth century.[43] *Mission and Evangelism* understood that the "present ecumenical movement came into being out of the conviction that the division of Christians is a scandal and an impediment to the witness of the Church."[44] Because of the scandal of divisions among Christian groups which gave a bad testimony to the world, the document accentuated the common confession of all Christians in Jesus Christ. Thus, the call to mission was a call to unity in Christ.

However, Shaull showed no interest in issues of religious pluralism or interreligious dialogue because his mission was to formulate and translate to his North American audience the theological developments in Latin American by liberation theologians. His contribution to the themes of unity came through the propagation of Latin American liberation theology and Brazilian Pentecostalism to North Americans in the final years of his life.

When Shaull returned to the United States after spending five months with the poor in Nicaragua, he began an evangelistic campaign describing various aspects of the Central American situation to the North American people. First, in the spiritual realm, Shaull was an interpreter of the theology of liberation as articulated by the poor, thus legitimizing their participation in the revolution. Second, he challenged the North American church to seek biblical alternatives for U.S. foreign policy.

41. Ibid., 29–49.
42. Bassham, *Mission Theology*, 98–103.
43. "Ecumenical Affirmation," 36.
44. Stromberg, *Mission and Evangelism*, 4.

Shaull's first job as a returned fraternal worker in the United States was sponsored by the Presbyterian Synod of Southern California. He was invited to be a theologian-in-residence at San Francisco Theological Seminary. The objectives of the Synod were the promotion of the Central American situation through the dissemination of information; and the promotion of theological and spiritual reflection and renewal and the advocacy for the people of Central America in the United States. The Synod had arranged an intensive and demanding schedule for Shaull. He offered a two-week course first on the campus of San Francisco Seminary and then at Pasadena and Anaheim, and to the San Diego Presbytery. All the presbyteries of Southern California requested one week of training with Shaull on the Central America situation.

On this tour, he preached eleven times in Presbyterian Churches throughout Southern California, typically using the same batch of sermons which he would present to different audiences, sermons such as: "Responding to the Cry of the Poor," "Christ's Presence among the Poor" and, "The Christ We may not Want to Meet." All of the sermons shared the same biblical text (Matthew 25:31–46), and they all presented the poor of Latin America as bearers of a new reformation. In these sermons Shaull described the inhuman condition in which the majority of the people of Central America were living. He pointed out, "the poor, who constitute the vast majority of people in almost every country, are nobodies and have no place. They are denied any sense of human worth or dignity; they are thrown off their land, left to starve without work in the urban slums, they have no resources whatsoever."[45]

After presenting the intolerable condition of human existence in Central America, Shaull continued with an affirmation of testimonies of people from the region who had encountered salvation in Jesus Christ. Mostly, Shaull's testimonies were of wealthy people who were transformed by the power of the Spirit and left their lives of opulence. For example, he talked about Teodulo Baez, a wealthy landowner whose land gave him an income of thousands per month. After having an encounter with Jesus Christ, Baez gave most of his land to the poor who worked for him.[46]

45. Shaull, "Responding to the Cry of the Poor" Sermon preached at the San Fernando Presbytery, March 26, 1984. The Richard Shaull Papers, Special Collections, Speer Library, Princeton Theological Seminary, Princeton.

46. Ibid.

After the testimonies of converted wealthy people, Shaull presented the revolutionary process as the only alternative that was working for the benefit of the poor. Shaull advised his audience that they should not be concerned with the Marxist tendencies of some Central American regimes (referring particularly to the Sandinistas); for "rather than finding a totalitarian Marxist-Leninist society, [he] experienced a country where the common people were free, unafraid and had hope."[47] The final section of the sermon described the apocalyptic judgment that Jesus declared in Matthew 25 against the nations that had not done good to the poor.

Shaull believed in the utopian manifestation of the Kingdom of God prepared from the foundation of the world to be a political reality on earth because it was what the world was created to become. Shaull's message was a call to radical discipleship, a call to obedience. Christians could be in solidarity with the poor and obtain life or reject the poor and face death.

In addition, Shaull led a synod retreat, keynoted in thirteen ecumenical activities, and made nineteen appearances at universities and seminaries in the area.[48] After this work for the Synod of Southern California, Shaull continued his evangelistic propaganda as guest speaker in many Presbyterian churches in the United States.

Throughout his life, Shaull tried to transmit to North American Christians the importance of the hermeneutical challenge which Latin America's poor presented to them. Shaull claimed that the poor of Latin America were the bearers of a new hermeneutical horizon, and such horizon represented a *kairos*, a moment of grace, for North American Christians. Shaull's dream in Brazil in the 1950s and 60s of Christians participating and leading the revolutionary process became a fulfilled prophecy. The Sandinista revolution was Shaull's legitimatization of his earlier work as a missionary in Brazil. For him God was present in the revolution through Christians who belonged to the church of the poor. The poor, according to Shaull, had rediscovered the biblical message of the God who is active in history on their behalf. The story of Exodus, the prophets, and Jesus of Nazareth became paradigmatic texts which

47. Ibid.

48. Report of the Theologian in Residence: Richard Shaull to the International Subsystem Service Program of the Presbyterian Church USA. The Richard Shaull Papers, Special Collections, Speer Library, Princeton Theological Seminary, Princeton.

invigorated in the poor the desire to live a better life. Shaull pointed out, "As the poor get together in small groups to study the Bible and pray together, they discover that in the eyes of God they are persons of worth, they begin to believe in themselves, work together to help themselves and join together to struggle for change."[49]

The Bible spoke directly to the poor and their condition. Its stories connected with their story: "When people in the base communities read the Bible together, they find that it relates to all aspects of their lives in the world. It describes their struggle in society and helps them articulate their hopes for a more human and just order."[50] New life was emerging from the depths of tragedy: a new life cemented in the dignity that God brings through God's redeeming activity in history.

Shaull's missiology continued to be rooted in God's redemptive actions in history based on the story of the Exodus—a story that presented a God who sided with the slaves, the down-trodden, and the despised. In the Exodus narrative, God had a distinctive concern for the slaves when God heard their cry in the midst of oppression and acted for their liberation. For Shaull, the same thing was happening in Latin America when poor people who were slaves to a political system found in the Bible a parallel story that helped them overcome their lot.[51]

The witness of the prophets in the history of Israel presented another stage of liberation in the lives of the poor and oppressed. Shaull saw the prophetic movement of Israel as the articulation of the insight of the Exodus narrative in which God commanded those who previously had been slaves to do justice in remembrance of the fact that they had once been slaves themselves. Shaull pointed out, "the prophets dared to confront the wealthy and powerful and declared that the historical devel-

---

49. Richard Shaull, "Christ's Presence Among the Poor," The Richard Shaull Papers, Special Collections, Speer Library, Princeton Theological Seminary, Princeton. Shaull was following the methodological guidelines traced by Gutiérrez in his theology of liberation. In *Heralds of a New Reformation* he barely quotes any liberation theologian, but the reader can perceived that he is in dialogue with them, at least following their methodological impetus to construct a theology of the people. For example, Gutierrez stated, "Speaking definitively, we will not have an authentic theology of liberation until the oppressed are able to express themselves freely and creatively in society and as a People of God." Gustavo Gutiérrez, "Freedom and Salvation," 87.

50. Shaull, "Basic Christian Communities," 10.

51. Shaull, *Heralds of a New Reformation*, 13–22.

opment of their nation had turned out to be one great failure."[52] The main concern for the prophets was issues related to social justice. In this sense, the prophets were called to desacralize the claims of the establishment when they were contrary to the will of God which was for the nation to practice justice.[53] For Latin Americans, this meant confronting a power structure that had been sacralized by the political sector. The church felt obligated to enter the world of the poor and serve as a prophetic witness against the political regimes that terrorized the majority of citizens, the poor.

The poor of Latin America were reminded that the central figure in the Bible was a poor man from Galilee. Shaull presented Jesus of Nazareth as the prophet who was called to establish a new humanity through his ministry. Jesus was the Messiah of the poor, continuing the prophetic tradition and embodying the values of the Kingdom of God as attested in the biblical tradition that ran from the Exodus, through the judges and the prophets. The Kingdom of God represented the aspirations of a new world order that would eliminate poverty, oppression, and marginaliza-tion: a place where human beings who had been victims would recover their dignity.[54] However, because of his message, Jesus of Nazareth was accused and sentenced as a subversive. As a subversive against the estab-lished order, he knew that the power of this age was imprisoning human beings to live in desperate situations. Latin Americans who were commit-ted to the principles of the Kingdom of God were experiencing the same lot as their Master. Thousands of Christians were repressed, tortured, and killed by the governments that were supposed to protect them. The poor in Latin America found in the Bible a message of liberation from their terrible condition but also one of empowerment through their trials.

Shaull understood that being poor was also a way of feeling, know-ing, reasoning, making friends, sharing life together, loving, believing, celebrating, and praying.[55] So Shaull recognized that commitment to the poor meant entering, and in some cases remaining, in that world. Shaull argued that this movement of solidarity was a second conversion,

52. Ibid., 25.
53. Ibid., 23–38.
54. Ibid., 39–57.
55. Shaull, *Heralds of a New Reformation,* 1–3.

a conversion to the poor.[56] This aspect of a spirituality of liberation was perceived by Shaull as the immanence of God who was present in history through Jesus of Nazareth, and now manifested in the neighbor through the Spirit.

The immanence of God erupted in history and was acting on behalf of those who suffer, the hungry, thirsty, the stranger, the ones with no clothes, the sick, the orphans, prisoners, the poor (Mt. 25:31–46).[57] Because of God's redeeming activity in history, liberation spirituality is action, a kind of action based in solidarity and love for the oppressed. God's concern for the poor makes them not only agents of their own liberation, but God's chosen agents to bring structural changes in accord with the Kingdom. After their encounter with the Bible, the poor became the new historical subjects determined to struggle against the structures of oppression for their total liberation. What validated their participation in the revolutionary process was their faith in the God of justice and their spiritual commitment to that God.

The Nicaraguan revolution and other revolutions occurring in Latin America in the 1980s represented a possible new beginning; those committed to it were determined to demonstrate to the world that the problems of the area could be solved in a way that would bring social peace with justice. The poor in the time of Somoza in Nicaragua only knew death at the hands of the National Guard. For Shaull in this context the term "liberation" expressed better than "revolution" the meaning of salvation as offered by Jesus Christ—the liberation of the poor from social, political, and economic oppression.[58]

### Who is the Enemy: Communist or Christian? Biblically-Based Alternatives to U.S. Foreign Policy

Denouncing the consequences of U.S. foreign policy to Latin America was not a new endeavor for Shaull. As we have seen, Shaull was one of the

56. Ibid., 86.

57. Shaull, "The Christ We may not Want to Meet," Sermon preached at Glendale Presbyterian Church. The Richard Shaull Papers, Special Collections, Speer Library, Princeton Theological Seminary, Princeton.

58. Shaull, "Christian Participation in Popular Movements in Central America," Lecture delivered at the University of Rochester, October 15, 1986: 1–3.

founders of NACLA, an organization dedicated to empirical studies about the imperialistic influence of the United States over Latin America. When Shaull arrived as a missionary to Latin America in 1942, he perceived the United States as the savior of civilization. He experienced the resilience of the American spirit in overcoming the most difficult moments of economic depression and experienced himself the American dream of going to college and securing better opportunities of existence through education. Such transfer of values were shattered after serving in Latin America for twenty-years as a missionary, where he came to understand that "the American dream was built, at least in part, on the suffering and exploitation of those people in the Third World, and required the persistent destruction of those movements for social justice."[59] Moreover, when he arrived in the United States in the early 1960s, Shaull realized that the American dream was never an option for some segments of society such as ethnic minorities and women.[60] From that moment on, Shaull began to apply to the North American reality the same principles of radical social transformation which he proclaimed in Latin America.

Shaull was convinced that the revolutionary process in Latin America had found its bedrock in the Sandinistas. To legitimize his claim, Shaull presented to North American Christians the way the poor constructed their spirituality in the midst of death. He maintained that it was precisely such a spirituality rooted in the liberating message of the Bible that empowered them to participate for the transformation of society. Shaull challenged North American Christians to participate in the new reformation by sharing their lives with the poor in their neighborhoods and to intervene against the government by developing biblically-based alternatives to U.S. foreign policy to Latin America.

One of the most intense propaganda efforts against the Sandinista revolution by the Reagan administration was driven by its claim that the Sandinistas were a Communist movement aligned with the Soviet Union. When the Republican Party took control of the nation under President Ronald Reagan in 1980, a new ideological and military war began in Central America. The Reagan administration blamed President Jimmy Carter's foreign policy and its emphasis on human rights as creating a lack of respect for the United States in the world. Dana Robert argued that

59. Richard Shaull, "The Death and Resurrection of the American Dream," 99.
60. Ibid.

the Maryknoll Sisters in the 1960s responded vigorously to the cry of the poor in Latin America as missionaries. In their capacity as missionaries, they were very influential in U.S. foreign policy to Latin America through Massachusetts Representative Tip O'Neill.[61] Serving as cultural and political bridges, the Maryknollers, through Mary Eunice Tolan, the aunt of O'Neill, gave the other side of the story. They publicized and denounced the abuses committed against the Nicaraguan people in a civil war strategized by the CIA.[62] However, the Reagan administration ignored the human rights violations in Central America and continued to arm those who tortured, raped, and killed their own people in the name of democracy and freedom.

Yet, according to the Reagan administration, the cases of Nicaragua and Iran were examples of a foreign policy that portrayed the United States as a weak nation. In his quest to revive the Cold War policy, Reagan began a bellicose campaign of arms buildup and accused International Communism for the problems of the world. Because Moscow and International Communism were the enemies, the Reagan administration pledged to back up any dictatorship in Latin America that was anticommunist.[63] To the Reagan administration Nicaragua's political situation was clear: Nicaragua was part of the expansionist intentions of the Soviet Union in Latin America. The Administration divided the struggle between two factions searching for human fulfillment: one was the democratic revolution that looked for constitutional democracy, and the other was a totalitarian Marxist-Leninist approach that led to tyranny and repression of the worst kind.[64]

In December 1981, the first sum of financial help ($19.5 million) to counter the Sandinista government was sent to anti-Sandinistas exiled in

61. Robert, "The Influence of American Missionary Women on the World Back Home" 73–74.

62. Ibid.

63. Schmitz, *The United States and Right-Wing Dictatorships*, 194.

64. Kirkpatrick, "Introduction" *Central America and the Reagan Doctrine*, xiii. Kirkpatrick was the most well-known critic of Carter's policy toward Nicaragua. She argued that the United States suffered a decline of power and prestige in the world because of its failure in the Vietnam War and "a posture of continued self-abasement and apology vis-à-vis the Third World." In particular, she blamed Carter's agenda of human rights for leading to the overthrow of U.S. allies like Nicaragua's Somoza family. 37.

Costa Rica, Honduras, and Miami.[65] President Reagan and the Religious Right baptized these Nicaraguan exiles as "freedom fighters" who received their military training and assignments from the CIA. Klaiber argued, "Under the legitimazing scope this official policy provided, the Pentagon put into practice the new concept of a war of low intensity."[66] But this war of low intensity would have tremendous repercussions for the poor peasants who were close to the borders of Costa Rica and Honduras as the *Contras* crossed the borders to perpetrate their terrorist acts against them. There are numerous testimonies of how the *Contras* raped, tortured, and killed thousands of peasants whose only sin was the dream of a better life.[67]

As the Reagan administration was sure that the FSLN was sponsored by a Cuban-Soviet proxy, they perceived the solution to be for them to implement and sustain the war against Nicaragua through their financial and military training support. To legitimize its claims that Nicaragua was a totalitarian regime, the Reagan administration embarked on an ideological battle to gain the hearts of the North American people by portraying Nicaragua's FSLN as a totalitarian regime. One of the tactics was to show how the Church was oppressed and persecuted by the FSLN.[68] The only problem with this interpretation was that the Administration completely ignored one crucial point: that the spark of the revolution came precisely from Christians committed to justice.

In Brazil, Shaull was advocating for Christians to embrace the revolutionary struggle in dialogue with Marxists committed to the cause of justice. In North America, he was defending the Nicaraguan revolution because it had nationalistic and religious elements ingrained in it. In this sense, now that Christians were participating in the creation of a new order in Central America, side by side with Marxist revolutionaries, Shaull needed to challenge policies that opposed the creation of a new order. Shaull argued for a God who was active in history to lead the way in the struggle of people at the bottom of society to liberate themselves and seek fullness of life. Therefore, the invitation was not to enter the world of the poor from a distance, but to change values and sides by looking and living

65. Berryman, *Inside Central America*, 47.

66. Klaiber, *The Church, Dictatorships, and Democracy*, 205.

67. Americas Watch, *Human Rights in Nicaragua*.

68. Stoll, *Is Latin America Turning Protestant?* 218–23.

in the world from their perspective, meaning from below.[69] In this sense, when North American Christians entered into solidarity with the world of the poor, they would experience a new conversion, a new way of looking at the world, which had redemptive qualities.[70] Therefore, because the poor were the new historical subjects creating a new social, political, and economic order in Nicaragua, Marxism was not used as a strict dogmatic philosophy, but rather it was a pragmatic and syncretized type of ideology integrating nationalism and Christian faith.[71]

Shaull denounced politicians for thinking they could sacralize their actions through religious language.[72] He pointed out,

> Policies are presented as dogmas not to be questioned and are defended with a spirit of intransigency reminiscent of religious fundamentalism. God is called to give divine sanction to what our nation is doing, while those conceived of as enemies are denounced as belonging to the kingdom of Evil. In this context a narrow view of national self-interest is portrayed as the Ultimate Good while those who question it can be branded not only as unpatriotic but as enemies of God.[73]

Shaull understood U.S. policy toward Central America as demonic in nature. He also saw how in the Bible, the story of the liberation of the oppressed was always followed by a reaction from the ones who enslaved them. This imagery from the Exodus and Paul's apocalyptic description of the "principalities and powers" Shaull used to pronounce judgment on the United States.[74] To Shaull, it was the "principalities and powers" that were guiding U.S. foreign policy in Central America. For that reason, he saw that the structures of society could be redeemed. As Christ exposed the "principalities and powers" as evil forces through his victory over death, so Shaull believed that once the powers and principalities directing foreign U.S. policy were exposed as evil, they would lose their grip

---

69. Shaull, *Heralds of a New Reformation*, 76–100.

70. Shaull, "The Redemptive Suffering of the Poor," 167–200.

71. Richard Shaull, *Naming the Idols*, 53–58.

72. Richard Shaull, "Third World Liberation or Continued United States Domination" lecture delivered at University of Pennsylvania, March, 1986.

73. Shaull, *Naming the Idols,* 42.

74. Shaull, "The Prophetic Challenge to Imperial America," 14–16.

on reality.[75] Shaull pointed out, "The God of justice is presented to us as the creator of the universe . . . the God whose determination to establish justice on earth constitutes the future toward which history is moving."[76] Shaull was convinced that terms such as "freedom and democracy" were used by the Reagan administration to absolutize its agenda in the Third World. Freedom and democracy were used as universalizing principles in the name of the free market which was becoming an idol that dominated the world.[77] As U.S. foreign policy absolutized its values, it needed to demonize its enemy—international communism.[78] But for Shaull the real enemies of civilization were the ones who perpetuated the enslavement of the oppressed. Because the Reagan administration preferred to authenticate and defend governments that repressed their own people, the U.S. was an accomplice to the crimes of repressive military or dictatorial regimes in Central America.

A Biblically-Based U.S. Foreign Policy

The Bible, for Shaull, was a book of "unfulfilled possibilities in and beyond the present moment."[79] His eschatological orientation guided him to read the Bible in light of the "new age" that was breaking into history through the presence of Christ in a new humanity. From the book of Exodus to the Apocalypse, according to Shaull, "we have the story of a people whose God calls them, time and again, to break out of bondage to the past and leads them in the construction of a radically new social order."[80] The Exodus was, one might say, a program for revolution in which the liberation of slaves was orchestrated by God, and in which God instructed them to construct a society based on egalitarian values. When Israel failed to accomplish the practice of justice, the prophets called the nation to judgment. The final outcome of the judgment would be seen in whether or not Israel repented from its sins. If Israel were not to repent, God would judge

75. Shaull, "Third World Liberation or Continual US Domination?" 14.
76. Shaull, *Naming the Idols*, 131.
77. Ibid., 38–39.
78. Richard Shaull, "Discord in the Americas," 5–11.
79. Shaull, *Naming the Idols*, 59.
80. Ibid., 91.

by tearing down the existing society and rebuilding a new society. Shaull pointed out, "The prophets find meaning in contemporary events not so much by analogies with what happened in the past as by looking forward to the events planned in the sovereign freedom of God."[81]

The life of Jesus of Nazareth called into question all the previous known moral, political, and religious standards. Using the gospel of Luke 1:51–53, Shaull understood that God was overthrowing those structures of power that benefited the rich, and supplanting them with new structures directed and promoted for the benefit of the poor.[82] The revolutionary character of Jesus' ministry in his identification with the poor and marginal placed him in a position of conflict with the religious leaders of the time. At the same time, his eschatological vision of the Kingdom of God as present among the disciples marked the terms for life right there. Shaull stated, "We can understand who we are only in the light of what we can become; the only social relationships that make sense or hold the promise of social stability and peace are those moving in the direction of God's Reign."[83] This was clearly seen in Paul's emphasis on the new age initiated by the death and resurrection of Jesus Christ. As exemplified in his own life, in his own transformation from persecutor to servant, Paul understood the importance of dying to the old nature and of being resurrected with Christ to a new age, the age of the Spirit. In this new age, all the structures that were preserved by injustice were called to die in order to be resurrected. Beyond the fall of the empire would come a new era characterized by the practice of justice to the poor.[84] But this eschatological perspective, which was apocalyptic in nature, did not offer anything new in Shaull's missiology as it was a repetition of his previous views while a missionary in Brazil. The only thing new was that now he was a missionary to his own country.

Shaull proposed a foreign policy based on the biblical theme of slavery and freedom. In this story, God was present in history forming a new era in which the poor would have a privileged position as the protagonists of their own destiny. Because the U.S. was backing a reign of death in Central America, its redemption would come when it took the cause of

81. Ibid., 96.
82. Ibid., 97.
83. Ibid., 98.
84. Ibid., 100–105.

the poor as its principal basis for foreign policy. Shaull felt the United States should enter into a partnership with the emerging leadership of the Central American countries who were striving to create a better society. It should not have to matter if they had a Marxist outlook, because the true measurement of their ideology would be judged by whether or not they followed the principle of establishing a new society. In this sense, Shaull was confronting the political loyalties of his fellow North American Christians while serving as an itinerant evangelist throughout the nation. His Calvinistic heritage came into its own under what Shaull considered to be repressive tendencies at home and abroad in U.S. policy, because it called him to stand up for God's sovereignty and order against the claims of any government wanting to usurp God's place.

# Conclusion

After more than forty years of experience in Latin America, Shaull was convinced that the world could be transformed through the power of the gospel of Jesus Christ. One thing that changed dramatically throughout his life was his conception of the United States. When he first arrived in Colombia, Shaull perceived the United States as the savior of modern civilization. That perception suddenly changed as he experienced the terrible consequences of some aspects of U.S. foreign policy to the region. Later in life, Shaull saw the United States as causing the devastating conditions the poor had to face in Latin America. Shaull became a critic of U.S. foreign policy to Latin America and denounced the policies of the Reagan administration through books, articles, lectures, and sermons.

Shaull was one of the most important and controversial missionaries of the second part of the twentieth century. The study of his life has revealed a myriad of connections with significant social, political, and religious issues of the day. Shaull based his missiology of social transformation in three overarching doctrines: the sovereignty of God, incarnation, and eschatology. One constant in Shaull's missiology was his understanding of the sovereignty of God in all affairs of human existence. Because God was guiding history to its final consummation in Jesus Christ, history had a goal: redemption. But redemption for Shaull was not only a futuristic stage where saints would enjoy the presence of God in "heaven." He was convinced that the message of salvation had implications for the transformation of society. Sin was not only personal, but also structural. Because the manifestation of sin happened in history, it was most revealed through the poor and oppressed of society. In this sense, redemption meant the elimination of oppressive structures in society through a continual revolutionary process. Shaull's theological standpoint on revolution was guided by his understanding of God as creator and ruler of the cosmos. His Calvinistic heritage of the sovereignty of God was interlaced with the incarnational event of Jesus of Nazareth in history and the eschatological significance of that event for the transformation of humanity.

There was an interrelationship between Shaull's missionary career and the development of contextual theologies. Shaull was convinced that the Gospel of Jesus Christ would address all realms of human existence. As one of the first contextual theologians, he constructed a missiology that took the contextual reality of the place in which he was involved and proclaimed the possibilities of life which were available to humans in that particular situation. Shaull influenced the field of contextual theology in at least two ways: the active participation of the theologian in the struggles of the poor, and the primacy of *praxis* over church doctrines.

Shaull was a missionary who insisted in constructing his theology in concrete situations of brokenness and despair. Shaull proposed a missiology that would be completely engaged in society. One of the areas for such engagement was the political realm. He was one of the first missionaries to Latin America who made the political question as religious in nature. His conviction that God was active in history led him to conclude that society would change through the political process as revolutionaries construct a better world. He understood the influence of Marxism as an ideology that gave the poor a sense of belonging and participation in the construction of a better society. In this sense, he was the first missionary in Latin America to identify the revolutionary ferment of the masses as a sign of God's intervention in the world and envision the meaning of such intervention in theological language. Thus, Shaull's contextual missiology of revolution was a by-product of his missionary experience with groups of marginalized people in Latin America. Shaull moved to a full-blown contextual methodology with major implications to the field of missiology in general. He departed from previous theological methods based on the absoluteness of metaphysics to an historical understanding of God's concrete actions. In Shaull's view, knowledge was acquired only through the existential involvement of the theologian in concrete situations of struggle for the liberation of humankind. Also, Shaull's method of theological education was praxis oriented. When he was a seminary professor, Shaull insisted that his students work in evangelistic centers like the Centro Obrero of Colombia or Vila Anastacio in Brazil where the gospel was incarnated to the social, economic, and religious reality of the poor.

Shaull's second contribution to contextual theology was his insistence that *praxis* overcomes church doctrines and denominational loyalties. As one of the foremost ecumenical leaders representing the World Council of Churches and the World Student Christian Federation in Latin America, Shaull was one of the first missionaries who established dialogues with Marxist and Roman Catholic leaders in Brazil. Shaull's ecumenism was inclusive in nature because he was looking for mutual cooperation between Protestants, Roman Catholics, and Marxists for the formation of a better society. In this sense, Shaull transcended and transgressed church doctrines and institutional loyalties. His main concern was not the transmission of a right doctrine, but the acceptance in faith that God was calling the church to participate with forces that were striving to create a better world. The future that transgressed against and transcended the present could be an ethical standpoint of solidarity with the world. Solidarity means entering and staying in the world of the less privileged, facing their struggles, and overcoming life together in the spirit of Jesus. Solidarity is entering the world of the other to face together the challenges of life. This requires from the church an act of self-denial. The church that wants to be a true instrument of God in the work of evangelism needs to enter into the world of the other and contribute with the means to improve the existing conditions of the community.

Solidarity could take the form of companionship and presence. Companionship and presence gives the church a true meaning and authority to proclaim the message of salvation in a way which seduces their audience. When the church is present accompanying those who suffer and struggle in life, she becomes incarnated in the image of God to those people. Therefore, the primary activity of the church is not just the proclamation of salvation, but rather through her incarnation she proclaims salvation by her mere presence among the oppressed. To fight and endeavor for a just world where there is no oppression, disfranchisement, and alienation is to proclaim the arrival of a new world order that signifies the Reign of God. The Reign of God is incompatible with any form of social injustice. Therefore, to work for the betterment of society is to work for the Reign of God. Even though the Reign of God and society are not equal the Church's responsibility is to improve society through the work of incarnational solidarity.

Shaull conceived the church as a missionary community called to continue the redemptive task of Jesus Christ in the world. Thus, the church as the body of Christ was in a special partnership with God to bring the eschatological culmination of all things in Christ. Shaull's ecclesiology was defined eschatologically in terms of God's goals for humanity. For him, the church lived where the new age was manifesting the kingdom of God. As Jesus Christ was the concrete manifestation of God in history, the church was called to incarnate the same reality while bringing the first-fruits of the kingdom. However, there was an apparent tension in Shaull's ecclesiology between the church as institutional and the church as the body of Christ.

Shaull was a vehement critic of the institutional church. For him the institutional church was part of the status quo and had scarce possibilities to be an agent of change to free humanity from the oppressive structures of the world. Since his first published article in North America, "Toward the Conversion of the Church" in 1947, Shaull believed that most of the structures in the church were part of the old age. Because the church as an institution was a supporter of the status quo through its structures such structures needed to be put under the judgment of God by the new transforming age of the Holy Spirit. Shaull envisioned the church as a *koinonia*, a group of believers sharing a common cause and goal in life: the establishment of God's *shalom*. As a true follower of the Reformation, Shaull believed that the church should be in a constant state of reformation, an *ecclesia reformata semper reformanda*. In this sense, when Shaull called for a sectarian option or for the dissenter to raise his/her voice, he was developing his missiology from a long history of public theology as attested by the Reformers.

## Postscript

Shaull spent the final years of his life in an unexpected place. Now in his late seventies and in deteriorating health due to a malignant cancer, Shaull became the associate pastor and missiological advisor for the Bryn Mawr Presbyterian Church in Pennsylvania. Bryn Mawr Presbyterian

Church was organized in 1873. From its humble beginnings, Bryan Mawr has become one of the twenty largest congregations of the Presbyterian Church U.S.A. with a membership of 3,500. Since 1873, four new buildings had been erected: a Sunday School Annex in 1874; a new sanctuary in 1927; an educational building in 1931; the Mary Catherine Pew Memorial Chapel in 1940; the Activities building in 1964; and in 1990, the Ministries Center which created offices and spaces for large groups. The church carried a strong missionary tradition since the 1880s when the first Presbyterian missionary, William Wanlass, was sent to Miraj, India to establish a hospital. Even today, the church continues its support of this work and allocates over 30% of the annual $4 million budget to benevolences.

One of those projects is the Richard Shaull Worldwide Ministries Award designed to fund new mission undertakings or provide support for remarkable mission leaders. The award is granted once a year to projects that represent the missionary life of Shaull in issues of justice and transformational ministry. In the final years of his life, Shaull guided the Bryan Mawr Presbyterian Church in its mission outreach program to craft new goals rooted on faith, justice, and mutual respect. Sam O. Folin, one of the associate ministers, said that Shaull helped the missionary program of Bryn Mawr not to be paternalistic but instead egalitarian.[1] Likewise, the senior pastor Dr. Eugene Bay, now president of Colgate Divinity School in New York, remembered Shaull's influence on the congregation: "He helped us understand that the primary benefactors of mission trips are not the so-called recipients of mission but those whose eyes are opened to what they see and experience in such trips."[2] Shaull organized three short term missionary trips to Brazil and one to Costa Rica while he was an associate at Bryn Mawr Presbyterian Church. He also helped to shape the mission strategy of the congregation through his missiological understanding of God's action in the world. In this sense, he prepared the official document for missionary outreach of the congregation.

In the Benevolence Task Force Review, Shaull laid down the theological rationale that would guide the mission outreach ministry of Bryn Mawr:

1. Sam O. Folim to Angel Santiago, email September 6, 2007.
2. Eugene Bay to Angel Santiago, email July 30, 2007.

> The life, death, and resurrection, and promised coming of Jesus Christ has set the pattern for the church's mission. His life as a man involves the church in the common life of humanity. His service to humankind commits the church to work for every form of human well-being. His suffering makes the church sensitive to all the sufferings of humankind so that it sees the face of Christ in the faces of the people in every kind of need. His crucifixion discloses to the church God's judgment on human inhumanity and the awful consequences of its complicity in injustice. In the power of the risen Christ and hope of his coming, the church sees the promise of God's renewal of human life in society and of God's victory over all wrong.[3]

It was clear that Shaull's missiological understanding was based on God's work through Jesus Christ's life, death, and resurrection and that from that experience of union with Christ the church was a continuation of Christ's ministry on earth through the power of the Holy Spirit. His missiology continued to be rooted in God's redemptive action in history through the church that was called to enter into solidarity with those suffering in the world. It was God who identified with human suffering and longed for the salvation of the world. Because God claimed the church to be the agent of reconciliation on earth, the community of faith was called to practice ministries of compassion, justice, and transformation—three characteristics descriptive of Shaull's own ministry throughout his life:

> If we want to experience the riches of life in Christ and be faithful disciples, we must find concrete ways of sharing in the lives of broken people. This includes living in communion with their religious experience and learning from it. We must be open to being transformed by them, to re-reading the Scriptures and church history, and to being surprised at how the Holy Spirit works when an old order is breaking down and a new order has not yet emerged.[4]

Shaull's willingness to enter into the religious world of the poor and learn from their experience with the Spirit convinced him that a spiritual awakening was the only solution to the recreation of human life and the problem of modern civilization. This was most evident in

3. Richard Shaull, "Report of Actions Referred to the Joshua Team" Minutes of the session Members of the Joshua Team, March 1, 2002. Mimeograph minutes provided by Sam O. Folim, Associate Minister of Bryn Mawr Presbyterian Church.

4. Shaull, "Renewed by the Spirit," 22.

Shaull's final sermon, at Bryn Mawr Presbyterian Church, "An Opening to Transformation" that was later published by *The Other Side.*[5]

"An Opening to Transformation" was a reflection on the aftershock that the attacks on September 11, 2001 brought to the United States and the world. When most North Americans were bellicose against the perpetrators of such carnage and wanted revenge by all means, Shaull saw the events as moments of revelation in which God was present "offering a way to bring life out of death." For him, "God's saving presence makes it possible for us to envision a new future. Our task is to discern what God is up to, then respond to God's leading."[6] As in the past when he perceived Communism as bringing judgment upon Christians for their complacency and inaction towards the world, now Shaull perceived the attacks on September 11, 2001 as an awakening call for Christians in the United States to formulate new ways and act according to the principles of steadfast love, justice, and righteousness.

Using Jeremiah 9: 23–24 that says "Let not the wise man boast of his wisdom or the strong man of his strength or the rich man boast of his riches, but let him who boasts boast about this: that he understands and knows me, that I am the Lord, who exercises kindness, justice, and righteousness on earth for in these I delight," Shaull called the United States to task for its continual boasting of being the wisest, strongest, and richest nation on earth.[7] Shaull insisted that instead of rushing to war to avenge its dignity because of the attacks on September 11, the U.S. should take the events as God's extension of God's mercy to turn the nation's course of direction, repent, and start to construct a better world: "A compassionate God may be offering us an extraordinary opportunity to foresee the dangers lying ahead if we persist along the road we are now traveling. This same God offers us the direction and the courage we need to begin envisioning a future that promises greater life and security for all of us, and to engage in the struggle to create it."[8]

Shaull's missiology of God's redeeming actions in history based on God's sovereignty and mercy continued to inform his life until the very end. One of the most fascinating attributes of long term missionaries like

5. Shaull, "An Opening to Transformation," 16–21.
6. Ibid., 16.
7. Ibid., 17–19.
8. Ibid., 18.

Shaull was his amazing and incredible sense of hope. Even though Shaull had seen the worst of humanity, his conviction that God was guiding history to its final consummation in Christ gave him faith and courage to persevere until the end.

Shaull perceived and predicted the continual spiral of violence that the United States would adopt through its political leaders in the perpetuation of war against the Middle East. Such a spiral of violence could lead to only one thing, he said: the widespread disintegration of society. Because the world was in such stage of chaos, Shaull called for a new Christian community to emerge and cultivate life in the power of the Spirit. Shaull had lost all confidence that the world could be fixed through political and social programs. He had spent a life struggling to construct a better world and used all means available to him to accomplish such task with few results. However, still holding to the utopian vision of the kingdom of God, Shaull continued to struggle with the recreation and transformation of human life through small Christian communities: "By their inner communal life and their work in the world, these new Christians will witness to the vision of a future in which our nation would at last create conditions for a full life at home and for overcoming exploitation and oppression abroad."[9] For him the reconstruction of human life was a religious task and only a church that incarnated itself in the realm of the Spirit and embraced those people at the margins of society would be triumphant in organizing new possibilities of human existence.

After a lifetime of missionary activities dedicated to the poor and oppressed of the world based on a conviction that God was actively redeeming history, Richard Shaull died at age 82 in his house in Ardmore, Pennsylvania on October 25, 2002. His memorial service was celebrated at Bryn Mawr Presbyterian Church on November 2, 2002. Today, Shaull's influence in the field of missiology and his commitment to the life of the Church is celebrated through different channels. As stated previously, the Bryn Mawr Presbyterian Church honored the missionary career of Shaull by creating The Richard Shaull Worldwide Ministries Award. This award was designed to reflect Shaull's witness to Christ in areas of mission and social transformation. The first recipient of the award granted in March 2006 was the Latin American Biblical University in San José, Costa Rica.

9. Ibid., 19.

The Latin American Biblical University proposed to work on a project dedicated to the marginalized in the community. In collaboration with local churches, the university was seeking to mobilize resources to help the less privileged of that neighborhood.[10] The second award was granted in May 2007 to Makunda Hospital of the Emmanuel Hospital Association of New Delhi, India. The hospital is located in a rural area of northeast India with a high death rate for women and newborns. The hospital is going to construct a labor ward, a delivery room, and prenatal and postnatal wards, along with the equipment for each space.[11]

Shaull's influence on Brazilian and Latin American Protestantism was substantial. Shaull took the everyday affairs of human beings in their respective contexts to construct a missiology that was always in touch with their reality. He was one of the first missionaries who took the social, economic, and political context of Latin America as the locus from which to understand God's activity in the world. His missiology was praxis-oriented toward the transformation of the world, and because of this, the *Igreja Presiteriana Unida do Brasil* honored him by naming their theological school in Vitoria, Espíritu Santo, the *Faculdade de Teologia Rev. Richard Shaull.* The *Faculdade* offers a bachelor's and advanced studies in theology. The *Faculdade* has twelve faculty members dedicated to the spiritual formation of a new leadership in the church who can respond to the challenges of the contemporary world through the good news of Jesus Christ.[12] The need to contextualize the Gospel, to make it at home everywhere, was the guiding principle in Shaull's life and ministry.

10. Telephone Conversation between Angel Santiago-Vendrell and Carol Smith, Director of the Bryn Mawr's Worldwide Ministry Council, February 21, 2008.

11. O. Sam Folin, "Worldwide Ministries 2007 Shaull Award to Emmanuel Hospital Association in India," 1–12 [3].

12. Brochure of the *Faculdade de Teologia Rev. Richard Shaull.*

# Bibliography

## Archival Sources

Flory, Margaret. Papers. Divinity Library Special Collections. Yale University Library, New Haven, CT.

Presbyterian Church in the USA. Board of Foreign Missions. *Colombia, 1833–1911.* Boston University School of Theology Library.

Presbyterian Church in the USA. Commission on Ecumenical Mission and Relations. *Brazil Mission, 1890–1965.* Presbyterian Historical Society, Philadelphia, PA.

Presbyterian Church in the USA. Commission on Ecumenical Mission and Relations. *Colombia Mission, 1882–1972.* Presbyterian Historical Society, Philadelphia, PA.

Shaull, Richard. Papers. Special Collections. Speer Library, Princeton Theological Seminary, Princeton, NJ.

## Works by M. Richard Shaull

### Books and Monographs

*Alternativa ao Desespêro.* São Paulo: Impresa Metodista, 1962.

"The Church as a Missionary Community: A Study of the Form of the Church's Life." PhD dissertation. Princeton Theological Seminary, 1959.

———. *Consumers or Revolutionaries?*, with Josef Smolik. Geneva: John Knox Association, 1967.

———. *Containment and Change*, with Carl Oglesby. New York: Macmillan, 1967.

*O Cristianismo e a Revolução Social.* São Paulo: UCEB, 1953.

*El Cristianismo y la Revolución Social.* México: Casa Unida de Publicaciones, 1955.

*Encounter with Revolution.* New York: Associated, 1955.

*Hacia una Revolución Responsable: Ensayos Sobre Socio-Ética Cristiana.* Buenos Aires: La Aurora, 1970.

*Heralds of a New Reformation: The Poor in South and North America.* Maryknoll: Orbis, 1984.

*Liberation and Change*, with Gustavo Gutierrez. Atlanta: John Knox, 1977.

# Bibliography

*Naming the Idols: Biblical Alternatives for U.S. Foreign Policy.* Oak Park, IL: Meyer-Stone, 1988.

*Pentecostalism and the Future of the Christian Churches: Promises, Limitations, Challenges,* with Waldo Cesar. Grand Rapids: Eerdmans, 2000.

"The Power of God in the Life of Man: A Study of the Protestant and Catholic Concepts of the New Life in Christ." ThM thesis. Princeton Theological Seminary, 1946.

*The Reformation and Liberation Theology: Insights for the Challenges of Today.* Louisville: Westminster John Knox, 1991.

*As Transformações Profundas á Luz de uma Teologia Evangélica.* Questões abertas 2. Petrópolis: Vozes, 1967.

## Pamphlets

*Consumers or Revolutionaries?,* with Josef Smolik. Geneva: Foger John Knox Association, 1967.

*Cuadernos de UCEB.* Rio de Janeiro, 1962.

*Los Evangélicos y las Elecciones.* Documento del Encuentro de Reflexión Evangélica, realizado el 4 de febrero de 1984, con la participación del teólogo evangélico Dr. Richard Shaull y del Presidente del Consejo de Estado, Comandante Carlos Nuñez Tellez. Managua: Cepres, 1984.

*The New Revolutionary Mood in Latin America.* New York: Committee on Cooperation in Latin America, Division of Foreign Mission, National Council of the Churches of Christ in the USA, 1962.

*Somos Uma Comunidade Missionaria: Oito Estudos de Prepareção para o Testemunho.* Rio de Janeiro: Secretaria Gerald da Mocidade Presbiteriana, 1957.

## Essays or chapters in books

"American Power and The Powerless Nations." In *What the Religious Revolutionaries are Saying,* edited by Edwyn A. Smith, 12–22. Philadelphia: Fortress, 1971.

"Centroamerica: Un Kairos para Estados Unidos?" In *El Kairós en Centroamerica,* edited by Jose Maria Vigil, 100–106. Managaua: Ediciones Nicarao, 1988.

"Christian Faith as Scandal in a Technocratic World." In *New Theology,* edited by Martin E. Marty and Dean G. Peerman, 123–34. London: Collier-Macmillan, 1969.

"The Christian in the Vortex of Revolution." In *Projections: Shaping an American Theology for the Future,* edited by Thomas F. O'Meara and Donald M. Weisser, 50–69. Garden City, NY: Doubleday, 1970.

"Christian Participation in the Latin-American Revolution." *Christianity Amid Rising Men and Nations,* 91–118. New York: New York Association Press, 1965.

"The Context of Personal Freedom and Maturity." In *Challenges of Change to the Christian College: Proceedings of the Fourth Quadrennial Convocation of Christian Colleges, June 19–23, 1966,* edited by Eliot D. Allen, 136–144. Council of Protestant Colleges and Universities, 1966."A Crise nas Igrejas Nacionais." In *Protestantismo e Imperialismo na America Latina,* edited by Waldo A. Cesar, 37–55. Petrópolis: Vozes, 1968.

"The End of the Road and a New Beginning." In *Marxism and Radical Religion: Essays Toward a Revolutionary Humanism,* edited by John C. Raines and Thomas Dean, 27-48. Philadelphia: Temple University Press, 1970.

"The Form of the Church in the Modern Diaspora." In *New Theology* 2, edited by Martin E. Marty and Dean G. Peerman, 264-287. New York: McMillan, 1965.

"And a God Who Acts and Transforms History." In *Social Justice and the Latin Churches,* 57-70. Consulta Latinoamericana de Iglesia y Sociedad, El Trabo, Chile, 1966. Translated by Jorge Lara-Braud. John Knox Press, 1969.

"Grace: Power for Transformation." In *Liberation, Revolution, and Freedom: Theological Perspectives,* edited by Thomas M. McFadden, 76-87. New York: Seabury, 1975.

"La Iglesia y la Situación Político-Ideológica de América Latina." In *La Naturaleza de la Iglesia y Su Misión en Latinoamerica,* edited by Gonzalo Castillo Cardenas, 154-65. Bogotá: Editorial Iquemia, 1963.

"Iglesia y Teología en la Voragine de la Revolución." In *De la Iglesia y la Sociedad,* 23-48. Montevideo: Tierra Nueva, 1971.

"The New Challenge before the Younger Churches." In *Christianity and World Revolution,* edited by Edwin H. Rian, 190-206. New York: Harper & Row, 1963.

"New Church, New Ministries." In *Struggles for Solidarity: Liberation Theologies in Tension,* edited by Lorine M. Getz and Ruy O. Costa, 95-103. Minneapolis: Fortress Press 1992.

"New Forms of Church Life in a New Society." In *Raise a Signal: God's Action and the Church's task in Latin America Today,* edited by Hyla Stuntz Converse, 108-126. New York: Friendship, 1961.

"Order, Power and Politics: Toward Responsible Government in a Revolutionary World." In *Revolution and Renewal: Christian Response to the Technological and Social Revolutions of Our Time. A Study Book for Churches in the United States in Preparation for A World Conference on Church and Society (July 12-24, 1966) Geneva,* edited by Walter W. Sikes, 37-42. Indianapolis: Christian Churches Disciples of Christ, 1965.

"Una Perspectiva Cristiana del Desarollo Historico y Social." In *Hombre, Ideología y Revolución en América Latina,* 78-91. Montevideo: ISAL, 1965.

"The Rehabilitation of Ideology." In *Religion and International Affairs,* edited by Jeffrey Rose and Michael Ignatieff, 99-107. Toronto: Anansi Toronto, 1968.

"Responding to the Challenge: Renewal and Re-Creation." In *Freedom and Discipleship: Liberation Theology in an Anabaptist Perspective,* edited by Daniel S. Schipani, 147-58. Maryknoll, NY: Orbis, 1989.

"Revolutionary Change in Theological Perspective." In *Christian Social Ethics in a Changing World,* edited by John C. Bennett, 23-43. Geneva: World Council of Churches, 1966.

"Rosenstock-Huessy: My Guide on a Lonely Journey." *Eugene Rosenstock-Huessy: Studies in His Life and Thought,* edited by Darrol M. Bryant and Hans R. Huessy, 191-202. Lewiston: Mellen, 1986.

"Technology and Revolution in Theological Perspective." In *Challenges of Change to the Christian College: Proceedings of the Fourth Quadrennial Convocation of Christian Colleges, June 19-23, 1966,* edited by Eliot D. Allen, 127-35. Council of Protestant Colleges and Universities, 1966.

# Bibliography

"Toward a Reformulation of Objectives." In *Protestant Crosscurrents in Mission: The Ecumenical-Conservative Encounter*, Norman A. Horner, 81-107. Nashville: Abingdon, 1968.

"A Theological Perspective on Human Liberation." In *When All Else Fails: Christian Arguments on Violent Revolution*, 52-63. Philadelphia: Pilgrim, 1970.

## Articles

"A ACA como uma Comunidade." *Testimonium* 2:3 (1954) 124-28.

"Blow the Connections: A Guide to Being Radical." *New* 3:2 (1968) 9-15.

"El Cambio Revolucionario en una Perspectiva Teológica." *Cristianismo y Sociedad*, 4:12 (1966) 49-69.

"The Challenge of Student Work in Brazil." *International Review of Missions* 44 (1955) 323-28.

"The Challenge to the Seminary." *Christianity and Crisis* (April 14, 1969) 81-86.

"Christian Initiative in Latin American Revolution." *Christianity and Crisis* 25 (January 10, 1966) 295-98.

"Christian Realism: Retrospect and Prospect. A Symposium." *Christianity and Crisis* (August 5, 1968) 175-90.

"Christian Theology and Social Revolution (I)." *Perkins Journal* 21 (Winter-Spring 1967-1968) 5-12.

"The Christian World Mission in a Technological Era." *The Ecumenical Review* 17:3 (1965) 205-18.

"Church and Culture in Latin America." *Theology Today* 13:1 (1956) 37-44.

"The Church and the Making of a Counter Culture." *The Chicago Theological Seminary Register* 61:4 (1971) 15-27.

"The Church in the World: Impatience in Latin America." *Theology Today* 20:3 (1963) 401-11.

"Community and Humanity in the University." *Theology Today* 23:1 (1964) 307-411.

"Containment and Change Revisited: A Conversation with Shaull." *American Report* (June 4, 1973) 6, 19.

"Desafío Revolucionario a la Iglesia y la Teología." *Marcha* (October-November 1966) 34-38.

"Desarollo Nacional y Revolución Actual." *Cristianismo y Sociedad* 6:17-18 (1968) 32-40.

"Deus Tem Falado" *Jornal Mocidade* 9 (1953) 9-12.

"The Devotional Life of Brazilian Protestantism," with Rubem Alves. *Student World* 49:4 (1956) 360-66.

"Discussion: Technology, Theology and the Christian Faith." *Union Seminary Quarterly Review* 21:4 (1966) 417-25.

"Does Religion Demand Social Change." *Theology Today* 26:1 (1969) 5-13.

"The Dominican Elections." *Christianity and Crisis* (May 16, 1966) 102-4.

"Entre Jesus e Marx: Reflexões sobre os Anos que Passei no Brasil." *Religiao e Sociedade* 9 (June 1983) 47-58.

"Evangelio, Espíritu Santo y Transformación Social." *Vida y Pensamiento* 15:2 (1995) 44–48.

"Evangelism and Proselytism in Latin America." *Student World* 46 (1953) 14–20.

"La Forma de la Iglesia en la Nueva Diáspora, *Cristianismo y Sociedad* 2:6 (1964) 3–17.

"The Form of the Church in the Modern Diaspora." *Princeton Seminary Bulletin* 57:3 (1964) 3–18.

"From Somewhere Along the Road," with Barbara Hall. *Theology Today* 29 (1972) 86–101.

"The Guerillas—Next Stage in Latin America?" *Worldview* 11 (April 1968) 15–16.

"Hacia una Perspectiva Cristiana de la Revolución Social-Nicolas Berdaiev." *Cristianismo y Sociedad* 3:6 (1965) 3–17.

"Ideología, Fe y Revolución Social." *Testimonium* 10:2 (1964) 41–47.

"Latin Ferment: Challenge to the US." *Christianity and Crisis* (August 9, 1965) 175–77.

"Liberal and Radical in an Age of Discontinuity." *Student World* 62 (1969) 350–58.

"Liberation through Transformation." *Communio Viatorum* 14:2–3 (1971) 85–106.

"Linhas Gerais da Orientação do Trabalho com Acadêmicos no Brasil." *Testimonium* 2:4 (1954) 167–72.

"Military Coup in Brazil." *Christianity and Crisis* 2 (April 27, 1964) 70–72.

"National Development and Social Revolution: Part I." *Christianity and Crisis* (January 20, 1969) 347–48.

"National Development and Social Revolution: Part II." *Christianity and Crisis* (February 3, 1969) 9–11.

"The New Humanity in a Technological Age." *Chimes: San Francisco Theological Seminary Commencement Addressed* 12:3 (1966) 6–11.

"The New Latin American Revolutionaries and the U.S." *Christian Century* 85 (January 17, 1968) 69–70.

"A New Look at the Sectarian Option." *Student World* 61 (1968) 294–99.

"The New Revolutionary Mood in Latin America." *Christianity and Crisis*, 23:5 (1963) 44–48.

"Next Stage in Latin America." *Christianity and Crisis* (November 13, 1967) 264–66.

"Nossa Tarefa Imediata em Face da Crise Iminente." *Testimonium* 1:1 (1953) 27–33.

"El Nuevo Espíritu Revolucionario de América Latina." *Cristianismo y Sociedad* 1:3 (1963) 30–42.

"O Dinamismo da Religião Cristã." *Testimonium* 1:2 (1953) 12–17.

"O Importante e o Ecumenismo de Base." *Contexto Pastoral* (May–June 1993) 3–4.

"La Opción de los Pobres por el Pentecostalismo." *Vida y Pensamiento* 15:2 (1995) 24–44.

"Our Third Conversion: Moving into the Religious World of the Poor." *Hospitality* 16:6 (1997) 1–2.

"Pastor Shaull: Temos Vivido Cegos a Miseria das Massas!" *Brasil Urgente* (1963) 6–12.

"A Personal Reflection." *Church and Society* 78 (November-December 1987) 51–56.

"Política e Revolução" *Jornal Mocidade* (September 1953) 6–9.

"The Political Significance of Parabolic Action." *Motive* (April 1968) 27–29.

"The Presence of God and the Human Revolution." *McCormick Quarterly* 20 (January 1967) 97–103.

"President Carter as Baptist Leader." *Sojourners* 7 (January 1978) 12–14.

"Protestantism in Latin America: Brazil." *Religion in Life* 27 (Winter 1957–1958) 5–14.

# Bibliography

"Questions about Process '67." *Wind and Chaff: A Journal of the University Christian Movement* 5:1 (1967) 14–15.

"Realism and Celebration." *Christianity and Crisis* 28 (November 1968) 272–73.

"Recientes Estudios Sobre el Desarollo Político en Asia, África, y América Latina." *Cristianismo y Sociedad*, 1:2 (1963) 43–50.

"The Reformation and the Sixteenth Century World." *The Reformed Church and the Mission of the Church in Latin America.* Lecture Series at Presbyterian Seminary of Campinas, Brazil, Lecture II (June 28–August 20, 1959) 1–5.

"Relatório do Primeiro Estágio de Evangélicos nas Fábricas Patrocinando pela União Cristã de Estudantes do Brasil," with Acyr Costa Araûjo. *Testimonium* 3:1 (1955) 41–48.

"Repression Brazilian Style." *Christianity and Crisis* (July 21, 1969) 198–99.

"Response to President Bennett." *Theological Education* (Winter 1967) 291–93.

"The Revolutionary Challenge to Church and Theology." *Theology Today* 25 (1968) 470–80.

"The Second Latin American Church and Society Conference." *Christianity and Crisis* (May 2, 1966) 89–91.

"Separating Hopes from Illusions." *Motive* (May 1968) 31–32.

"Some Aspects of the Human Situation in the Sixteenth Century." *The Reformed Church and the Mission of the Church in Latin America.* Lecture Series at Presbyterian Seminary of Campinas, Brazil, Lecture I (June 28–August 20, 1959) 1–5.

"The Struggle for Economic and Social Justice." *Social Action and Social Progress* (January–February 1966) 27–30.

"Testemunhas de Cristo num Mundo em Transformação." *Revista de Mocidade Presbiteriana* 15 (July-September 1954) 32–35, 44.

"A Theological Perspective on Human Liberation." *New Blackfriars* 49 (July 1968) 509–17.

"Theology and the Transformation of Society." *Theology Today* 25 (1968) 23–36.

"Toward the Conversion of the Church." *Theology Today* 3 (1947) 502–11.

"University Education for World Responsibility." *Federation News* (1968) 21–25.

"The Van Leeuwen Thesis: a Review of Christianity in World History." *Study Encounter* 1:2 (1965) 68–71.

"What Does the Lord Require of You?" *Church and Society* 77 (May–June 1987) 6–15.

## Secondary Sources

Abrecht, Paul. *The Churches and Rapid Social Change.* Garden City, NY: Doubleday, 1961.

———. *Las Iglesias y los Rápidos Cambios Sociales.* México City: Casa Unida de Publicaciones, 1961.

Ahlstrom, Sydney E. *A Religious History of the American People.* New Haven: Yale University Press, 1972.

Alvarez, Carmelo. "La Iglesia en Diaspora de Ricardo Shaull: un aporte protestante a la teología de la liberación." *Vida y Pensamiento* 10:1 (1980) 43–53.

Alvarez, Eliseo Perez. "Richard Shaull, Sobre la Marcha." *Lectura Alternada: Revista de Literatura Cristiana* 1:3 (1997) 20–24.

Alves, Rubem. "Toward a Theology of Liberation." PhD diss., Princeton Theological Seminary, 1969.

———. "Su Cadaver Estave Lleno de Mundo." *Religião e Sociedade* 23 (2003) 91–94.

———. *Protestantism and Repression: A Brazilian Case Study*. Maryknoll, NY: Orbis, 1985.

Araûjo, João Dias de. *Inquisição sim Fogueiras: Veinte Anos de Historia da Igreja Presbiteriana do Brasil, 1954–1974* [*Inquisition without Burnings: Twenty Years of the History of the Presbyterian Church of Brazil, 1954–1974*]. Sao Paulo: Instituto Superior de Estudos da Religião, 1976.

Arias, Mortimer. "El Itinerario Protestante: Hacia una Teología de la Liberación." *Vida y Pensamiento* 8:1 (1988) 49–59.

Barreiro, Julio. "La Naturaleza del Hombre en Marx." In *Hombre, Ideología y Revolución en América Latina*, 19–41. Montevideo: ISAL, 1965.

Barreto, Raimundo C. "Facing the Poor in Brazil: Towards an Evangélico Progressive Social Ethics." PhD diss., Princeton Theological Seminary, 2006.

Bassham, Roger C. *Mission Theology: 1948–1975 Years of Worldwide Creative Tension, Ecumenical, Evangelical, and Roman Catholic*. Pasadena, CA: William Carey Library, 1979.

Bell, George K. A., editor. *The Stockholm Conference 1925: The Official Report of the Universal Conference of Life and Work Held in Stockholm, 19–30 August, 1925*. Oxford: Oxford University Press, 1926.

Bennett, John C. "Theological Education and Social Revolution." *Theological Education* (Winter 1967) 283–90.

Berryman, Phillip. *Stubborn Hope: Religion, Politics, and Revolution in Central America*. Maryknoll, NY: Orbis, 1994.

Bidegaín, Ana María. *Iglesia, Pueblo y Política: Un Estudio de Conflictos de Intereses— Colombia, 1930–1950*. Bogotá: Pontificia Universidad Javeriana, 1985.

Borda, Orlando Fals. *La Violencia en Colombia: Estudio de un Proceso Social*. Bogotá: Ediciones Tercer Mundo, 1962.

Bosc, Jean. "Secularisation et revolution." *Foi et Vie* 68:5–6 (December 1969) 47–56.

Bosch, David. *Transforming Mission: Paradigm Shifts in Theology of Mission*. American Society of Missiology Series 16. Maryknoll, NY: Orbis, 1991.

Boston, Bruce. "Report from A Theological Community in the Meantime." *Colloquy* 5:10 (November, 1972) 34–39.

Brunner, Emil. *The Theology of Crisis*. New York: Charles Scribner's Sons, 1929.

———. *Natural Theology: Comprising Nature and Grace and the Reply No! by Karl Barth*. London: Centenary, 1946.

Brusco, Elizabeth E. *The Reformation of Machismo: Evangelical Conversion and Gender in Colombia*. Austin: University of Texas Press, 1995.

Bushnell, David. *The Making of Modern Colombia: A Nation in Spite of Itself*. Berkeley: University of California Press, 1993.

Cavalcanti, H.B. "Political Cooperation and Political Repression: Presbyterians under Military Rule in Brazil (1964–1974) *Review of Religious Research* 34 (1992) 97–116.

———. "Human Agency in Mission Work: Missionary Styles and Their Political Consequences" *Sociology of Religion* 66 (2005) 381–98.

# Bibliography

Cesar, Waldo. *A Conferência do Nordeste: Cristo e o Processo Revolucionário Brasileiro II Volumenes.* Rio de Janeiro: Setor de Responsibilidade Social da Igreja, 1964.

————. *Final Report. Pentecostal Response in Brazil to the Suffering of the Poor: An Interdisciplinary Study of Recent Theological Developments.* New Haven, CT: Overseas Ministry Study Center, 1996.

————. "Church and Society—or Society and Church?" in *Revolution of the Spirit: Ecumenical Theology in a Global Context. Essays in Honor of Richard Shaull,* edited by Nantawan Boonprasat Lewis, 133–48. Grand Rapids: Eerdmans, 1998.

*Christian Work in Latin America.* Vol. 1: *The Inceptior and History of the Congress. Survey and Occupation. Message and Method. Education.* Reports of Commissions presented to the Congress on Christian work in Latin America, Panama, February, 1916. New York: Missionary Education Movement, 1917.

Cleary, Edward. *The Struggle for Human Rights in Latin America.* Westport, CT: Praeger, 1997.

Clebsch, William A. *Perspectiva Contemporanea sobre a Palavra, o Mundo e os Sacramentos.* Rio de Janeiro: Cuadernos de UCEB, 1965.

Comblin, José. *The Church and the National Security State.* Maryknoll, NY: Orbis, 1979.

*Congress on Christian Work in Latin America, Panama, February, 1916.* Vol. 1. New York: Missionary Education Movement, 1917.

Cook, Guillermo. *New Face of the Church in Latin America: Between Tradition and Change.* Maryknoll, NY: Orbis, 1994.

Costas, Orlando. *Theology at the Crossroads in Contemporary Latin America.* Amsterdam: Rodopi, 1976.

Cunha, Carlos and Jose Bittencourt Filho. *De Dentro de Furação: Richard Shaull e os Primordios da Teología da Libertação.* São Paulo: Sagarana, 1985.

Dayton, Donald W. *Theological Roots of Pentecostalism.* Metuchen: Scarecrow, 1996.

D'Antonio, William V., and Frederick B. Pike, editors. *Religion, Revolution, and Reform: New Forces for Change in Latin America.* New York: Praeger, 1964.

Derby, Marian. *Latin American Churches and North American Organizations.* Four Addresses presented at the Study Conference of the Committee on Cooperation in Latin America, Buck Hill Falls, PA, 1961.

De Vries, Egbert. *El Hombre en los Rápidos Cambios Sociales.* México City: Casa Unida de Publicaciones, 1962.

Dulles, John W. *Unrest in Brazil: Political-Military Crises 1955–1964.* Austin: University of Texas Press, 1970.

Escobar, Samuel. *La Chispa y la Llama: Breve Historia de la Comunidad Internacional de Estudiantes Evangélicos en América Latina.* Buenos Aires: Certeza, 1978.

————. *La Fe Evangélica y las Teologías de la Liberación.* El Paso: Casa Bautista de Publicaciones, 1987.

Faria, Eduardo Galasso. *Fé e Compromiso: Richard Shaull e a Teología no Brasil.* São Paulo: ASTE, 2002.

Filho, William S. "Seis Fenomenos na Vida do Protestantismo Brasileiro." *Cruz de Malta* (June 1958) 36–49.

Gillette, Gerald. "John A. Mackay: Influence on My Life." *Journal of Presbyterian History* 56 (Spring 1978) 33.

Goés, Paulo de. *Do Individualismo ao Compromiso Social. A Contribuicao da Conferencia Evangelica do Brasil para a Articulacao de uma Etica Social Crista.* Grau de Mestre en

Ciencias da Religiao: Instituto Metodista de Ensino Superior Sao Bernardo Campos, Brasil, 1989.

Goff, James. "The Persecution of Protestant Christians in Colombia; 1948 to 1958, with an investigation of its background and causes." ThD diss., San Francisco Theological Seminary, 1966.

Green, John W. *Gaitanismo, Left Liberalism, and Popular Mobilization in Colombia*. Gainesville: University Press of Florida, 2003.

Grenholm, Carl-Henrie. *Christian Social Ethics in a Revolutionary Age: An Analysis of the Social Ethics of John C. Bennett, Heinz-Dietrich Wendland and Richard Shaull*. Acta Universitatis Upsaliensis. Uppsala: Tofters, 1973.

Gutiérrez, Gustavo. *A Theology of Liberation: History, Politics, and Salvation*. Maryknoll, NY: Orbis, 1971.

———. "Toward a Theology of Liberation." In *Liberation Theology: A Documentary History*, edited by Alfred T. Hennelly, 62–76. Maryknoll, NY: Orbis, 1990.

Hamblin, David W. "A Social History of Protestantism in Colombia, 1930–2000." PhD diss., University of Massachusetts at Amherst, 2003.

Hoekendijk, Johannes. "The Call to Evangelism" *International Review of Missions* 39:2 (1950) 162–67.

———. "The Church in Missionary Thinking" *International Review of Missions* 41 (1952) 324–36.

———. "Christ and the World in the Modern Age" *The Student World* 54 (1961) 75–82.

Hogg, William Richey. *Ecumenical Foundations: A History of the International Missionary Council and its Nineteenth-Century Background*. New York: Harper & Brothers, 1952.

Houtart, Fracois, and Emile Pin. *The Church and the Latin American Revolution*. New York: Sheed & Ward, 1965.

Hutchinson, William R. *American Protestant Thought: The Liberal Era*. New York: Harper & Row, 1968.

Inman, Samuel Guy. *Latin America: Its Place in World Life*. Chicago: Willett, Clark, 1937.

———. "Missions and Economics in Latin America." In *Christianity and the Growth of Industrialism in Asia, Africa, and South America. Report of the Jerusalem Meeting of the International Missionary Council*, 117–45. London: Oxford University Press, 1928.

International Missionary Council. "Christ the Lord of All of Life." In *Christianity and the Growth of Industrialism in Asia, Africa, and South America. Report of the Jerusalem Meeting of the International Missionary Council*, 181. London: Oxford University Press, 1928.

Johnson, Douglas. *A Brief History of the International Fellowship of Evangelical Students*. Lausanne: The International Fellowship of Evangelical Students, 1964.

Klaiber, Jeffrey. *The Church, Dictatorships, and Democracy in Latin America*. Maryknoll, NY: Orbis, 1998.

Labrunie, Claude Emmanuel. "Richard Shaull—Mestre, Profeta e Amigo." *Religião e Sociedade* 23 (2003) 62–63.

Latourette, Kenneth Scott. *World Service*. New York: Association, 1957.

Laubach, Frank C. *Toward World Literacy: The Each One Teach One Way*. Syracuse: Syracuse University Press, 1960.

———. *Forty Years with the Silent Billion*. Old Tappan, NJ: Revell, 1970.

Lavine, Daniel H. *Churches and Politics in Latin America.* London: Sage, 1979.

Leber, Charles T. "A Young Man Worth Watching." In *New Frontiers for Old*, 49–55. New York: Board of Foreign Missions of the Presbyterian Church of the United States of America, 1946.

Lehmann, Paul. *Ethics in a Christian Context.* New York: Harper & Row, 1963.

Lehtonen, Risto. "The Story of a Storm: An Ecumenical Case Study" *Study Encounter* 8:1 (1972) 1–16.

———. *Story of a Storm: The Ecumenical Student Movement in the Turmoil of Revolution.* Grand Rapids: Eerdmans, 1998.

Levering, Ralph B. *The Cold War, 1945–1987.* 2nd ed. American History Series. Wheeling, IL: Harlan Davidson, 1988.

Levine, Robert M. *Father of the Poor? Vargas and His Era.* Cambridge: Cambridge University Press, 1998.

Lipset, Seymour Martin, and Aldo Solari. *Elites in Latin America.* New York: Oxford University Press, 1967.

Longfield, Bradley J. *The Presbyterian Controversy: Fundamentalists, Modernists, and Moderates.* New York: Oxford University Press, 1991.

Mackay, John A. *The Latin American Churches and the Ecumenical Movement.* Address Delivered at the Study Conference of the Committee on Cooperation in Latin America, Bulk Hill Falls, PA, 1961.

———. "The Role of Princeton Seminary." *The Princeton Seminary Bulletin* 31 (November 1937) 1.

———. "The Evangelistic Duty of Christianity." In *The Christian Life and Message in Relation to Non-Christian Systems of Thought and Life*, Vol. 1: *The Jerusalem Meeting of the International Missionary Council, March 24–April 8, 1928*, 383–90. New York: International Missionary Council, 1928.

———. *That Other America.* New York: Friendship, 1935.

Marcuse, Herbert. *The New Left and the 1960s: Collected Papers of Herbert Marcuse.* Edited by Douglas Kellner. London: Routledge, 2005.

Martinez, Pastor. "Obstacles in the Way of National Evangelical Union." *La Voz de Tolima* (March–April 1946) n.p.

Martz, John. *Colombia: A Contemporary Political Survey.* Westport, CT: Greenwood, 1962.

Matos, Alderi S. "The Life of Erasmo Braga, A Brazilian Protestant Leader." ThD diss., Boston University, 1996.

———. *Os Pioneiros Presbiterianos do Brasil (1859–1900) Missionarios, Pastores e Leigos do Seculo 19.* São Paulo: Cultura Cristiana, 2006.

Maury, Philippe. *Cristianismo y Política.* Buenos Aires: Metropress, 1964.

Melano, Beatriz. "The Influence of Dietrich Bonhoeffer, Paul Lehmann, and Richard Shaull in Latin America." *Princeton Seminary Bulletin* 22:1 (2001) 64–84.

Míguez Bonino, José. *Faces of the Church in Latin America.* Grand Rapids: Eerdmans, 1997.

Muelder, Walter G. *The Idea of the Responsible Society.* Boston: Boston University School of Theology, 1955.

Mueller, George A. "Theology of Revolution." *New* 3:2 (1968) 2–8.

Neely, Alan. "Protestant Antecedents of the Latin American Theology of Liberation." PhD Catholic University of America, 1977.

Newbigin, Lesslie. "The Nature of the Christian Hope." *Ecumenical Review* 4 (1952) 284.

——. "Can Churches Give Common Witness?" *Theology Today* 9 (1953) 512–18.

——. "The Present Christ and the Coming Christ." *Ecumenical Review* 6 (1954) 119.

——. *One Body, One Gospel, One Church.* London: Carling, 1958.

——. "Mission to Six Continents." In *A History of the Ecumenical Movement, 1948–1968*, vol. 2, edited by Harold E. Fey, 171–97. Geneva: World Council of Churches, 1970.

Niebuhr, Reinhold. *Christian Realism and Political Problems.* New York: Scribner's Sons, 1953.

——. "Ideology and the Scientific Method." In *The Essential Reinhold Niebuhr: Selected Essays and Addresses*, edited by Robert McAfee Brown 205–7. New Haven, CT: Yale University Press, 1986.

Nuñez, Emilio A. *Teología de la Liberación: Una Perspectiva Evangélica.* San José: Caribe, 1986.

O'Keefe, Mark. "An Analysis and Critique of the Theory of Revolution in the Theology of M. Richard Shaull." Licentiate in Sacred Theology, The Catholic University of America, 1985.

O'Neill, William L. *The New Left: A History.* Wheeling, WV: Harlan Davidson, 2001.

Orchard, Ronald K., editor. *Witness in Six Continents: Records of the Meeting of the Commission on World Mission and Evangelism of the World Council of Churches Held in Mexico City, December 8th to 19th, 1963.* New York: Friendship, 1964.

Ordoñez, Francisco. *Historia del Cristianismo Evangélico en Colombia.* Medellín: Tipografía Union, 1956.

Opoçenský, Milan. "Profile of a Teacher of Theology." In *J. L. Hromadka: The Field is the World*, 11–26. Prague: Christian Peace Conference, 1990.

Pierson, Paul. *A Younger Church in Search of Maturity: Presbyterianism in Brazil from 1910 to 1959.* San Antonio: Trinity University Press, 1974.

Potter, Phillip, and Thomas Wieser, *Seeking and Serving the Truth: The First Hundred Years of the World Student Christian Federation.* Geneva: WCC Publications, 1997.

Ramalho, Jether Pereira. "Buscando Novidades no Trabalho do Espírito." *Religião e Sociedade* 23 (2003) 69.

Ramos, Jovelino. "Voce nao Conhece o Shaull." *Religião e Sociedade* 23 (2003) 27.

Restrepo, Jose. *La Iglesia en Dos Momentos Difíciles de la Historia Patria [The Church in Two Difficult Moments in the History of the Country].* Bogota: Kelly, 1971.

Rian, Edwin H. *The Presbyterian Conflict.* Grand Rapids: Eerdmans, 1940.

Rycroft, Stanley W. *Religion and Faith in Latin America.* Philadelphia: Westminster, 1938.

——. *The Ecumenical Witness of the United Presbyterian Church in the U.S.A.* Board of Christian Education of the United Presbyterian Church USA, 1968.

Robert, Dana Lee. *American Women in Mission: A Social History of Their Thought and Practice.* The Modern Mission Era, 1792–1999. Macon, GA: Mercer University Press, 1997.

——. "Extending the Kingdom: The Universal Visions of Student Christian Movements, 1855–1939." Lecture delivered on Febreary 17, 2006, at the University of Birmingham, Sponsored by the Christian Youth Movement and the Royal Historical Society. Unpublished paper.

——. "The Influence of American Missionary Women on the World Back Home." *Religion and Culture: A Journal of Interpretation* 12:1 (2002) 59–89.

# Bibliography

——. "World Christianity as a Women's Movement." *International Bulletin of Missionary Research* 30:4 (2006) 180–88.

Roche, Barbara Anne. "Initiating and Sustaining Ecumenical Ministries: A Study of the Ministry of Margaret Flory, 1951–1980." DMin Thesis, San Francisco Theological Seminary, 1984.

Rosen, Fred. "NACLA: A 35 Years Retrospect." *NACLA Report on the Americas* 16:3 (2002) 14.

Santa Ana, Julio de. *Protestantismo, Cultura y Sociedad: Problemas y Perspectivas de la Fe Evangélica en América Latina.* Buenos Aires: Nueva Imagen, 1973.

——. *Hacia una Iglesia de los Pobres.* Buenos Aires: La Aurora, 1979.

——. "The Influence of Bonhoeffer on the Theology of Liberation." *Ecumenical Review* 28 (April 1978) 188–97.

——. "ISAL: Un Intento de Encarnación." *Cristianismo y Sociedad* 5:14 (1967) 113–19.

——. "ISAL, Un Movimiento en Marcha." *Cuadernos de Marcha* 29 (Septiembre 1969) 49–57.

——. "La Insatisfacción de las Masas en América Latina." *Cristianismo y Sociedad* 2:5 (1966) 26–35.

Santos, Áureo Bispo dos. "Shaull Mudou o Projeto de Vida de um Jovem Seminarista." *Religião e Sociedade* 23 (2003) 58.

Segundo, Juan Luis. *Liberación de la Teología.* Buenos Aires: Lohle, 1975.

Sherman, John W. *Latin America in Crisis.* Boulder, CO: Westview, 2000.

Silva, Heterson. "O Movimento Ecumenico e a Igreja Presbiteriana do Brasil." *Revista Teologica* 58:46 (1997) 7–17.

Skidmore, Thomas E. *Politics in Brazil, 1930–1964: An Experiment in Democracy.* New York: Oxford University Press, 1967.

Smolik, Josef. "Josef Lukl Hromadka." In *Christian Existence in Dialogue: Doing Theology in All Seasons. In Memory and Appreciation of Josef L. Hromadka,* 7–10. Geneva: World Council of Churches, 1990.

Uribe, Eugenio Restrepo. "El Protestantismo en Colombia." PhD diss., Universidad Javeriana de Bogotá, 1944.

Van Leeuwen, Arend Th. *Christianity in World History.* London: Edinburgh House, 1964.

Verkuyl, Johannes. *Contemporary Missiology: An Introduction.* Grand Rapids: Eerdmans, 1978.

Visser't Hooft, William A. "The Historical Significance of Stockholm 1925." In *The Gospel for all Realms of Life,* edited by William A. Visser't Hooft, 1–16. Geneva: World Council of Churches, 1975.

Wagner, Peter C. *Latin American Theology: Radical or Evangelical?* Grand Rapids: Eerdmans, 1970.

WCC. *The Witness of a Revolutionary Church: Statement Issued by the Committee of the International Missionary Council, Whitby, Ontario, July 5–24, 1947.* New York: International Missionary Council, 1947.

WCC. *The Church for Others: Two Reports of the Missionary Structures of the Congregation.* Geneva: World Council of Churches, 1967.

WCC. *Common Witness: A Study Document of the Joint Working Group of the Roman Catholic Church and the World Council of Churches.* Geneva: World Council of Churches, 1984.

Xing, Jun. *Baptized in the Fire of Revolution, The American Social Gospel and the YMCA in China: 1919–1937*. Bethlehem, PA: Lehigh University Press, 1996.

Yates, Timothy. *Christian Mission in the Twentieth Century*. Cambridge: Cambridge University Press, 1996.

# Index of Names

# Index of Names

# Index of Subjects

apocalyptic, 136, 160, 167, 169

Campinas Theological Seminary, 46–53, 60, 104, 114

Centro Evangelico Obrero, 22–23

Church,
  as *koinonia*, 33, 78, 90, 110, 123–26, 143, 158, 174
  local, 1–7, 12–15, 17–21, 24, 30, 54, 60, 72, 83, 85, 150, 179
  Roman Catholic, 2n7, 31, 34–34, 37, 39, 53, 68, 70, 106–7, 149–50, 153, 155, 193
  base communities, 148, 156–57, 161
  Presbyterian USA, 1–4, 11, 19, 23, 28–30
  in Colombia, 35, 41n100, 146–51, 163, 174–80, 181
  in Brazil, 48, 54–55, 59–60, 76–77, 80, 83, 90, 104, 107, 114, 140
  International Subsistence Program, 147
  Mission Volunteer International Program, 147–58

Civil Rights Movement, 131–32

Communism, 3, 57, 68, 70–71, 73, 86, 96, 118, 165, 168, 177

Confederação Evangélica do Brasil, 56

contextualization, 128

eschatological, 62, 83, 99, 103, 113, 121, 132, 135–36, 139–40, 168–69, 172

eschatology, 107, 171

evangelism, 15, 22–25, 36, 52, 58, 68–70, 87–91, 158, 185
  industrial evangelism, 9, 20–23
  evangelism through literacy, 26–29
  preparation of national leaders, 29–31

First Ecumenical Conference: Edinburgh, 1910, 24, 70

Great Depression, 11, 19

hermeneutical, 83, 100, 160

ideology, 18, 34, 49, 67, 76, 88, 95–99, 134, 136, 140, 167, 170, 172, 190, 191

Iglesia y Sociedad en America Latina, 84–96, 195, 200
  Huampaní, Peru, 1961, 85–95
  El Tabó, Chile, 1966, 93–104

Incarnation, 56, 65, 83, 87, 89, 91–92, 100, 125, 128, 157, 171–74

International Council of Christian Churches, 67

Kingdom of God, 5, 33, 35, 56–58, 63, 67, 75–76, 81, 123, 129, 138–39, 146, 160, 162, 169, 174, 178

Latin American Liberation Theology, 84, 100, 150, 152, 158

Lordship of Jesus Christ, 86, 94–99

metaphysics, 100, 112, 126, 130, 139, 140, 143

missio dei, 111

missiology, 4–7, 9, 29, 31, 41–43, 50, 57–61, 63, 74, 80, 88–89, 94–95,

34597196R00126

Made in the USA
Lexington, KY
25 March 2019